Santería

Santería

THE BELIEFS AND RITUALS OF A GROWING RELIGION IN AMERICA

Miguel A. De La Torre

William B. Eerdmans Publishing Company
Grand Rapids, Michigan / Cambridge, U.K.

© 2004 Wm. B. Eerdmans Publishing Co.

Wm. B. Eerdmans Publishing Co.
255 Jefferson Ave. S.E., Grand Rapids, Michigan 49503 /
P.O. Box 163, Cambridge CB3 9PU U.K.

Printed in the United States of America

09 08 07 06 05 04   7 6 5 4 3 2 1

Library of Congress Cataloging-in-Publication Data

De La Torre, Miguel A.
  Santeria : the beliefs and rituals of a growing religion in America /
  Miguel A. De La Torre.
    p.   cm.
  Includes bibliographical references and index.
  ISBN 0-8028-4973-3 (pbk. : alk. paper)
  1. Santeria. I. Title.

  BL2532.S3D4 2004
  299.6'74 — dc22

                                        2004050601

\#55534764

www.eerdmans.com

To my son Vincent *May your curiosity about different cultures and religions increase with age as you apply yourself to reach your full potential in life*

Contents

Tables

Figures

Preface

Throughout the 1950s, the character of Ricky Ricardo in the popular television sitcom *I Love Lucy* entertained viewers with his signature song, *Babalú-Ayé*. Desi Arnaz, playing Ricky, beat his conga drums and strutted around the stage to the amusement of a predominantly Anglo audience. The audience delighted in the Latin beat that came from Ricky's drum, conjuring up images of a more exotic culture. But what most television viewers failed to realize was that Ricky Ricardo was singing *to* Babalú-Ayé, one of the deities, called *orishas*, of an Afro-Cuban religion known as Santería. They were unaware of what the Latino community recognized: he was engaged in a sophisticated choreography that descended from the African civilization of the Yoruba, which was established long before Europe was ever deemed civilized.

Santería, from the Spanish word *santo* (saint), literally means "the way of saints." This religious expression has been a part of the American experience for some time even though the majority of the dominant Euroamerican population fails to recognize its existence. Today, as since the days of slavery, it is probably the most practiced religion in Cuba. Over time the religion made its way to the United States, in part due to the 1959 Castro revolution, which over a period of forty-five years sent about a million Cubans north seeking refuge. With each forced migration — from Africa to Cuba and then from Cuba to the United States — believers brought their gods with them. But all too often, when compared to the normative Eurocentric manifestation of Christianity, Santería is presented to the world through Hollywood movies and the news media as idolatrous, dangerous, or a product of a backward people. Some, operating from their anti-Hispanic prejudices, have used the religion to "prove" that the Latino community is indeed primitive. Others caricature the religion as simply something exotic to titillate the dominant culture's imagination. Missing from most analyses is a desire to respectfully learn about, and learn from, a religious expression that comes from the margins of society.

The word "Santería" itself originated as a pejorative term used by Catholic clerics in Cuba to denote what they considered a heretical mixture of African religious practices with the veneration of the saints. The term became popular during the 1940s in the Cuban cities of La Habana and Matanzas where large concentrations of Yoruba settled, although few of the older practitioners during this time accepted or used the term for self-description purposes. Several contemporary scholars, in an attempt to break with the name imposed on the religion by white Christians, have rejected the term, preferring instead *Lucumí* (Friendship)[1], *Regla de Ocha* (Rule of Ocha), or *Ayoba*. But the average person who practices or who is familiar with this religion knows it as Santería, and so I will continue to use this name throughout the book. Likewise, the priests of the faith are by some referred to as *oloshas* or *babaloshas* (for men) and *iyaloshas* (for women); however for the same reason they will be referred to as santeros or santeras.

Santería originated when the Yoruba were brought from Africa to colonial Cuba as slaves and forced to adopt Catholicism. They immediately recognized the parallels existing between their traditional beliefs and the ones newly imposed on them. Both religions consisted of a high god who conceived, created, and continued to sustain all that exists. Additionally, both religions consisted of a host of intermediaries operating between the supreme God and the believers. Catholics called these intermediaries saints, while Africans called them orishas. In order to continue worshiping their African gods under the constraints of slavery, they masked their deities behind the "faces" of Catholic saints, identifying specific orishas with specific saints. These gods, now mani-

---

1. The term *Lucumí* is used to refer to any characteristic of Yoruba culture, including the language. Some scholars believe that the word is derived from the Yoruba greeting *oluki mi* which literally means "my friend"; others believe it refers to an ancient Yoruba kingdom called Ulkumi.

fested as Catholic saints, were recognized as the powerbrokers between the most high God and humanity. They personified the forces of nature and had the power to impact human beings positively or negatively. Like humans, they could be virtuous or exhibit vices, doing whatever pleased them, even to the detriment of humans. Like humans, they expressed emotions, desires, needs, and wants.

Basically, modern believers in Santería worship these African gods, masked as Catholic saints, by observing their feast days, "feeding" and caring for them, carefully following their commands, and faithfully obeying their mandates. Complete submission, without question, is required of devotees, who are usually motivated by a mixture of fear and awe of the gods. Believers are not to question or argue with the gods or with priests of the faith. The only response is obedience. Disobedience implies a lack of respect that can lead to a total loss of guidance and protection. In return for obedience, believers learn the secrets by which natural and supernatural forces can be influenced and manipulated for their benefit. Rain can be summoned, seas calmed, death implored, fate changed, illnesses healed, and the future known, if such things will help individual followers come closer to their assigned destiny.

Santería is comprised of an Iberian Christianity shaped by the Counterreformation and Spanish folk Catholicism, blended together with African orisha worship as it was practiced by the Yoruba of Nigeria and later modified by nineteenth-century Kardecan spiritualism, which originated in France and became popular in the Caribbean. But while the roots of Santería can be found in Africa's earth-centered religion, in Roman Catholic Spain, and in European spiritism, it is neither African nor European. Christianity, when embraced under the context of colonialism and/or slavery, has the ability to create a space in which the indigenous beliefs of oppressed groups can resist annihilation. And while many elements of Santería can be found in the religious expression of Europe and Africa, it formed and developed along its own trajectory. In fact, different unique hybrids developed as the religious traditions of Yoruba slaves took root on different Caribbean soils. The vitality of Yoruba religiosity found expression through French Catholicism as *Vodou* in Haiti and New Orleans, and through Spanish Catholicism as *Shango* in Trinidad and Venezuela, *Candomble* in Brazil, *Kumina* in Jamaica, and of course, Santería in Cuba.

It should be noted that Orisha worship is not limited to a synthesis of Catholicism with the Yoruba religion. Examples of this African faith combining with Protestantism can be found in the Jamaican groups *Revival* and *Pocomania.* A similar example can be noted in the Trinidadian group known as Spiritual Baptists or Shouters, in which the Yoruba faith found expression through Christian fundamentalism. Furthermore, religion need not be the only lens through which to view Santería. Some of Cuba's atheist Marxists embrace its traditions. For them, Santería expands and enriches Marxism; they maintain that for Marxism to function in Cuba, it must incorporate Cuban reality as defined by the traditions of Santería.[2]

As the faith system of a marginalized people, under persecution throughout its history, Santería has always been an underground religion in Cuba and the United States. Only recently has it become recognized as a legitimate religion in the States. On June 11, 1992, the United States Supreme Court ruled that the followers of Santería had a constitutional right to sacrifice animals in connection with their rituals. Although it is impossible to document the exact number of orisha worshipers, some scholars estimate that about one hundred million are identified with the religion of Santería in the Americas, of which anywhere between half a million and five million are located in the United States. If this is true, there may be more practitioners of Santería than of some of the mainline U.S. Protestant denominations. Of course, given the lack of central organization of the religion, this number could be substantially higher or lower. In reality, there is no actual accounting system available. Nonetheless, one thing is clear, while the number of orisha worshipers is declining in Africa due to the missionary ventures of Muslims and Christians, the number of orisha believers is growing in the Americas. And even though the religion's African roots would suggest its adherents to be predominantly black, many believers and even priests are white, from middle-class backgrounds, and college-educated.

Still, as already mentioned, few Euroamericans know that such a religion even exists. And for many who have come into contact with the religion, specifically with its animal sacrifices, the tendency exists to

2. For more on the way this is played out in the art world, see Luis Camnitzer, *New Art of Cuba* (Austin: University of Texas Press, 1994), especially 211.

view its followers as primitive. One Florida mango farmer who found three decapitated chickens close to his mailbox offered a stereotypical assessment: "These queer people are of a lower culture than you or I."[3] Such comments are indicative of the pervasive ignorance of most Euroamericans toward Santería. Even within academic institutions it is seldom mentioned in books on comparative religion. Most college courses on world religions ignore spirituality with African roots, relegating it to a modern manifestation of primitive superstitious belief— though this no doubt reveals the outdated biases of those academics more than it does anything else!

What makes the study of Santería difficult is its lack of a central dogma or strict orthodoxy to regulate the rituals and practices of believers. In fact, dogma can be altered to suit new experiences or situations faced by the faith community. Individual priests are free to subjectively reinterpret the belief system, introducing new variations to old myths and practices based on their knowledge and on the faith community's needs. But what the religion lacks in orthodoxy, it makes up in ritual. Santería is highly ritualistic, and believers do not achieve the outcomes they desire based on the fervency of their prayers, or on the good intentions of their hearts, but rather on faithfully fulfilling the prescribed ritual or sacrificial procedure. Thus it is not a belief system composed of doctrines and creeds; rather it is one marked by a recognition of the existence and power of the ultimate god Olodumare and the subordinate deities known as orishas. Their reality is not accepted on faith, but based on how they have manifested themselves, spiritually and physically, to their followers. Although no doctrinal statement of belief or creed exists, if there were one it would confess that Olodumare, the owner of everlasting abundance, the one almighty creator, the everlasting God who is beyond maleness or femaleness and cannot be associated with human form, is to be worshiped through nature and nature's intrinsic polarities.

Researching Santería can prove difficult for the scholar for many reasons. First, there is no body of beliefs, sacred text, or ritual practice on which there is universal agreement. Since there is no central author-

3. Sonia L. Nazario, "Sacrificing Roosters to Glorify the Gods Has Miami in a Snit — But Adherents of Santería Must Keep Their Orishas from Getting Riled Up," *Wall Street Journal* (October 18, 1984).

ity, all worship is individualized and community-based. Second, there are spiritual leaders within the faith who deliberately provide false information, at times reinforcing stereotypes, in an attempt to prevent outsiders from discovering the secrets of the faith. Finally, practitioners of Santería interviewed by scholars are usually themselves recent inductees whose testimonies are unreliable since life within the faith is a gradual learning experience in which the deeper mysteries are revealed over time based on one's commitment to the orishas.

Further complicating the research process are the numerous books written about the religion. A few claim to reveal the secrets of Santería, yet, in spite of the reticence the religion has developed as a survival tactic, its practices are hardly secret. Some present the religion as truth not to be questioned. Still others examine it from a social location vastly different from the majority of its devotees — many, for example, are written by middle- and upper-class Euroamericans who ignore the cultural significance the religion has for the poor living a marginalized existence. Some books portray Santería as an exotic religion, not realizing that to believers, Santería is not exotic, but rather common; for those who worship the orishas, the Western European religions are the ones that appear exotic. Others portray it as a religious fusion, the product of a confusion of Christianity and Yoruba beliefs in the minds of believers, not recognizing that it is a cultural fusion more than a religious one. All of these difficulties prevent any one book — including this one — from being an authoritative or definitive treatment of the religion. The most we can hope to accomplish is to share how different believers understand Santería, hoping that such experiences resonate with others who have been involved in the religion and create for outsiders a window through which the religion can be observed.

While many of the books that fall into the above categories are of top-notch scholastic rigor (indeed many were invaluable to my research for this book), it must be recognized that all of them, as well as this one, are limited by the social location and beliefs of their authors. Santería cannot be understood only in terms of anthropology or sociology. All too often the trained scholar focuses on commonly held beliefs and analyzes how said beliefs are products of a given social background. While such approaches are helpful, they fall short of capturing the faith experience of the religion's adherents. Furthermore, adherents of other religions often study Santería with the ulterior motive of converting its followers, and they therefore expend their energies seeking any inconsistency to prove that the religion is "wrong." Unfortunately these same individuals seldom analyze their own beliefs for their own inconsistencies. Finally, some of the more prolific writers on Santería are themselves converts to the religion, at times writing with the typical zeal of a new believer, which, unfortunately, again gives a slant to the material and avoids the rich dynamics existing between Santería and Christianity.

Let me therefore lay out my own position. Unlike most others who have written on this subject, I will approach Santería from the social location of a former believer. It is not my goal either to condemn or to condone this faith system. Rather, I want to examine this important part of the Latino/a consciousness, which I claim influences all Hispanics from the Caribbean islands, even those who choose not to participate in the faith. I find that although many Latino/as who participate in a liberationist style of Christianity insist on doing their theological reflection from the perspectives of marginalized groups, the indigenous spirituality of Hispanics (whether manifested as Santería or as any other orisha-based form of religious expression) is usually ignored in favor of a Eurocentric Christian perspective. I maintain that if Hispanic scholars truly desire to do grassroots theological reflection, then they are obligated to consider Santería, a Latino/a form of popular religiosity. And I believe that much can be learned from Santería — not just by Latina/os, but also by the dominant Euroamerican culture. I contend that all who call themselves Christians, regardless of their ethnicity, are able to learn more about their own faith as they learn about and contemplate the religious expression of marginalized groups.

This book is geared toward the individual who possesses little, if any, knowledge about this growing religious movement practiced in the homes of many Hispanics throughout the United States, especially those of Cuban descent. Its goal is to explain the religion in a fashion accessible to the person who until now has never heard of Santería. To be understood successfully, it must be studied as the faith of a people. Thus, special attention is given to Santería's worldviews, myths, rituals, practices, and belief systems from the perspective of one who for two and a half decades was an "insider." Additionally, the book will critically analyze the faith tradition from the perspective of one who is now an "outsider," paying close attention to the role and function the religion plays in the life of the typical devotee. The result, I hope, is a book that provides the lay reader with a basic understanding of what Santería is. Yet the work goes beyond a simple description, such as might be found in an encyclopedia, by providing a cultural analysis of the faith — specifically, by examining what it means to its average believers, who historically have been disenfranchised. I hope the book will explore what Christians can learn about their own faith system through a consideration of this different religious expression.

It would be erroneous to assume that this book is the product of one individual. Numerous people have shared their wisdom, knowledge, and help while it was being written. I specifically want to thank Hope College for providing me with the Faculty Fund for Faith summer writing grant. I am also indebted to Allen Verhey for his assistance in getting this book to a publisher. Additionally, I wish to thank Santería priest Ernesto Pichardo for the hours he spent answering my many questions about the faith, and my Religion Department secretary Pamela Valkema, who spent just as many hours transcribing recorded interviews. The insights of scholar and believer Andrés I Pérez y Mena, who read several chapters of the book, have been invaluable. My research assistants Elinor Douglass, Allison Sanders, and Sarah Wilkinson provided a great deal of help, as did librarian Anthony Guardado of Hope College. Jonathan Schakel provided proofreading assistance and Andrew Hoogheem provided editing, for both of which I am deeply appreciative. Finally, I am indebted to my mother Mirta and to Santería priest Nelson Hernández for obtaining some of the photos which appear in this book.

I would be remiss if I did not mention my wife Deborah, and my two children Victoria and Vincent, whose constant love provided the strength to get this project finished. Last, but certainly not least, I thank the many unnamed santeros and santeras who influenced my overall spiritual development while I was growing toward adulthood. If we are all influenced by our social contexts, then these individuals have left a permanent mark on my spiritual being, even though I no longer participate in this religious tradition. Of course, my parents Miguel and Mirta, priests of this faith system, had the greatest impact.

Chapter 1

Santería: What Is It?

I grew up as a believer in Santería, in a home where both parents minis-
tered to the needs of our faith community. Memories of streams of
people visiting our modest apartment to consult the saints about the
problems they were facing remain vivid in my mind. These individuals
were mostly marginalized people, Latinos and Latinas, mainly Cubans,
struggling to survive in the United States. They were Catholics, Protestants, and followers of the orishas. They came to our home expecting
miracles to occur. As for myself, I was an *hijo de Elegguá* (child of
Elegguá, one of the orishas) destined to someday become a priest. My
family and I followed the precepts of the orishas; paradoxically, I also
went to a Catholic elementary school in Queens, New York. I took my
first communion, participated in weekly confession, and was confirmed at Blessed Sacrament Church, even though at night, crowds
would visit our apartment to consult the gods.

There was never any confusion in my mind, in my parents' minds,
or in the minds of those visiting our house-temple regarding the difference between what was done at the Irish church down the street and
what was done in our apartment. From an early age, my parents explained to me that the rituals we participated in could not be revealed
to the priests or the nuns because they were "confused" about how God
works, and if they found out that we had *el conocimiento* (the knowledge), I would be expelled from the school. Yet when I asked what we
were, they would reply without hesitating, as if by rote: "We are apos-
tolic Roman Catholics, but we believe in our own way."

Those of us raised in this spiritual environment survived the alienation of living in a new country because of the shared sacred space created by the tension existing between Christianity and Santería. For my family and myself, Santería became a source of comfort, community, and empowerment for those who, like us, were refugees navigating the difficulties and struggles of trying to survive and adapt to exilic life. While there was no confusion among those of us practicing Santería concerning the difference between us and the priests and nuns, still an ambiguous religiosity developed, fusing the elements of these diverse traditions in order to resist what was perceived to be the danger of assimilating into the dominant Euroamerican ethos.

The Faith of a People

The elaborate belief system of the Yoruba became part of the Cuban experience when Europeans in colonial Cuba began to import African slaves to develop urban centers and to work in mines and on sugar plantations. Over half of all Africans who made the perilous journey to the Americas found themselves on sugar plantations throughout the Caribbean islands. Many of these Africans were noble patricians and priests who had been disloyal to the ascendancy of new rulers, specifically in the kingdoms of Benin, Dahomey, and the city-states of Yoruba. The vicissitudes of monarchic power struggles resulted in the enslavement of those opposing the new hegemony. Prisoners of war were routinely enslaved, but slavery was also imposed as a debt payment for a period of time or as punishment for committing a crime. Whichever the individual slave's case, forced expatriation was often a more profitable alternative than imprisonment or capital punishment. Possible rebels and undesirables were thus eliminated from African society by being sold to Europeans, who in turn made these individuals their slaves.

Torn from their ordered religious life, Africans were compelled to adjust their belief system to the immediate challenges presented by colonial Cuba. Central to life in Cuba was Roman Catholicism with its belief in Jesus as the son of God. (Ironically, one of the slave ships that brought Africans to the Western Hemisphere for a life of servitude was named the *Jesus.*) Prior to being led away from their homeland forever,

Africans were forced to pass under a Catholic priest, who usually sat on an ivory chair baptizing these chained "heathens" in the name of Jesus. Throughout the Middle Passage, these slaves would see pious captains holding prayer services twice a day and singing famous hymns about the sweet name of Jesus or the amazing grace of God. These Africans being led to a life of bondage, like so many of their descendants, saw no reason to turn to the white Spanish Jesus of the dominant culture. Prevented by their masters from worshiping the gods of Africa, these slaves simply masked their gods with the clothing of Catholic saints. It thus appeared to priests, sea captains, and slaveholders that slaves were praying to Saint Lazarus, for example — but unbeknownst to these oppressors, the slaves were continuing the worship of the orisha Babalú-Ayé.

Thus Santería became the religion of an oppressed people. To truly understand the worldview of Santería, it is crucial that it is approached on these terms. We begin by recognizing that followers of Santería are not interested in proselytizing, nor in justifying their beliefs to outsiders. Only those who are willing to take a step toward the orishas are entrusted with more in-depth information. The closer one moves toward the orishas, the more the mysteries of Santería are revealed.

Membership

When attempting to explain or understand another world religion, Christians seem to have a tendency to emphasize the similarities between that other religion and their own. That is, the unfamiliar religion — in our case Santería — is described in Christian, and therefore Western, terms. Generally Christians have understood Santería as primitive, magical superstition, or as simply a variation on "respectable" Western Christianity. Unfortunately, by forcing Santería to be understood through Western Christian paradigms, an analysis is produced which differs from the reality of its practitioners. This is best illustrated by Christians' attempts to understand it by exploring its beliefs, its doctrines.

In most Western religions, membership is clearly demarcated by doctrinal boundaries. What individuals claim to believe usually determines which faith community they belong to. With Santería, on the other hand, neither correct doctrines nor homogeneous belief systems are as important as the rituals practiced. Unlike other world religions, in which belief is central to belonging (consider, for example, Judaism's belief in a monotheistic God; Christianity's belief in Jesus Christ as the savior of the world; or Islam's belief in Muhammad as the prophet of God), in Santería one either has gone through the ordination ritual, or one has not.

Though rooted in Africa, Santería is not limited to those of African descent. Anyone and everyone is welcome to honor and worship the orishas because the natural forces they represent are present everywhere in the world. In fact, as Santería continues to take root in North American soil, it is becoming more common to find Euroamerican santeros and santeras. One becomes a devotee not according to ethnicity or race, nor because of a profession of faith, but rather because of an action taken during a ritual.

Santería is composed of a highly decentralized religious body lacking any central institutional structure. There is no headquarters where elders, bishops, or other leaders maintain doctrinal purity, represent the faithful to the media and the government, or coordinate the rituals occurring among the multitude of believers. Each house-temple is an entity unto itself, with little or no responsibility to other house-temples. In fact, neighboring *casas de santos* ("houses of saints") can very easily have divergent practices and different interpretations of those practices. Although a vast informal network exists through which devotees can be referred to santeros and santeras throughout the United States, no formal instructional structure is in place. For Westerners, the absence of a national church council, board of elders, or presbytery can lead to the assumption that Santería is not really an organized religion because of its lack of a centralized governing body.

Purpose

Santería's main purpose is to assist the individual, regardless of their religious background or affiliation, to live in harmony with their assigned destiny by ensuring they possess the necessary rituals to navigate life's difficulties. Hence it begins with the believer's problems, for the problem is an obstacle preventing the individual from reaching their full potential. Unlike Western religions whose starting point is an almighty, all-knowing God, Santería's point of origin is a frail, hurting person. "Where there is no human, there is no divinity," states a Yoruba proverb. The individual is the starting point of the religion, responsible for any and all actions taken — actions which produce positive or negative consequences. The basic mission of Santería is to help with the normal, everyday trials and tribulations of ordinary life, including basic problems dealing with health, love, or money. To address these physical problems, the believer turns to the spiritual world for answers and solutions. It is insufficient to simply invoke the name of a deity; rather, the individual must seek the spiritual force that can best resolve whatever dilemma is faced, then provide said force with the necessary energy (either through a lit candle or a sacrifice) so that help can be provided.

For believers, the physical universe emerged from the invisible spiritual realm. Thus, when these two realities are aligned, the physical and the spiritual, harmony exists. Those who understand that the two realms are closely connected and are willing to pursue the mysteries of the spiritual realm will find the answers and solutions that can bring healing to life's difficulties. For example, the problem with modern medicine, according to Santería, is that it attends to only physical ailments, totally ignoring the spiritual. Complete cure must extend to both realms of reality; thus, the first step toward healing must be divination, the process by which the will of the orishas is discovered so that harmony can once again be established between the physical and spiritual worlds. While the medicine can provide a cure for the physical ailment, Santería provides healing for the root of that ailment, spiritual disharmony.

The physical elements of existence, air, fire, water, and earth, each have their spiritual counterpart. Air, which literally creates the sky, is associated with the orisha Obatalá. Fresh air resolves ethical dilemmas, contributing to spiritual growth. As wind, air blows away unwanted negative energy, bad emotions, and harmful spirits. Fire, associated with the orishas Aganyú and Changó, contains the power to burn away impurities, leading to a spiritual transformation. Through the testing of fire, character is built, steel becomes iron, resolve is strengthened. Water cleanses. It washes away dirt, as well as evil energy, cleansing both the physical and the spiritual. Fresh water, the domain of the orisha Oshún, becomes the source of fertility. Salt water, on the other hand, under the rule of the orisha Yemayá, symbolizes the maternal,

5

the source of all life. Stagnant water, such as that in a lagoon, represents spiritual death — which is a prerequisite for new life. And finally, the earth, the fourth element, provides the necessary resources for survival. The orisha Oggún provides the tools for survival. Eliminating obstacles with these tools leads to physical survival and spiritual growth.

Because the physical elements of existence reflect spiritual principles, believers are assured that they do not exist in a universe that lacks reason or direction. Rather, all that is, whether it be seen or unseen, exists as part of a system in which valiant orishas protect all of creation. The orishas also provide guidance and security to humans, whom they adopt as their children. It is the orishas who provide structure to reality, and without them, human existence simply cannot develop.

Syncretism?

In a sense, all religions are syncretistic — that is, all religions are transformed as they pass through and assimilate elements from different cultures. As new religions interact with new social contexts, both the culture and the religion are transformed to enable them to coexist. At times the changes are dramatic; at other times they are modest, even unnoticeable. Regardless of the degree of change, however, one thing is certain: neither the religion nor the culture ever remains the same; both become new expressions. To this extent, all religions are syncretistic.

Take, for example, Christianity. Originally a Jewish sect, it began to differentiate itself from Judaism as it took root among the Greeks. Greek philosophical concepts like the dichotomy of the body and soul became absorbed into Christian thought.[1] As Christianity expanded into the Roman world, it organized itself along the lines of the Roman government.[2] While its core beliefs remained the same, it was strongly

---

1. For example, the original Christian understanding of the afterlife encompassed the belief of the resurrection of the body, as illustrated by belief in the physical resurrection of Jesus Christ. Greek philosophy, on the other hand, taught that upon death, the body decayed while the soul lived eternally. Today, a majority of Christians believe that souls enter heaven, leaving the body behind.

2. The early church fashioned itself along Roman political structures. The office of the Pope was analogous to the office of the Emperor (who was often considered a deity); cardinals were the equivalent of Roman senators; bishops were like the governors; and priests like the centurions.

influenced by whatever culture it moved through. This continues today: it is not hard to see the mega-churches run by well-paid senior pastors who are assisted by a ministry staff resembling capitalist corporations run by well-paid CEOs who are assisted by a board of directors. For religions to survive, they must constantly be changing to adjust to new struggles and to the circumstances faced by believers. Such changes do not invalidate the religion of the forebears; instead, the ability of the religion to evolve prevents the faith from become irrelevant to each new generation of followers.

Now, if all religions are in some ways syncretistic, why is Christianity seldom referred to as syncretistic while that label is almost invariably used to describe Santería? Could it be that the syncretistic label implies an impure mixture? To single out Santería as a syncretistic religion may make it easier for Eurocentric minds to categorize, but to do so, in effect, subordinates it to the self-perceived "purity" of the dominant culture's religion. By masking the syncretism of the dominant religion while accenting the syncretistic nature of the marginalized one, the dominant culture imposes a value system upon these religions in which the former is viewed as a purer representation of the truth while the latter is perceived as a distortion. We are left to wonder if the very concept of syncretism is in reality a Eurocentric intellectual invention, a product of racism. Andrés Pérez y Mena said it best: "Syncretism is a model of analysis that denies the enslaved a consciousness of their predicament in the New World."[3]

Racism has caused followers of Santería to face religious persecution throughout Cuba's history. Official Christianity portrayed the Afro-Cuban religions as the principal cause for Cuba's problems. Slavery was a curse, not because of its maltreatment of Africans, but because it contaminated whites with the barbarism of nonwhites. Prostitution, laziness, superstition, and criminality were said to have originated with Cuba's blacks.

In addition to being Eurocentric, it is simplistic for Christians to explain Santería as a syncretistic phenomenon caused by the merging of Catholic and African belief systems in primitive and confused

3. Andrés Pérez y Mena, "Cuban Santería, Haitian Vodun, Puerto Rican Spiritualism: A Multiculturalist Inquiry into Syncretism," *Journal for the Scientific Study of Religion,* Vol. 37, No. 1 (March 1998): 15.

minds. In reality, the disguising of African gods in the clothes of Catholic saints was a very shrewd maneuver on the slaves' part. When slaves publicly worshiped the orishas, participated in possessions, or conducted consultations, the Catholic officials moved quickly to stop them, fearing that such demonstrations of fidelity to the African gods frustrated attempts to evangelize and convert the slaves to Catholicism. But when believers in the orishas connected them, however superficially, to Catholic saints, the problem was quickly solved. All the power, characteristics, fetishes, and due devotion which belonged to a particular orisha were now transferred to the Catholic saint. To all appearances, and to the satisfaction of the Catholic clerics, the slaves were now worshiping Saint Barbara; in reality, the slaves who bowed their knees to the image of the saint recognized that they were truly worshiping Changó in his European manifestation as St. Barbara. In fact, the devotees of Changó saw the learned Catholic clerics as naive, if not ignorant, about the true essence of St. Barbara; only the orisha devotees had the fuller knowledge of the spiritual world.

The masking of the orishas behind Catholic saints continues to this day for the good of those who come to santeros and santeras seeking guidance. I recall how my father would explain to a Catholic, unfamiliar with the nuances of Santería, the results of a consultation. During the divination ritual, my father would never say, "Obatalá understands the pain and suffering you are undergoing. Obatalá loves you and has committed himself to embrace and assist you through this difficult time. If you light a white candle to Obatalá each day for the rest of the week, you will see how by this time next week, your problem will be solved." Had he done this, the Catholic seeking guidance would probably have wondered, "Who in the world is Obatalá? Is this some type of demon? What am I getting myself into?" If the primary function of the consultation is to restore harmony in the life of the seeker, then what is needed is not a dissertation on the Yoruba pantheon outlining the different African deities. Rather, what is needed is the resolution of the seeker's dilemma. For this reason, my father would communicate the divine message in a language which the Catholic would understand. He would say something like, "You know our holy mother Mary, Our Lady of Ransom. Well, she was originally known in Africa as Obatalá. She loves you and embraces your pain, and commits to resolve your problem if you venerate her and light a white candle to her every day." The seeker, now understanding the message, is able to do what is required without necessarily feeling conflict with their Catholic faith.

If, after this initial problem was solved, the seeker continued to come to my father for more help, then, little by little, he would help them begin to understand the powers residing behind the Catholic masks. The concept of Our Lady of Ransom would recede as the seeker gradually began to learn about Obatalá. With time, the seeker would come to appreciate the image of Our Lady of Ransom as an important symbol to ease the transition into a new faith, but an image no longer maintains its usefulness in seekers' lives as they begin to direct their worship toward Obatalá. In reality, they would eventually know, Our Lady of Ransom had nothing to do with resolving the seeker's first problem. But only the seeker who has matured in faith is at a level to understand better the dynamics of the spiritual realm.

This process of transition may take years, if not decades. A person who grows up Catholic and converts to Santería in adulthood, even to the point of becoming a santera or a santero, might never make the full transition from Catholicism to Santería. Such a person's worldview may be so grounded in the Catholic faith that it is impossible to distinguish between Our Lady of Ransom and Obatalá. If researchers or scholars interview them in their role as a priest or priestess of Santería, they conclude that the religion is obviously syncretistic. But it is not the religion that is syncretistic. It is the individual who has yet to mature in his or her newfound faith.

One particular santero had his house full of statues of Catholic saints, making him the envy of many local Catholic churches. The instruments of the Santería faith were kept out of view. His reasoning for de-emphasizing his faith and emphasizing Catholicism was based on his realization that even though the trapping of statues was unimportant to the faith, the people who sought him for a consultation needed a point of reference. They had no concept of what Santería was about. Even though the santero believed that his work with these people was meaningful as their problems found resolutions, he recognized that they would never seek help if they could not find a common language. Hence he never referred to the orishas by their African names, but would always use their Catholic equivalents. Had he not done so, these people might have concluded that this was some sort of strange cult and fled, never finding resolution to their problems. Therefore, for their sake, this particular santero made his home resemble a Catholic church so that seekers would feel comfortable in what appeared to be a familiar environment. Here again, doctrinal purity is unimportant. What is important is resolving the seekers' dilemma. With time, as the seekers' trust is gained, as they see for themselves the power of the orishas, and as they seek to have a deeper understanding of the faith, they too will discover the unimportance of all the Catholic statues in the house as they begin to focus their worship and adoration on the orishas.

How Santería presents itself to the world depends to a very large degree on the level of knowledge or interest of the seeker. A first-time visit to a Santería worship festival might reveal many statues of Catholic saints with candles before them as worshipers pray to the saints in Spanish. African elements may also be seen, like an African-style statue behind the door, or bead necklaces around worshipers' necks, leading the casual observer to dismiss these peculiarities as some form of syncretism. Yet as this observer becomes a seeker, committed to the way of the orishas, the African images are uncovered and the prayers are said in Lucumí, the language of the Yoruba. It becomes less important which saint corresponds with a particular orisha. What matters is that the proper orisha be worshiped. In fact, the Catholic saints begin to be discarded as the believer's understanding of the orishas' mysteries deepens.

For this reason, many Catholic priests who are aware of the faith see their role as correcting followers of Santería regarding their doctrinal errors so that they can reenter the official faith of the Church. Others voice harsher criticism, claiming Santería adulterates the true (mostly white) form of Catholicism. For evangelical Protestants, especially Pentecostals, Santería is a demonic cult, a form of sorcery like that condemned by the apostle Paul in Acts 13. In this story from the Christian New Testament, Paul goes to the isle of Cyprus preaching the resurrection of Jesus Christ. There he meets a sorcerer named Elymas. When Elymas attempts to interfere with Paul's preaching, the apostle says, "You son of the devil, you enemy of all righteousness, full of all deceit and villainy, will you not stop making crooked the straight paths of the Lord?" Immediately Elymas is struck with blindness. For many Protestant ministers, santeros and santeras are no different from Elymas, or from any of the other magicians and sorcerers opposed by the apostles. For example, one Baptist minister in Hialeah, Florida, whose congregation worshiped in a neighborhood where many participated in Santería, described Santería as an attempt on the part of believers to manipulate God, a form of "old world spiritualism."

Similarly, Victorio García-Barbón, a former follower of Santería who presently serves as pastor of a nondenominational Protestant church in Hialeah where about 75% of the members are former believers, insists that Santería is the opposite of all that is Christian. While Christians claim Christ's sacrifice on the cross was done once and is sufficient for all, Santería must constantly rely on animal sacrifices. He asserts that there really is no power within Santería, because there is only one power, the God of the Bible. Despite this alleged lack of power, he views Santería as satanic because he believes that it leads people away from the true God, replacing an abundant life with a superstitious one, full of unfounded fears.

I believe Santería can best be understood as a different religion from Christianity, not a distorted variation of it. As a new cultural reality, can it be faithful to the Christian tradition of the Gospels as reflected in the community of Christian believers? Robert Schreiter, writing to a Catholic and liberal Protestant audience from a missionary background, provides five criteria for distinguishing Christian identity. These criteria, when taken together, are helpful in attempting to determine whether a given faith is "Christian." For a religious expression to be Christian it must first adhere to a "hierarchy of truth" in which the role of Jesus as the definitive revelation of God's salvific presence in history is primary. Second, what is expressed in the faith community through worship, prayer and sacrament must express the presence of God. Third, the actions of the community must reflect a credible Christian essence. Fourth, the openness of the faith community to the judgment of other Christian churches must exist. And finally, the challenge from the faith community to other Christian churches must be present.[4] While an argument can be made that Santería meets the second, third, and fifth criteria of Schreiter's paradigm, it would be difficult to maintain such a position for the first and fourth. The absence of Jesus playing a central role within Santería's cosmology and the arcane nature of the religion prevent it from being defined as a Christian religion. Indeed, even if it met four or five of Schreiter's requirements,

---

4. Robert J. Schreiter, *Constructing Local Theologies* (Maryknoll, N.Y.: Orbis Books, 1996), 117-21.

it seems doubtful that a Christian designation is necessary for Santería. The faith has reached sufficient maturity to discard any syncretistic label. Such a label may have originally been helpful in elucidating Santería's genesis, but it hinders understanding it as a present-day religion. Santería expresses a worldview on its own terms.

For this reason, santeros and santeras, Catholic priests, and Protestant ministers all agree on one thing: one cannot be a Christian and a follower of Santería. They are two different religions. The idea that Santería is a syncretistic blend of Christianity and African religion is a misunderstanding, perpetuated in large part by scholars and interviewers relying too strongly on the testimonies of new believers lacking in religious depth or maturity. Santería is neither "confused" in its beliefs, nor the product of confused imagery. Santeras and santeros have always recognized the difference between their own religion and Catholicism.

Ashé: The Energy of Existence

In Santería, Ashé is a sort of primal energy that comprises the power, grace, blood, and life force of all reality. It is amoral, neither good nor bad, unable to be seen or personified, a neutral cosmic energy undergirding every aspect of existence. All that has life or exhibits power has ashé. The blood of living creatures, the moving wind, the growing plants, consuming fire, and flowing water all expend ashé.

It is because everything that exists contains ashé that Santería believes the orishas can manifest themselves in other religions. In a sense, this leads to a type of "anonymous Santería" similar to Karl Rahner's "anonymous Christianity," in which individuals who do not profess Christianity may be followers of Christ unawares.[5] Santería's internal structure allows for the incorporation and assimilation of new deities. When a seeker is unable to comprehend a concept because she or he lacks a Catholic background, the santero/a may substitute for a saint a compatible icon of the seeker's own religious tradition. For example, if

---

5. For more on this, see Karl Rahner, *Theological Investigations,* trans. David Bourke (London: Darton, Longman & Todd, 1973), 46; and, Karl Rahner, *Foundations of Christian Faith: Introduction to the Idea of Christianity,* trans. William V. Dych (New York: Seabury Press, 1978), 119-23.

a seeker were Roman Catholic, the creator of the world, Obatalá, could be presented as the Virgin Mary, the Mother of God (our Lady of Ransom), and the war-orisha, Oggún, could manifest himself as St. Peter. However, if the seeker were Hindu, then Obatalá could just as easily be understood as Brahma, the creator, and Oggún as Shiva, the destroyer. According to Santería, the seeker is enlightened not by rejecting their old faith, but by developing new insights into it.

"Anonymous Santería," as I call it, allows worshipers to participate in other religious traditions. Many, of course, participate in Catholic services. In fact, it is required by many house-temples that the believer be baptized within the Catholic church and attend the masses for the dead. Others attend church on the feast days of the saints worshipped in Santería, or to obtain holy water for incantations. In the mind of the believer, participating in a Catholic worship service does not constitute an inconsistency in religious thought. Praying before a Catholic statue is understood as praying to the orisha that the particular statue represents. For the believer, there is a recognition that ashé flows through all worldly religions — however, the Catholics lack the knowledge or understanding of what exactly is spiritually occurring during the mass.

In other words, anonymous Santería means that every human who worships the Divine through their different religious expressions is in reality worshiping the orishas. And although some people may consider themselves to be both Catholics and worshipers of the orishas, to the exasperation of clergy in both faiths, it is ashé that allows them to worship any deity through any religious structure, and still be able to worship the forces of nature personified as the orishas from whom ashé flows.

Absolutes: Some Fundamentals of Santería

The idea of absolute truth is foreign to the mindset of believers in Santería. For them, no one religion has a monopoly on absolute truth. All religions contain truth, and thus require respect. When Olodumare, the supreme God, created all that exists, the wisdom relied upon to create was distributed throughout all of creation, and hence all peoples, all creatures, all nature contain Olodumare's truth. The Christian, the

Jew, the Muslim, the Hindu, the Buddhist, in effect every religious person regardless of their faith tradition, has a piece of the truth in their sacred writings, in their worldview, and in their holy rituals. Their perspectives cannot be ignored, for they contain elements essential to understanding the spiritual realm. The believer in Olodumare and the orishas does not condemn other religious faiths, nor attempt to invoke the wrath of their supernatural entities. Instead, through diplomatic conversations, santeros and santeras attempt to learn from others' religious experiences.

An Earth-Centered Religion

In a very real sense, Santería is a terrestrial religion, firmly rooted in the earth. While Western religions tend to emphasize a heavenly place, or stress the placement of the stars and planets to determine the course of human events (remember that a shining star over Bethlehem was said to signify the birth of Jesus), Santería is shaped and formed by earth-centered forces of nature. These forces are personified as the deities known as orishas. The orishas are gods of earthly forces — for example thunder (Changó), the harvest (Oko), and the sea (Yemayá). Its rituals utilize earthly things — stones, herbs, water, plants, trees, soil, seashells, and so on all become sacred objects. Seldom do devotees of Santería look to the stars or to the movement of planets to determine the will of the gods; rather, they look to the earth for the answers to all conceivable questions.

The religion teaches that the earth provides all that is needed to live a full and abundant life. As the oceans are able to support and sustain all life that exists in its waters, so too is the earth able to support and sustain all life that exists on its land. This abundance becomes evident as we learn to live in harmony with nature. Shortages occur when we attempt to impose our own will upon the fair and natural distribution of nature's resources according to the needs of the people.

Sacred Text

In Santería, the main sacred text is known as the Corpus of Ifa. In short, Ifa teaches about gods and humans. It consists of a collection of poetry, history, legends, myths, folktale, verses, and proverbs. Unlike the Bible of Christianity and Judaism, or the Qur'ān of Islam, a final version of the Corpus of Ifa does not exist in writing. While the scriptures of Western religions are believed to be complete, containing all truth necessary, the Corpus of Ifa is more of a reference manual. No complete or final version can ever exist. Each priest adds his or her own life journey and experiences to the text, passing it down to disciples who incorporate their teacher's wisdom as part of the body of wisdom. Thus the text never remains stagnant, but grows and adapts to each succeeding generation of believers.

The only similarity between the sacred texts of Western religions and the Corpus of Ifa is that they all require the interpretation of the reader; however, all interpretations of the Corpus of Ifa are specific to the individual. No collective meaning for all people at all times exists. The writings which make up the Corpus of Ifa are transmitted from one generation to the next, originally orally, but in more recent times by means of having new santeros and santeras handwrite them into notebooks known in Spanish as *libretas*.

But even after it is transcribed into a libreta the Corpus of Ifa is incomplete. Because it is a written version of an oral tradition, its practices, traditions, and stories differ from one location to another. One can expect inconsistencies in both the practices and the stories of the orishas. These differences become obvious when comparing Santería as practiced in Miami, for example, with Santería as practiced in New York or La Habana. No central ecclesiastic structure exists to arbitrate, regulate, or impose "correct" doctrine. In short, a lack of dogmatism exists. Variations in beliefs and rituals can easily be detected within different house-temples existing within the same city or town, with each house believing in the authenticity of its own teachings. In spite of these differences, some generalizations can be made, and I will attempt to concentrate on those areas of similarities, cognizant that, at times, all views may not be fully expressed.

Ethics: Seeking Harmony

Believers in Santería cannot simply do as they wish, but are required to live according to a set of ethical principles that determine morality among the faith community. But unlike Western religious traditions, Santería does not have a bipolar concept of good and evil. In fact, there are no personifications of evil or good, as in the case of Satan or God. All orishas represent concepts that are pure and all contain contradictions. Terms like good and evil are relative, dependent on the situation. What is morally imperative for one individual may not be for another. For this reason, santeros and santeras do not necessarily pass moral judgment upon their clients.

Santería does not teach that misfortune is punishment, a result of angering God or the gods. It is better described as the natural outcome of disregarding the laws inherent in nature. For example, if we pollute our streams and rivers, we create disharmony by destroying the ecological balance of our planet. The consequences of such pollution might include a contaminated drinking source, which in turn could cause illnesses. Spiritually speaking, we can say that Oshún, goddess of the rivers, is offended and is punishing the people. She will be placated only by restoring harmony — that is, by learning to live in respect and awe of our natural resources. This can be understood as making sacrifices to Oshún to pacify her anger and learning to live in respect of Oshún, which in turn means respecting the forces she manifests, in this case, the rivers.

Hence believers seek to find harmony with the seen and unseen world and with those with whom they share the planet. If harmony is maintained between the physical and the spiritual realms, then those who dwell on earth experience enlightenment, prosperity, peace, and good health. If, however, disharmony and imbalance prevail, then ignorance, scarcity, violence, and malady will plague the earth. Santería seeks the power required to struggle efficiently against these types of oppressive forces, specifically in areas of societal subjugation, physical diseases, and relational difficulties.

The santero Raul Canizares provides an interesting hypothetical case that adequately demonstrates this concept and is worth repeating here:

A Roman Catholic priest in a small Latin American town cuts down a tree to which local santeros give offerings. The priest feels he is helping his neighbors by eliminating a temptation to practice idolatry, a mortal sin. The santeros, however, feel that the Catholic priest has caused a very serious imbalance. One santero consults an oracle, which indicates that the Catholic priest will suffer the consequences of having caused this imbalance. That night, the priest suffers a heart attack and dies. Christians denounce the santeros as belonging to a satanic cult that used magic to harm a saintly man.[6]

To Catholics, the priest, adhering to doctrinal truth, destroyed the root of evil, idolatry, by cutting down the tree. To santeros and santeras, the misguided actions of the priest, however good his intentions, disrupted harmony by committing a belligerent act against a sacred object, thus bringing upon himself the wrath of the orisha.

What ethical actions, then, lead toward harmony? Like most religions, stealing, hypocrisy, lying, and covenant-breaking are condemned, while speaking the truth is considered a virtue. Behavior is expected to be modeled after what Christians call the "Golden Rule" — to do unto others as you would want them to do unto you. Each believer is responsible for seeking the greatest good for the entire community, even when that good conflicts with what is best for the individual. Hence selfishness is frowned upon. The story is told about the orisha of divination, Orúnla, who used to be very selfish. One day he fell into a deep pit and was unable to climb out. By the third day he heard the footsteps of town members walking by. He cried out for help, only to be rebuffed. The townspeople, glad to be free of him, insisted he should stay where he was so that he could enjoy the consequences of his selfishness. After this, the orisha renounced greed.

In spite of the orishas' own shortcomings, justice is reserved for the gods to enact. Retaliation is thus forbidden; however, those who are wronged know it is likely that an orisha will deal with an evil cast by reversing the spell back to the one who perpetrated it. In this sense, the Yoruba ethics have a sense of karma, in which to commit evil is to invite evil upon oneself and one's descendants.

But while proper ethical behavior is advocated and desired, these moral considerations are actually secondary to the more important process of getting the orishas to support and empower the believer. Regardless of the person's moral standing, if they feed the orishas, placate them with their favorite offerings, and offer the respect due them, then the orishas will act favorably even if what is asked for is ethically ques-

---

6. Raul Canizares, *Cuban Santería: Walking with the Night* (Rochester, N.Y.: Destiny Books, 1993), 5.

tionable. For this reason, individuals whose morality is questionable — as in the case of drug dealers, pornographers, or adulterers — are not necessarily admonished, as in other religious traditions. In fact, it is not unheard of for such people to have entered the faith to obtain assistance from the orishas in carrying out their antisocial activities.

Also, as in so many religions, sexism is ethically justified. Men are called on to protect the "weaker sex." Sexual prohibitions are usually reserved for women, who are expected to remain virgins until marriage, not a requirement for men. Once married, the avoidance of adultery is limited to the wife, while the man is only limited by the taking of another man's woman, implying, of course, that women are the property of men.

One major difference between Christian ethics and the ethics of Santería deals with the issue of redemption. For Christians, God is thought to offer the sinner divine grace. The concept of divine grace does not exist in Santería. Instead, the orishas demand perfect performance. Rather than being offered grace, the sinner must supplicate for mercy, making offerings to placate the offended orisha. Meriting forgiveness depends totally on the whim of the orisha, which may grant or withhold grace irrelevant to the sincerity of the sinner's remorse.

Consciousness and Reincarnation

Practitioners of Santería believe that all that exists in the universe contains the image of God, the very essence of Olodumare, placed there when he formed the universe. Accordingly, all of creation, in all of its manifestations, has the ability to transform itself, to experience rebirth. For humans, this process of rebirth is reflected in each individual's spiritual journey, the ability each individual has to live in harmony by remembering the original reason for existence. To live a life contrary to the original reason for existence is to live a life full of misery, malady, and mental illness.

The worldview of Santería recognizes that human beings are physical creatures infused with the spiritual. The concept of the *ori* functions similarly to the Christian notion of the soul. Literally, the word means "head," but thinking of it simply as the physical head is misleading. It refers more essentially to the source of sensation, the seat of consciousness, encompassing both the rational and spiritual aspects of human thought. According to legend, the head was the last attachment to the human body, bringing human creation to completion.

But ori is not limited to humans. All forces of nature also have it: trees, plants, minerals, winds, mountains, animals. Every element and force of nature is spiritual and self-aware. And because all elements of the universe contain the spark of Olodumare within the ori, everything that physically exists is inherently sacred. So restrictions within Santería are not viewed as capricious demands made by the orishas, but as guidelines designed to align one's ori, or consciousness, with ashé, cosmic force. The end product of such an arrangement is spiritual growth, health, prosperity, and the development of wisdom, all leading to abundant life.

Interestingly, Olodumare created only a certain, finite number of ori. This means that, once a creature's body dies, its ori can be reincarnated into another body, usually that of a descendant. It is widely believed in Santería that grandchildren contain the ori of their deceased grandparents — hence the importance of honoring and respecting both children and ancestors. More broadly, each orisha is believed to be a founder of a people, of a clan, of a community, meaning that everyone on earth, whether they know it or not, is the child of an orisha who guides and protects and, when necessary, punishes them. When an individual dies, their ori returns to Olodumare, who causes the ori to be reborn until its destiny on earth is fulfilled. In the days of slavery, some Africans in America responded to their tragic circumstances by committing suicide. The act of killing their own body was meant to deprive the slaveholder of "property," but, more importantly, it was also intended to free the slave's ori from the confines of the body so that it could be reincarnated in Africa.

Santería teaches that at the beginning of time, before the birth of humanity, every ori prostrated before Olodumare, the creator, to negotiate its assigned fate on earth. Each ori received a specific destiny from the creator, a "potential" destiny designed to unfold itself through the multitude of lives it would experience. Ergo, no person's life is an accident; individual destiny is preordained. Remembering the destiny originally negotiated for becomes the ultimate responsibility of each person and the purpose of their spiritual journey. But while destinies are preordained, they are not determined. They can be changed by appealing to the orishas. Happy destinies can be safeguarded and unhappy ones can be rectified by consulting Orúnla, the orisha of divination, who knows each ori's assigned fate because he was the only orisha present when every individual received a personal destiny from Olodumare. He can warn against evil spells or spirits designed to wreak havoc on an otherwise satisfying destiny; he can also warn how a person's own deteriorating character will create negative consequences in the future. Also determined before birth is which orisha will serve as each believer's mother and father. Every human is the child of an orisha, even if they live their entire life without recognizing to whom they belong. Neither nationality nor ethnicity nor religious affiliation matters to the orishas; they claim all human lives and will guide, protect, and if necessary, discipline their children.

Once an individual's fate and heavenly parent are chosen, the orisha of all heads, Obatalá, finishes shaping the child in the womb. No child's conception is an accident in the worldview of Santería; rather, all births are fated and part of the continuous evolution of the ori. Prior to birth, the ori embraces the tree of forgetfulness so that, once born, the new person has no memory of what occurred prior to birth or what destiny awaits.

Not only are individuals claimed as children of the orishas before birth, but every aspect of human life is controlled by certain orishas. Issues of love fall under the jurisdiction of the orisha Oshún. If a woman is pregnant, Yemayá is in control. Divination belongs to the orisha Orúnla. The santero or santera is able to affect any aspect of human existence by invoking the corresponding orisha. For example, if a person needed protection against death, they would make an offering to Oyá, who is in charge of cemeteries. Through the religion's priests, life and the phenomena that affect it can be altered. Those who are not santeros or santeras may also alter life's course by appeasing the orishas — through offering a sacrifice, making a vow, or simply lighting a candle in the color of the orisha.

Reincarnation in Santería is understood to include multiple "souls." The most important is a kind of guardian angel, known as the *eleda,* which is associated with the ori. While some claim the eleda is a guardian spirit, others believe it is the spirit of a dead person, while still others insist it is the spiritual force of the individual. The eleda must be kept fed — usually with coconut milk, although it prefers the blood of guinea fowl and pigeons. It is believed that while individuals sleep, the eleda sometimes leaves the body and roams about. At the end of each individual's time on earth, the eleda returns to its source to await reincarnation.

Egun: The Dead

Santería recognizes that there can be no orishas without the dead, the *egun*. Thus no ceremony in Santería can ever be conducted without first thanking the spirits of the ancestors or appeasing the egun. Their permission to use the knowledge handed down from generation to generation is required before any ceremony. They become the first to be questioned in any divination ritual. Though no specific festival is held for the dead, they are typically honored on the Day of the Dead, November 2nd.

Historically, the salvation of the individual has been the primary concern of Christianity. Thus the individual has been the most basic unit within the historically Christian society. This is not the case with Santería, in which the family — comprised of the living, future generations, and dead ancestors — is regarded as the basic unit. Death does not separate a person from their community; rather, the dead remain tied to and part of the faith community of which they were a part in life. The egun are therefore in a position to continue to help their loved ones and bring harm to their enemies. In Santería the dead can interact with the living. Such interactions are not perceived as evil or frightening, as they tend to be portrayed in Hollywood horror movies; instead, they are a natural aspect of existence, an existence in which the physical and spiritual converge and intermingle to the benefit of both realms. To be visited by an ancestor is a blessing for any household, for the egun may provide guidance, warn of impending dangers, grant fertility, reveal hidden opportunities, insure health, dispense wisdom, reprimand unseemly behavior, serve as an intermediary for the orishas, or instruct in spiritual growth.

Any practitioner of Santería may communicate with the dead. At times this may simply mean remembering a departed loved one and using the remembrance of the dead as a model for living: "What would father, if he were still alive, do in this situation?" This speculation, which can lead an individual to take a particular course of action, is an example of how the dead communicate and guide the living. In other cases, the dead may appear in a dream, reawakening old memories or providing other information needed to make a decision. Of course, more elaborate rituals exist by which a person can directly communicate with the dead and receive their reply. One such form of communication is the yes-and-no questions asked through the divination system known as the *Obi*, which will be discussed in greater detail in Chapter Five. The egun as spirit guide need not be a deceased family member, though they often are. They might also include Old Congo slaves, Native Americans, and Gypsies.

Communication with and care for ancestors are both a privilege and a responsibility. When the egun are prayed to, and care is taken for their advancement in the spiritual world, then they will provide protection and serve as the foundation for the individual's journey through the levels of Santería. But they have needs as well, which are met in the form of offerings. Generally speaking, these are modest: a lit candle, a bit of the foods they enjoyed in life, and a small cup of black coffee are enough to keep an egun content. If an egun's progeny refuse to offer prayers and light candles, these souls cannot advance in the spiritual world, thus binding them to the earth — and causing unconscious harm, in the form of sickness, misfortune, and death, to the egun's living descendants.

Although communication with ancestors is considered a blessing, communication with some ancestors is best avoided. Individuals who lived ruinous, unethical lives should not be relied on in death any more than in life. And those who underwent violent and sudden deaths, such as, for example, those killed in car crashes, may not fully comprehend that they are dead. Their confusion will cause their assistance to be unreliable for the living who seek guidance.

At times the egun may initiate contact with the physical world that is less than welcome. The emotions of love and hate can be so strong, so powerful that they transcend death. When the passion of lovers or enemies is interrupted by the death of one of the persons, the departed soul may begin a quest for the object of that passion within the spiritual world, a quest that may last for centuries. Unfortunately, the seeker may find that the soul they have been seeking is reincarnated in another body. Rather than losing the object of their passion again, the searching spirit will sometimes attach itself to the unsuspecting person. If the motivating passion is hatred, the person will begin to have bad luck in everything they do — business dealings, family relationships, and so on. If, however, the motivating passion is love, which quickly turns to jealousy, the person will experience failure in all romantic relationships. At times, the frustrated egun may attempt to have sexual relations with their former lover, somewhat like the legends of incubi or succubi which were popularized during the Middle Ages in Europe. At other times, the desire to be reunited with the object of the egun's passion may be so strong that it may attempt to bring the person to an early death.

Ikú

Ikú is death, a quasi-deity whose function is to dispose of life, a parallel to the Grim Reaper of Western lore. Ikú can usually be found in the graveyard, where he abides under the jurisdiction of the orisha Oyá, who is in charge of cemeteries. Anyone wishing to work with death must do so through Oyá.

Every individual has a fixed number of days of life on earth before they must return, through death, to the source of all life. The day of death cannot be extended, but it can be shortened. Suicide, the wrath of an orisha, an evil spell or curse, accidents, or the harassment of a troubled spirit can all reduce the number of days destined for life. Those who are killed prior to their allotted time remain on earth as ghosts until their original time expires, while those who live out their allotted days go directly to a type of heaven for judgment upon death. This is why oracles are so important: they warn of impending danger and seek to restore harmony so that the individual can fulfill their allotted time on earth. At times, Ikú can be cheated. When a person is facing death before their appointed time, a santero or santera can try to divert Ikú's attention. If they succeed, the infirm may live to see another day.

As has been implied, death does not indicate the cessation of life, but rather a new phase of existence. When a person dies their ori stands before Olodumare, who calls upon the individual's guardian orisha. This orisha gives an account of the faithfulness of the individual in fulfilling their destiny, in maintaining the rituals of the religion, and in keeping secret its mysteries. Olodumare and Orúnla are charged with passing judgment upon the good or bad deeds of humans. If an individual has yet to fulfill their assigned destiny, they are reincarnated into the body of a new human being and provided the opportunity of succeeding to please the orishas in this new life. In Santería there is no stigma associated with reincarnation; rather, it is considered a joyful and blessed event. Neither guilt nor curse is associated with a return to earth. Individuals are deemed unworthy only if they lived a base or self-indulging life, if they did not evolve into a self-realized person. These may be sent to a bad heaven, where they are forever forbidden from reincarnating. They are the ones who become the evil spirits that wreak havoc, aligning themselves with witches and sorcerers.

Prior to reincarnation, the ori goes to a good heaven *(orun rere)*, where the egun experience complete consciousness and contentment. Wrongs are righted, families separated by death are reunited, and existence is eternally full. This eternity is not measured by time; it is rather a dimension outside time and space in which the egun are united to the source of creation. Many in Santería also believe in an invisible realm beneath the earth, or in the ancient city of Ilé-Ifé. But the underworld is not a place of punishment. Rather, it is a womblike place of regeneration where the ori become egun, where souls become ancestral spirits. And the primeval city of Ilé-Ife, which means "House of Origins," is an invisible spiritual realm where the egun work with the orishas in maintaining cosmic harmony.

The cycle of birth and death and rebirth is not without its potential complications. For example, infertility is considered a curse because it prevents the reincarnation of ancestors, which is considered to be a woman's duty. In some cases, a woman may give birth to successive children who are either stillborn or who die in infancy. It is believed by some in Santería that she is repeatedly giving birth to the same ori; the problem is that the ancestral guardian soul, preferring heaven where they maintain the form of a child, is granted a very short lifespan by Olodumare. Others believe the ori in such a case must be possessed by a transient spirit known as an *abikú*. The abikú is known to choose a womb with an unborn child in it so that it too can be birthed, usually living for a short period. When the child dies, the abikú returns to the same womb, bringing death to future children that come forth from that womb. If a child is discovered to have an abikú, it becomes important to "chain" the child's life to earth so that the abikú will not depart and take the child's life with it. So the spirit is literally chained: a small iron anklet is placed on the child's left ankle after it is gently spanked with a small wooden broom. In rare cases, the abikú is threatened with having a finger or toe cut off, or with burning, in order to scare it into remaining on earth.

The life cycle thus elucidates the connection between consciousness and destiny. Every step toward self-realization requires death: death of the old self so that a new creature can be born. The reincarnation process continues until the individual has proven their faithfulness to their destiny, that is, until they have achieved perfect harmony between their ori and the destiny originally negotiated with Olodumare.

Itutu: A Ritual for the Time of Death

When a santero or a santera dies, a ritual called an *itutu* is performed to ease the transition of the departed to the next phrase of existence, thus ensuring their eventual reincarnation. The ceremony is intended to tranquilize, reassure, and refresh the dead person — and to ensure that their spirit does not return to torment or punish those still living for not conducting an itutu. On the day the person dies, a group of santeros or santeras gather at the funeral home. Through the casting of shells, it is determined how the sacred stones and other ritual paraphernalia of the deceased are to be disposed of; they can either be returned to nature (generally by being cast into a river or ocean) or given to another, depending on the will of the dead person's orisha. The deceased is dressed in the full regalia worn during their ordination into the faith, and the hair that was cut when the deceased originally became a priest of Santería, along with the scissors and comb used during the ordination ritual, are placed in the bier (the portable framework on which their coffin is placed).

Additionally, a sacrifice — corn leaves, vegetable coal ash, herbs, and a black chicken whose head was crushed against a floor — is placed in a small jar. Prior to interring the body, the elements of the sacrifice are thrown into the front of the grave. At a closed-door ceremony, the ritual continues with the singing of songs and hymns to the different orishas, culminating in praises to Oyá, the owner of the cemetery. Later, after a year has passed, a ritual known as the *levantamiento del plato* (the raising of the dish) takes place. An animal is sacrificed to the deceased's soul and a *bembe* (dance festival) is conducted to honor the dead person along with all others who died in the previous year. It is believed that the deceased drinks the blood of the sacrifice. The ceremony is intended to bid a final farewell to the deceased.

Evil

When I was a child, people of different Latino ethnicities would visit our apartment to consult the orishas. Their visits did not concern me; I usually ignored them and went about the normal activities of a ten-year-old. But I remember the visit of one woman because she was not Hispanic but Italian-American. She had heard of my parents' reputation and had come seeking their help. My parents' poor command of English and her inability to speak Spanish meant that I was to serve as interpreter. After my father warned me of the importance of accurately translating everything that was to be said, I entered the *cuarto de los santos,* the room in our apartment that was reserved for the orishas. After casting the cowrie shells a few times my father asked me to tell the woman that she was sleeping with a married man who had two small children. She was obviously embarrassed to hear me repeat my father's words in English. Then my father threw the shells again and asked me to tell her that she wanted him to cast a spell that would cause the man to leave his family and marry her. The woman confirmed what my father divined. At that point my father ended the session by informing the woman, through me, that Santería exists to do good, not evil, and that breaking up a home was evil. There would be no charge for the consultation. The woman left disappointed. Then my father turned to the other santeros and santeras in the room and said that she would no doubt find someone who would willingly do what she asked.

To practitioners of Santería like my parents, the orishas control the forces of good; death, disease, curses, fighting, prison, loss, and so on are not their domain. Evil is better understood as the result of society's excess, caused by disrespect for the laws of humans and Olodumare. It is true that if ashé can be manipulated to bring about good, then those who are tempted by power or lured by riches can also manipulate it to bring about evil. But even though individuals within the faith do not always use it that way, Santería is viewed by the vast majority of its followers as a force for good in the world.

Brujería

Before concluding this section on what some call the "dark side of Santería," we should look briefly at another kind of spirituality with connections to the faith. These developed mostly in the Congo culture of central Africa and have typically been associated with *brujería* or *bilongo,* the Spanish words for witchcraft. The most popular manifestations are known as the *Reglas de Congo* (Rule of the Congo): *Palo* and its variations *Palo Monte* and *Palo Mayombe.*[7] Although an entire book could be written on each one of these manifestations, and while each has its own internal nuances and variations, we can make a few generalizations here.

All of them are very secret societies, neither proselytizing for new converts nor attempting to interact religiously with other groups. They are extremely reticent concerning their rituals and their belief systems. Probably their secrecy is rooted in the oppression they underwent (and continue to endure) in Cuba. Cuban children in the last century were commonly frightened or threatened with stories of being kidnapped and cannibalized by the black practitioners of brujería; its practitioners became the Cuban equivalent of the North American "bogeyman." Because brujería's myths center upon death, it was believed that this form of spirituality specialized in works that bring harm or death to others through the use of spiritual powers.

Those who become santeras or santeros cannot be ordained into Palo because of the higher prestige associated with Santería. However, a person can begin by first entering Palo and then progressing to Santería. The ordination ritual for Palo requires the initiate to wear clothes that have been buried in a grave for three weeks, and culminates in the acquisition of a human tibia wrapped in black cloth. This bone is used as a scepter to rule over the forces of darkness. Unlike

---

7. The Ekoi people of the Calabar Coast in Africa formed a network of all-male secret societies known as *Abakuá* when they were brought to the Americas. Often considered another permutation of brujería, though not a variation of Palo, Abakuá has a reputation for redressing even small offenses with violence and is therefore feared.

Santería, human remains, especially bones, are a component of many rituals. Depending on where they live, readers may have seen newspaper headlines reporting the desecration of graves from which parts of corpses have been stolen for ritual purposes. For example, on October 8, 2002, two men, a father and son, were arrested in Newark, New Jersey, when a search of their home revealed stolen body parts believed to have come from area mausoleums and cemeteries, which had experienced a rash of robberies. Three human skulls and an assortment of other bones (legs, arms, and feet) were found in a ceremonial cauldron set up in the basement of the men's three-family home.

Because of rituals like this, the Reglas de Congo have been labeled the "dark side of Santería." According to Baba Oloye Ifa Karade, a Yoruba priest, "Palo Mayombe is a mutation of Yoruba in much the way that satanism, which sprang from Christianity, is a misguided mutation. It is more oriented towards spells and does not bring forth a level of salvation in its practitioners."[8]

Central to the belief system of Palo is human association with certain spirits of the dead. One practice of its followers is to find a restless spirit, usually the soul of a criminal or mentally ill person that was condemned to the bad heaven and forbidden reincarnation. Such a spirit, filled with hatred, envy, and anger, will be susceptible to manipulation by a human by whom it might profit. For the cost of a few copper coins and a white candle, a disembodied spirit can be hired to serve as a guide through life for the follower of Palo, informing them about what is occurring both in the spiritual and physical dimensions. Such a guide can reveal upcoming dangers or opportunities of which the individual can take advantage.

Additionally, a spirit might be hired to torment or to visit harm on a particular person. In such a case the victim, suspecting from the negative turn of events that something is wrong, would have to consult a santero or a santera to determine the cause of their misfortune. Once it is discovered that the person is being tormented by an evil spirit, a long process of sacrifices and *dispojos* (cleansing) must take place to get rid of the spirit. (While santeros and santeras may refuse to do harm, it is important for them to know how to counteract evil spells. They are

8. Ronald Smothers, "Two Accused of Robbing Graves for Cult's Rituals in Newark," *The New York Times* (October 9, 2002).

not responsible if, in the reversal of a spell, the person who originally cast the spell meets the fate intended to befall the victim.)

Movies and television have exposed most Euroamericans to the concept of the voodoo doll: some evildoer makes a rag doll, sticks some pins into it, and their enemy suddenly experiences sharp pain in the same body parts where the pins have been stuck. This Hollywood image has some basis in real Palo rituals. A doll may be fashioned from old clothes worn by the intended victim or a wax image of them may be made and then dressed in scraps of their clothes. In either case, the doll is given the same name as the target. Oyá, the orisha of the cemeteries, is then invoked on numerous occasions to claim this person. Eventually, the doll is buried in the cemetery. With time, according to Palo, so will the person the doll represented.

Central to the follower of Palo's power is the *nganga*, also known as the *prenda*. This is a small bag or cauldron containing ingredients which represent the elements of the world. Among the stones, sticks, soil, insects, bird or animal carcasses, herbs, and so on, are human remains — again, usually a piece of bone, ideally a human skull with remains of the brain still present. The remains of a murderer or lunatic are especially prized because their spirits will be willing to carry out bad acts without reservations. In any case, the bone is used to capture the spirit of the deceased. This spirit becomes the source of the individual's power in return for the blood of sacrifices by which the prenda is kept fed.

Although the general population perceives Palo as witchcraft, its practitioners insist that it can be used for both good and evil. In fact, those who do good works, operating with the spirits of good people, are sometimes referred to as *nganga cristiana* (Christian nganga), while those who do evil works and operate with the spirits of criminals and the insane, are referred to as *nganga judía* (Jewish nganga). The good manifestation often uses the symbol of a crucifix, while the malevolent one usually uses a railroad spike. It is hard to ignore the anti-Semitism common among the Latin American culture as these terms are imposed to distinguish good from evil. No doubt the connection of the word "Jewish" to the evil practice of nganga is due to the spurious accusation that the Jews killed Jesus. Nevertheless, what is termed nganga cristiana constitutes practices designed to cure the sick, bring peace and harmony, and help those who are distressed, while the practices of nganga judía attempt to extract vengeance, or humble, humiliate, and domesticate one's enemies. Such practices can cause illness, break up marriages, create financial difficulties, even bring death to one's enemy. For the practitioner of nganga judía, the religion is primarily about power. Moral consequences of the spells cast onto the intended victim are unimportant, as there is no concept of a final reckoning at which one must justify one's actions, no concept of karma where negative acts will return to those who commit them, and no concept of eternal punishment. All that exists is power, and to learn how to manipulate it ensures survival in life.

While some classify these religious expressions as sects of Santería, or simply think of them as one and the same, the Santería faith community does not regard them as legitimate expressions or manifestations of itself. Santería insists that its purpose is to do good, creating harmony among humans and their environment, regardless of the abuses committed by those who are disenfranchised seeking power and security in this lifetime.

Chapter 2   **Creation**

The Western "religions of the book" — Judaism, Christianity, and Islam — rely on their sacred texts to understand God, God's revelation to humanity, and the practical implications of that revelation. But whether one turns to the Hebrew Bible, the New Testament, or the Qur'ān, interpretation of the text is of central importance. For example, did the world come into being in a way similar to the creation account in the book of Genesis, or is that story best understood as the mythology of pre-modern individuals attempting to understand God's creativity? When the text claims that creation occurred in six days, must those days be construed as literal twenty-four-hour periods, or can a day be understood to be a million, if not a billion years? Conservatives tend toward more literal interpretations of the texts; liberals often advocate more symbolic ones. At times dissension about issues such as these has led to schisms, perhaps best illustrated by the numerous denominations existing within Christianity.

In Santería, the orishas' lives are recounted as legends known as *patakis*. For most santeros and santeras, such stories are not interpreted literally; whether a particular pataki is history or myth is not important. The purpose of the story is to provide guidance and practical help for believers in the here and now. According to anthropologist Clifford Geertz, legends or myths can provide both a model *of* reality and a model *for* reality. While they inform the day-to-day dynamics of life, they are also capable of shaping those dynamics.[1] When a pataki is re-cited, each orisha, person, animal, herb, sacred tree, and object con-tains symbolic meaning, pointing to a truth that exists beyond its lit-eral meaning. The stories become reference points that provide divine revelation on the particular life issue being faced by the person seeking the orishas' assistance. Or, to put it another way, the issue being faced by the individual imploring the orishas becomes the context by which the pataki is interpreted. Hence the same story can be interpreted to-tally differently depending on the circumstances of the individual for whom the story is recited.

The patakis preserve the collective memory of displaced people. Cultural norms, traditions, and customs are thus passed down from one generation to the next. Because each new generation hears the patakis in a social context very different from those of their ancestors, the patakis must be reinterpreted to address contemporary spiritual di-lemmas, needs, and concerns. In a sense, the patakis of the faith cannot be rendered dogmatically, for stagnant interpretations lead to lifeless religiosity, which is useless to the believer in a religion based on coping with the struggles of reality. The myths and stories of Santería require new readings through the eyes of each succeeding generation, that is, from the social location of the one doing the reading. Only in context do the patakis become real and significant to the believer.

To read a pataki out of context, disconnected from a questioner dealing with a specific issue, makes interpretation difficult. Unlike Ju-daism, Christianity, and Islam, which begin with the text, Santería be-gins with the context of the believer who approaches the orishas with a specific area of concern. The orishas then reveal a pataki to be inter-preted by the santero or santera. Consequently, there is no one inter-pretation applicable to all individuals at all times. Interpretations are highly individualized.

Because the stories themselves are less important than the con-texts in which they are told, accuracy in details or contradictions within the stories may become the source of lively debate among fol-lowers of Santería, but are ultimately unimportant in verifying belief. In fact, inconsistency is to be expected given the different contexts of

---

1. Clifford Geertz, *The Interpretation of Culture: Selected Essays* (New York: Basic Books, 1973), 124.

believers. For example, patakis told in the Western Hemisphere differ somewhat from those told in Africa. In the West, all the orishas are blood-related, while in Africa such family ties do not necessarily exist between them. One explanation for this difference is that the vastly different tribal origins of slaves in the Caribbean kept them separated, if not enemies. By making the orishas interrelated, historically separate (if not hostile) African nations who found themselves expatriated were able to see themselves united as brothers and sisters, one nation, one religion, against a common oppressor. Even within the West, the stories differ between nations. The orishas as understood in Cuba through Santería differ substantially from how they are understood in Voodoo in New Orleans or Haiti. A great deal of disparity can even exist between house-temples within the same nation, if not the same city or town, again emphasizing that the present life situation of a devotee is the point of departure in understanding the pataki.

Keeping these inherent ambiguities about patakis in mind, we now turn to the legends of Santería, cognizant that the stories as they are presented here mean little because they are not directly connected with the needs of a particular person seeking the orishas for power to overcome their circumstances and restore them to harmony with their destiny. Nevertheless, by reading the patakis accepted by most santeros and santeras, the reader will be able to better understand the orishas, and thus Santería.

In the Beginning

In the beginning was ashé, pure cosmic energy. Ashé was with Olodumare, and ashé was Olodumare. The beginning of ashé can be traced to the moment when time and space came into Being. Through ashé all things came into being, and all things will return to ashé, the source, which provides the strength and power to fulfill the purpose of each created thing. Olodumare, the supreme God, is above all else that exists (see Table 1 on p. 34). It matters little whether one worships the Muslim manifestation of Olodumare known as Allah, or the Hebrew manifestation known as Yahweh, or the Christian manifestation known as God. These different masks worn by Olodumare still exhibit his awesome power and justice, punishing those who disobey his mandates and re-

Table 1: Spiritual Hierarchy of Ashé

Olodumare
orishas or santos
egun — the dead
humans
animals and plants
charms and talismans

warding those who are faithful. It matters still less if worship occurs in a mosque, a synagogue, a cathedral, or in a forest. What matters is that the Supreme Being be recognized.

Olodumare exists without form, having neither beginning nor end. He is the universe with all of its elements. All that exists is an expression of Olodumare (a concept best understood by Eurocentric theologians as pantheism). Because every aspect of creation contains the essence of Olodumare, humans who listen carefully to the rocks, trees, animals, and so on can hear the resonating word of God, and thus learn how to live life from every manifestation of creation. Ashé, the substance of Olodumare, is a transcendent world force or "current" that undergirds all that comprises the earth. It is a force that while incomprehensible can still be understood. Those who discover ashé's mysteries are able to use it for the betterment of humans. This sacred energy becomes the power, grace, blood, and life force of all reality, embracing mystery, and divinity. Ashé is absolute, illimitable, pure power, non-definite and non-definable. It is what some scholars would call a non-anthropomorphic form of theism.[2]

Olodumare can be understood as the Prime Mover, the Ultimate Source, the First Cause, the Designer of all that exists. Neither created

2. Pierre Verger, "The Yoruba High God: A Review of the Source," *Odu: Journal of Yoruba and Related Studies*, Vol. 2, No. 2 (1966): 36-39.

Table 2: Names of Olodumare

Name	Appellation	Function
Alaaye	the Living One	Gives life to all of creation
Elemi	Owner of Life	Provides nourishment to creation
Olofi	God on earth	Serves as humanity's personal God
Olojo Oni	Controller of daily actions	Guides humanity's daily activities
Olori	Universal Soul	Dwells in each individual's soul
Olorún	Owner of the Heavens	Provides light and energy as the sun

nor begotten, Olodumare is the origin of all creation. As creator, ruler, and judge, Olodumare is immortal, omniscient, omnipotent, and beyond the total comprehension of mortals. Within him are many different facets or persons. He is Elemi, owner of life; Olorun, owner of the sky, typically identified with the sun; and Olojo Oni, controller of daily occurrences. However it is as Olofi that Olodumare is humanity's personal god (see Table 2 above). Believers in Santería most commonly worship Olofi, the personification of Olodumare. To them, Jesus Christ is the mask of Olofi. Olofi is coequal with two other aspects of Olodumare, Nzame and Baba Nkwa. Christians will see parallels here with the Holy Trinity of their faith, but while there are similarities we need to be wary of imposing Christian paradigms on Santería in order to make it more palatable to Western sensibilities.

At first, there was only sky above and a watery, marshy waste below. No land existed for humans to dwell upon. Supreme in the sky was Olodumare the almighty, the owner of all destinies, the God that is above all gods. Now, it was Nzame as Olodumare who created all that exists. In four days, all was completed, leaving the fifth day set apart for rest and for the worship of the Supreme Being. After bringing into existence the planets, stars, plants, and animals, Nzame asked Olofi and Baba Nkwa what they thought of his handiwork. Although impressed, they noted that his creation lacked an intelligent being to rule over all. Agreeing, Nzame formed the first man, in his own image, out of mud. When finished, he breathed immortal life into this man, whom he called Omo Oba.

With time, Omo Oba became conceited because of his beauty and strength, believing himself to be equal with Olodumare. Offended, Nzame, using lightning bolts, set out to destroy all life on earth, forgetting that he had made Omo Oba immortal. So even though all life on the planet was destroyed, Omo Oba was unharmed. He attempted to find refuge in the bowels of the earth, where he became trapped by the smothering fire of Nzame's fury. Yet he did not die, and every so often he is able to escape his fiery confinement to tempt humans to abandon the ways of Olodumare.

The Second Creation

The total destruction of the first creation reduced the world to a scorched desert. For centuries, nothing existed on earth but smoldering fire. Smoke filled the skies, forming dense, impenetrable clouds. According to one version of this second creation story, Olodumare eventually desired to re-create the earth. So he converted the clouds into water, which fell on the fire and extinguished it. Where the fires burned most fiercely, the grounds were left with lower elevation. As the rains fell, these low points filled with water, creating the great oceans we see today. Here, in the huge crevices between the cooled rocks, the orisha Yemayá was born. Yemayá laid her body across the earth and exclaimed, "My womb is hurting!" Then from her womb came forth all the rivers, orishas, and creatures great and small.

Another pataki tells of Olodumare — again as Nzame, Olofi, and Baba Nkwa — creating new life forms. They created a being to rule the earth; however, this being was not given the gift of immortality. His name was Obatalá. Olofi took charge of this new creation, while Nzame and Baba Nkwa went to other parts of the universe to start new marvelous works. Realizing that Obatalá would need companionship, Olofi gathered numerous smooth stones and projected his ashé upon them, thus birthing the orishas. Among the first orishas created were Orúnla the diviner and Olocun, queen of the ocean's depths. These new orishas all lived in heaven — with the exception of Olocun, who made her abode in the depths of the water-covered earth. Some claim Olocun is androgynous, manifested as a mermaid; others claim she is a great marine serpent or a siren. Regardless, before long she was in constant battle with Olorun (that is, Olodumare in his sky god aspect) for the domination of the earth. Every time Olorun would send something to earth in hopes of establishing a foothold, Olocun's waters would swallow it up.

This saddened Obatalá, who desired to see life. With Orúnla serving as counselor, he set out to establish the foundation of what today is the earth. For this reason it is Obatalá who represents the force by which the universe is created. Hanging from a gold chain, Obatalá spilled some loose soil he had stored in a snail's shell. As soon as the soil touched the water he let loose a five-toed chicken, which immediately started to dig into the spilled earth. Wherever this earth was dispensed, solid ground appeared and the water could not flood it. The larger piles of soil became mountains while the lower stretches became valleys. After a while, enough solid ground existed that Obatalá could let go of the golden chain and descend to earth. In this fashion he appropriated some of Olocun's domain. The first firm ground established was the city of Ilé-Ife.

For as far as Obatalá could see, only dry land existed. So he dug a hole and planted a palm nut. Within seconds, a fully grown tree sprung up from the ground. From this palm tree with sixteen branches located in the center of Ilé-Ifé, the creation of the world spread outward. The mature tree immediately dropped palm nuts on the ground; these in turn immediately grew to maturity. In this fashion, the land was quickly forested. With time, the other orishas became curious with this new land created by Obatalá. One by one, they left their domain in the sky and began to follow him to the earth.

A third version of the creation story holds that as different parts of creation were brought into being by Olofi, different orishas were born. For example, when the volcanoes were formed, the orisha in charge of them, Aganyú, was born. As grass, herbs, plants, and trees spouted, the orisha who cares for them, Osain, was born. When the orisha Oko was born, crops began to develop and yield produce. And as the rivers took form, so did Oshún. Shortly after creating Obatalá, Olofi created a wife for him named Oddudúa; the two of them begat several orishas. In the beginning the orishas were powerless, but with time, Olofi became weary with his responsibilities and bestowed upon them aspects of his powers.

Eventually the time came to create humans. There are two basic stories of how this came about. In one, Olofi fashioned human beings out of mud and breathed life into them. But he did not make heads for them. These humans straggled aimlessly throughout creation. Obatalá was asked to complete the creation of humans by forming and giving them heads. He did so, and for this reason Obatalá is considered the Lord of human heads. In the second version of the story, Obatalá was commissioned by Olofi to create humans. While forming the bodies of humans, Obatalá would take short breaks and refresh himself with palm wine, and as time passed he started to become intoxicated. After a while, the bodies started to reflect deformities, which is the explanation for those born with physical disabilities. Repentant, he forsook alcohol and became the patron of those born deformed.

Once created, these new people began to build huts like Obatalá, and with time, Ilé-Ife became a prosperous city-state. All people were equal before Olofi and they lived together as equals in Ilé-Ife. Nevertheless, they were eager for there to be differences among themselves. Some began to demand larger properties from Obatalá; others asked for more cattle; still others requested either darker or lighter skin pigmentation. The orisha soon tired of all these requests, so he decided simply to give everyone what they wanted. He also created different languages so that they could truly be different from one another. Unfortunately, those who received more land began to look down at those who had smaller plots. The same held true for those who received larger herds. People whose skin color or language differed became suspicious of each other. Soon people began to group themselves by skin tone and language. These groups left Ilé-Ife, seeking lands that they could inhabit without having to share. Thus the entire earth came to be populated, and thus people with different languages and ethnicities distrust one another.

To read this story explaining physical disabilities literally leaves the reader with the impression that Obatalá is an unreliable and flawed deity, a drunkard whose intoxication brought imperfection to humanity. To read the Yoruba myths in this fashion justifies Eurocentric scholars in their dismissal of African spiritualities as primitive if not savage. Yet such a reading is simplistic, ignoring the deeper truth of the story. The purpose of the story is not to comment on Obatalá's drunkenness; rather, it is to highlight a truth about reality. In this world, the possibility for imperfection exists; sometimes it comes in the form of physical disabilities. But regardless of these imperfections — perhaps even because of them — Obatalá cares for and protects those who suffer from disability. And those who wish to take advantage of those born disabled need to beware, for he sides with the disabled, serving as their patron.

Whichever creation story a practitioner of Santería prefers, it is invariably Olodumare who animates human beings by breathing the breath of life into them. Hence each creation story reveals that the source of physical existence and human consciousness is Olodumare.

Marriage

According to some very old African legends, men and women lived separately, seldom coming together. Each group established its own communities and lived independent of the opposite sex. When the men felt the urge to reproduce, they would invade the lands of women, gratify their sexual instincts, and then return to their own lands. The women would eventually give birth to the product of these unions and take on the full responsibility of raising the children. One day the women, understandably less than happy with this arrangement, hid from the men who had invaded their territories seeking amorous liaisons. Unable to gratify their needs, the men returned to their territories unsatisfied. In their frustration, they declared war on the women. Prior to entering battle, the men consulted Obatalá for guidance. The great orisha listened patiently to the men's diatribe against the women. He requested an offering from the men to ensure their success, but several among them came to the conclusion that offerings were unnecessary to overcome women in the battlefield. All that was needed to bring the women into submission was a beating.

Meanwhile, the women discovered what the men were planning to do. They too went to Obatalá for guidance. Again, the great orisha requested offerings. Unlike the men, the women, in humble submission, made offerings to Obatalá. On the night before the battle, torrential rain fell upon the encampment of the men, soaking their wooden weapons and rendering them useless. The rains soon created flooding, placing the men in great peril. They began to cry out to the women for help. The women agreed to help, each taking one of the men into her home. The next day Olofi decreed that each man was to take as his wife the woman in whose house he found refuge. Thus marriage was established to bring an end to the battle of the sexes.[3]

The Commandments

Inherent within creation are ethical principles by which human life should be fashioned. To guide humanity in conducting their lives, Olofi, through Obatalá, gave humans eleven commandments to follow. They are:

1. You shall not steal.
2. You shall not kill, except self-defense.
3. You shall not eat the flesh of humans.
4. You shall live in peace with your neighbors.
5. You shall not covet your neighbor's possessions.
6. You shall not use the name of your God in vain.
7. You shall honor your mother and father.
8. You shall not ask for more than what I have provided, and you shall be content with your fate.
9. You shall neither fear death nor commit suicide.
10. You shall keep and respect my laws.
11. You shall teach my commandments to your children.

The Great Incest

With time, disharmony fell upon the house of Obatalá. Whenever he was away, his new wife Yemmú and son Oggún, orisha of iron, had sex-

---

3. It is interesting to note that, despite the women's obedience to Obatalá and their benevolence toward the men, marriage in Yoruba society was extremely patriarchal. Unlike women, men were free to marry as many women as they could support and protect. Divorce was not common. Families arranged marriages, usually for the benefit of the entire group. The marriage procedure was established on four main principles: (1) the couple's parents had to know one another; (2) the bride, as possession, was understood to be a gift given by her father; (3) the couple was required to agree to the arrangement; and (4) in the event of the husband's death, his brother was obligated to marry the widow if she had no children.

ual relations. Some in Santería claim that the relationship was consensual; others claim Yemmú was the victim of rape. Eventually the sexual encounter became a daily occurrence and was found out by Elegguá, Oggún's brother. Unable to bear the shame caused by his brother and mother, yet aware he lacked the strength to overcome his more powerful brother, he decided to trick his father Obatalá into coming home early. The next day, when Oggún and Yemmú were together, Elegguá ran to his father imploring him to come quickly home, for he thought he heard his mother crying and feared for her safety.

Obatalá ran home, only to catch his son and wife copulating. Fearing his father's wrath, Oggún begged for mercy, asking that he himself be allowed to utter his own curse. Obatalá relented. Oggún decreed that he would never again know peace or rest, but would work day and night for all eternity. Furthermore, he would divulge the secrets of making iron to humanity so that he would no longer rule over anything, not even the metal. Still enraged, Obatalá turned to his wife Yemmú. Rather than cursing her directly, he cursed her next child, swearing to bury it alive.

Some time later, Yemmú gave birth to Orúnla. Obatalá, true to his word, ordered Elegguá to bury his brother alive. Elegguá, the trickster, found a gigantic ceiba tree and buried his brother up to his neck in the tree's dark shadow. As time went on, Orúnla learned the secrets of divination from the ceiba tree. His fame as a diviner spread, and people came from miles around to have their fortunes told. In exchange, they fed and cared for the buried Orúnla. With time, Obatalá, thinking his son was dead, repented for having his son buried and regretted his harsh judgment. When Elegguá heard this, he took his father to see Orúnla, very much alive although buried up to his neck. With reunion all was forgiven, and Orúnla was released from his grave. But he did not wish to leave the tree that had served as his mother. In compliance with Orúnla's wishes, Obatalá turned the tree into a round wooden tray, which Orúnla has used ever since in determining futures.

The Departure of Olodumare

At first, all creation lived in relative harmony. But with the passage of time, humans began to make war among themselves. Olofi had difficulty understanding the ways of humans. As the very embodiment of peace, he was puzzled with human strife, competition, and fighting. Although it had been easy for him to create the earth, he struggled to ensure that it functioned efficiently. He was further disturbed by Ayáguna, the orisha of pendency, who seemed to encourage discord among humans. When Olofi reproached Ayáguna, the orisha explained that for the world to develop and progress, there must be competition. When two individuals fight for the same thing, the one who is more capable will succeed, ensuring the forward movement of civilization. Disillusioned by Ayáguna's response, yet convinced of the truth uttered by the orisha, Olofi thought it best if he ceased to interfere in the matters of humans.

So Olodumare as Olofi decided to depart from the earth, a decision also motivated by the orishas. The orishas began to tax Olofi, demanding more and more ashé. Some even plotted to dethrone Olofi. The orishas conspired to challenge Olofi as master of the world, believing he was becoming too old and weak, even though they were all afraid of directly confronting him. One day, while a group of them were discussing how to overcome him, they remembered that Olofi was deathly afraid of mice. They decided to trap him in a house full of mice, convinced that he would either die of fright or run away forever. As they plotted, though, they did not notice that Elegguá, who was not part of their cabal, was hidden by the door, as he often was. When the day on which they decided to kill Olofi came, the orishas invited him to a party. As soon as he entered the house the doors shut behind him and mice were released. Unable to escape, Olofi tried to hide, but with every door he opened, more mice appeared. But when it seemed that all was lost, Elegguá appeared and began to eat all of the mice, one by one, thus saving Olofi from certain death.

Though this plot failed, Olofi was tired of being involved in the affairs of humans. So he left the earth, giving it over to the orishas. He is seen today as a kind of retired or absentee landlord, never coming down to earth. Because the universe is so vast, he no longer has the time or the inclination to become directly involved in the affairs of humans. As the supreme Creator of all that exists, he still demands and expects the awe, respect, and veneration of his creation. He is still mentioned in every prayer, and still holds the secrets to creation; he has simply relegated all earthly matters to the orishas. He dispenses his ashé to the orishas, but none of them will ever become his equal.

Santeras and santeros neither worship nor offer sacrifices to Olodumare, for the supreme God is too great, holy, and high to intermingle with the pettiness of human affairs. Besides, why offer sacrifices to a God that needs nothing from humans? For this there are the orishas, who have a need for sacrifices and to whom humans have recourse. Olodumare, on the other hand, is distant; he created an abyss between his home and this world when he abdicated his earthly involvement to search for his own happiness. In fact, no one in the universe knows where he resides except for two orishas, Obatalá and Elegguá.

The Flood

After Olofi left the earth, Obatalá was left to reign as supreme orisha. As he had done before, he continued to expand the amount of solid ground on the earth. In doing so he encroached on the domain of the powerful Olocun, the orisha of the ocean's depths (see Figure 1 on p. 44). Olofi had made the error of entrusting Olocun with considerable power, and one day she began to challenge Obatalá's supremacy by reclaiming the territory she had lost to the land Obatalá created. Enraged that humanity ignored and neglected her, she endeavored to destroy all human life by creating a great worldwide flood. She summoned the waters to rise, creating a flood that covered the entire earth. During this great world flood, the great ceiba tree was the only thing not covered by the rising waters. Those who found refuge there, whether animal or human, survived. Thus all life was not destroyed, and for this reason the ceiba is considered sacred. The orishas, along with a handful of fortunate humans and animals, found refuge from the flood in the heavens, climbing a silver ladder sent down by Obatalá, who happened to be visiting Olofi when the flood occurred.

It turned out that Olocun in her anger was indeed too powerful for Obatalá. She would have succeeded in destroying all life if Olofi had not intervened. In spite of his commitment not to interfere in the affairs of humans, he assisted Obatalá in regaining his authority. Together they shackled Olocun to the bottom of the sea with seven iron chains. Although chained, she still makes her anger known today, attempting to reclaim the land in the form of tidal waves and rough seas that overturn boats, cause shipwrecks, and drown sailors. Additionally,

Figure 1. The image on the left is Olocun, the androgynous queen of the ocean's depths, dressed in blue and wearing the beads that correspond to her. On the right is the image of Changó, the orisha who rules lightning, thunder, and fire, dressed in red, carrying his double-edged wooden ax.

Photo taken by author at *la casa de los orishas* (House of the Orishas) in La Habana, Cuba.

Olocun did make a request of Obatalá, which he granted her: every day, one human life would be given to her. Those who drown are believed to be those whom Olocun claims per the terms of her agreement with Obatalá.

The Orishas

But who are these powerful entities ruling the world in the Supreme Being's stead? Loosely speaking, Santería recognizes the existence of one God, Olodumare. Orishas, by contrast, are secondary gods, created by Olodumare as Olofi, who rule certain parts of nature for him, communicating the ultimate wishes of the creator to his creation. They personify these forces of nature, and to worship an orisha is to give reverence to the force it represents. These orishas are the receptacles of Olodumare's ashé, and they manipulate the ashé they have been given within the cosmic forces they govern.

Together the orishas form the Yoruba pantheon, similar in many respects to the pantheons of Greek and Roman mythology (see Table 3 on p. 46). The exact number of orishas is not certain; some sources list over 1,700 while others list 400 plus one (400 being a mystical number symbolizing a multitude). Regardless, only a handful are renowned in the Western Hemisphere. The eighteen most worshiped orishas in Santería are Obatalá, Elegguá, Orúnla, Yemayá, Osain, Changó, Ochosi, Oggún, Babalú-Ayé, Oshún, Oyá, Olocun, Aganyú, Oko, Inle, Ósun, Obba, and the twins, the Ibeyi. Of these, the first six are considered major orishas. The primary difference between the Yoruba pantheon and those of Greece and Rome is that devotees of Santería are capable of communicating with their gods. Through the reading of oracles and through spiritual possession by orishas, an intimate relationship is created between the gods and their followers, one in which communication occurs both ways.

The orishas serve in this way as "guardian angels" to human beings. But in a very real sense, humans and the orishas exist in a codependent relationship. Humans need the ashé of the orishas, manifested as guidance and protection, while the orishas need to be fed by humans the ashé of sacrifices. If humans were denied ashé, their lives would be meaningless; they would fumble aimlessly with no way to un-

Table 3: Comparison of Yoruba Methodology to Greek and Roman

Function	Greek	Roman	Yoruba
Ruler of the Gods	Zeus	Jupiter	Obatalá
The Gods' Messenger	Hermes	Mercury	Elegguá
God of Divination	Apollo	Faunus	Orúnla
God of Thunder	Gebeleizis	Fulgora	Changó
God of the Hunt	Artemis	Diana	Ochosi
God of War	Ares	Mars	Oggún
God of Healing	Asklepios	Aesculapius	Babalú-Ayé
God of the Sea	Poseidon	Neptune	Yemayá
Goddess of Love	Aphrodite	Venus	Oshún
God of the Underworld	Hades	Pluto	Oyá
God of Nature	Pan	Inuus	Osain
God of the Volcano	Hephaestus	Vulcan	Aganyú
God of Agriculture	Demeter	Ceres	Oko
God of Science	Athena	Minerva	Inle
God of Wifely Role	Hera	Juno	Obba
Heavenly Twins	Kastor & Polydeukes	Castor & Pollux	Ibeyi

derstand their destinies. If the orishas were denied ashé, on the other hand, they would cease to exist. Orishas, unlike Olodumare, can go out of existence, and their survival depends on humans' offerings of ashé. So without humans, there could be no orishas. If there are no blood offerings, then there is no power to work for the benefit of human devotees. When offerings are given, the orishas can and usually do become responsive to the needs of the individual making the offering.

When an animal is sacrificed, for example, to the orisha Babalú-Ayé, the practitioner is in fact making an offering to the part of Olodumare exemplified in this particular orisha. Another way of understanding this is that the orisha Babalú-Ayé manifests Olodumare's ashé through the action of healing. Every major activity, every natural phenomenon, every type of human characteristic, and every living thing contains ashé, and falls under the authority of a patron orisha. When a person pleases an orisha, the ashé the latter supervises can be channeled for the benefit of the person. The ultimate goal of believers is to acquire more ashé so that they can obtain what they desire — usually health, love, or wealth (see Table 4 on pp. 48-49). Ashé is offered to the orisha (through means of a sacrifice, food offering, or lit candle) who rules over the cosmic sphere that governs the object of desire. In return, the orisha is strengthened by the ashé of the offering and will grant the worshiper's petition. But what offering is acceptable? Through the oracles humans are able to determine what offering needs to be made.

The prestige and power of any orisha is directly proportionate to the prestige and power of the community that worships it. Such power is reciprocal. In Africa, strong city-states were believed to be protected by powerful orishas, while weaker city-states were protected by minor ones. Prior to the movement of the Yoruba religion to the Western Hemisphere, inhabitants of each Yoruba city-state served as priests to a sole orisha. As Africans of different communities were thrown together to create one slave community, all the orishas began to be worshiped by the entire community. Still the reputation of the orishas is dependent on those who provide worship. An orisha failing to provide results to its devotees can be discarded in favor of a more powerful one. In this sense the believer in the orishas does have some leverage. Prayers can contain strongly-worded pleas for help, reminding the god of the reciprocal nature of their relationship. Veiled threats of abandonment by the devotee can motivate the orisha to grant the request.

Yet making offerings does not automatically guarantee blessings from an orisha. Unlike the God of Christianity, Judaism, and Islam, the orishas are morally ambivalent — more like humans, or like the gods of Greek and Roman myth. In Santería there is not one being to personify

Table 4: Influence of the Orishas

Orisha	Has power over	Patron of	Personal characteristics
Obatalá	all things pertaining to human heads; bones; all things white	fatherhood	regal; wise; peaceful; pure; serene; patient
Elegguá	crossroads; fate	doorways; messengers; tricksters; justice	playful; unscrupulous; clever; mischievous; childlike
Orúnla	human destiny	the oracles of Ifá	wise; sagacious
Changó	fire; thunder and lightning; semen	revenge upon enemies	passionate; sensual; risk-taking; arrogant; prone to violence
Ochosi	hunting; jails; courtrooms	those seeking legal justice	impartial; quick-witted; alert
Oggún	war; employment; hospitals; minerals; iron and other metals	all human effort	militant; belligerent; hardworking; strong
Babalú-Ayé	smallpox and other illnesses	beggars; the sick; the disabled	gentle; compassionate; humble
Yemayá	ocean	womanhood; motherhood	maternal; dignified; nurturing

Orisha	Has power over	Patron of	Personal characteristics
Oshún	gold; rivers; lower abdomen; fertility	eros; love; marriage	seductive
Oyá	cemeteries; death; wind; human respiratory system	Niger River in Africa; ancestors	tempestuous; violent; sensual; authoritarian
Osain	nature; forests; herbs	houses	solitary; rational; chaste
Aganyú	volcanos; earthquakes	those with high blood pressure and fevers	fiery; violent; muscular
Oko	agriculture	delicate matters	peacemaker
Inle	fertility of water to produce crops	fishermen; healing of human illnesses	studious; scientific; calculating
Obba	Oba river	human ears and bone structure	neglected wives; virtuous; gullible
Ibeyi	good luck; childhood illnesses	children	innocence

the ideal good. Instead, good and evil coexist in balance within the same beings. The orishas exhibit human shortcomings like rage, greed, lust, revenge, pettiness, and so forth. They can be tender and loving; they can also willingly bring about great suffering. They can be generous to the point of overindulgence; they can also be childishly unforgiving. Among themselves, they sometimes make war and commit incest and adultery and acts of cruelty. But the unwholesome behavior in which the orishas at times participate does not mean that they are evil. It simply accommodates the fact that bad things happen. Practitioners of Santería contend that it would be difficult for a sinless god to understand the experiences and urges of mere humans; the flaws of the orishas provide them with a better understanding of the human experience. In this way camaraderie develops between imperfect humans and less than perfect gods.

There are numerous stories of orishas lashing out at devotees for slights both real and imagined. One believer recalls an incident she witnessed: at a festival, the orisha Oshún took possession of a devotee. Even though the devotee was a man, the characteristics of the feminine and seductive Oshún began to manifest themselves in him; he was laughing, joking, and flirting in an effeminate way. Another man attending the festival slapped the rear end of the man who was being possessed by the orisha, accusing the man of being a closeted homosexual. Insulted, Oshún faced the man who had slapped "her," predicting that both he and the devotee whose body she was possessing would die in five days' time. Within five days, both men died of intestinal troubles. (The number five and the abdominal region are both associated with Oshún.) Few were surprised at their deaths.[4]

Of course we who were not there cannot say whether this is exactly how the event occurred; it might be tempting to think of the story as an exaggeration or a strange coincidence. But the pressing issue is the punishment meted out for the offense. Was the punishment of the slapper excessive? Is death an appropriate punishment for his lapse in judgment? Might not chastisement have been sufficient? Granted, his act was disrespectful — but do the actions of Oshún betray a self-absorbed, vain deity? What about mercy? Forgiveness? Even loving

4. Migene González-Wippler, *The Santería Experience* (Englewood Cliffs, N.J.: Prentice-Hall, Inc., 1982), 60.

chastisement? And what about the person who was possessed by the orisha? Surely he did nothing wrong; in fact, being possessed means that he had no control over his actions because the orisha had fully taken over his body. Why then was he also punished — and so severely? Are these questions simply those of Judeo-Christian minds that cannot comprehend Santería, or should santeros and santeras be as concerned about them as anyone else? Whoever asks them, these questions all come back to the fact that the orishas can strike out at anyone for whatever actions offend them, even when the person is not responsible for the offense. And once the anger of an orisha is inflamed, even when at times no reason can be found to justify that anger, little can be done for the object of the orisha's wrath. Even though santeros and santeras attempt to appease the offended orisha with sacrifices and ceremonies, in many cases it will choose not to be pacified.

Another story popular among different santeros and santeras that raises similar questions concerns a celebration at which one of the priests of Oggún was possessed by the orisha. A woman with an ulcer on her leg was brought before the possessed santero. He, as Oggún, kneeled before the woman, wrapped his mouth around the ulcer, and began to suck out the infirmity. A woman who walked by saw the procedure. Becoming sick to her stomach, she literally vomited before the possessed priest. Although Oggún cured the woman with the ulcer, he struck the vomiting woman with tuberculosis for offending him. Like the previous story, it matters little whether this story is fact or fiction. What is interesting is how swiftly punishment falls upon those who offend an orisha, even when the offense is caused by an involuntary physical reaction to what many would agree to be an unorthodox medical procedure (see Table 5 on p. 52).

In spite of stories like these, Santería claims that human beings are children of loving orishas. Literally every person is believed to be the spiritual child of an orisha and, upon becoming a follower of Santería, the believer learns who is his or her spiritual parent. Once this knowledge is revealed, the "child" can begin to cultivate a relationship with the orisha, petitioning it for guidance and assistance and engaging in activities that please it, such as offering sacrifices and dressing in the colors that please it (see Table 6 on p. 53).

Like humans, the orishas are complex beings. They can have multiple *caminos* (literally "paths"), that is, ways of manifesting themselves

Table 5: Most Likely Form of Discipline from an Orisha

Orisha	Identity	Most Likely to Punish by
Obatalá	sculptor of human form	paralyzing or blinding the offender
Elegguá; Ochosi; and Oggún	warrior deities	causing accidents, hemorrhages, or anything else involving blood
Orúnla	god of wisdom	inflicting mental illness
Changó	god of fire and thunder	causing death or suicide by fire
Babalú-Ayé	god of infectious diseases	causing infectious diseases, especially skin ailments and venereal diseases
Yemayá	god of the ocean and motherhood	causing intestinal disorders or tuberculosis
Oshún	god of love	inflicting the lower abdomen or genitals
Oyá	god of strong winds	causing windstorms or electrocution

to humankind, and in this way they reflect the diversity of existence. For example, the orisha of love, Oshún, has five caminos. As Oshún Yeyé Moró, she signifies the sensuous saint, knowledgeable in the art of love-making, akin to the Greek Aphrodite or the Roman Venus. She is the goddess of love capable of bringing men and women together. But as Oshún Kolé Kolé she is the saint of poverty, the owner of one faded yellow dress who eats only the scraps brought to her door by a vulture. In this aspect she represents and defends the suffering of all women at the hands of abusive men. In these two caminos, Oshún epitomizes both joviality and seriousness. She signifies frolicking, enjoying nightlong dancing, and parties, as well as domesticity, sewing, and keeping house. She is diverse and multifaceted as life itself (see Table 7 on pp. 54-55).

Table 6: Colors of the Orishas

Orisha	Color
Obatalá	purest white
Elegguá	red; black
Orúnla	green; yellow
Changó	red; white
Ochosi	lavender and black; green and black
Oggún	green; black
Babalú-Ayé	light blue; royal purple
Yemayá	white; blue
Oshún	red; green; yellow; coral; amber; violet
Oyá	maroon
Osain	green; red; white and yellow
Ósun	white; blue; yellow; red (primary colors)
Aganyú	red
Oko	lilac; pink; blue
Inle	blue; yellow; aquamarine
Obba	pink
Ibeyi	red and white (male); blue and white (female)

Table 7: Identities of the Orishas

Orisha	Corresponding Catholic Saint	Common Emblems
Obatalá	Our Lady of Ransom	fly whisk (beaded horse tail); all white substances
Elegguá	Anthony of Padua; Martin of Porres; Benito, the Holy Infant of Prague; or Holy Child of Atocha	whistle; hooked staff painted red and black
Orúnla	Francis of Assisi; St. Phillip; St. Joseph	Table of Ifá
Changó	St. Barbara; St. Mark; St. Jerome; St. Elijah; St. Expeditus; St. Bartholomew	double-edged wooden ax; cup; thunderbolt; castle; spear
Ochosi	St. Norbert; St. Albert; St. Hubert; St. James	bow and arrow
Oggún	St. Peter; St. James (in Santiago); St. John the Baptist; St. Paul; the Archangel Michael	metal weapons; iron objects; knife
Babalú-Ayé	Lazarus	crutches; reed; cowrie shell; dog
Yemayá	Our Lady of Regla	fan; seashell; canoe; coral; the moon
Oshún	Our Lady of Charity	peacock feather; fan; mirror; boat
Oyá	Our Lady of Candelaria; St. Teresita	fire; lance; black horse tail; copper crown with nine points

Orisha	Corresponding Catholic Saint	Common Emblems
Osain	St. Sylvester; St John; St. Ambrose; St. Anthony Abad; St. Joseph; St. Benito	pipe; twisted tree branch
Aganyú	St. Christopher; Archangel Michael (in Santiago); St. Joseph	double-edged wooden ax covered with red, yellow and blue beads; two bull horns
Oko	St. Isidro	gardener's tools, especially an iron hoe ornamented with cowrie shells
Inle	Angel Raphael	silver fish hook with net; two entwined snakes on a staff
Obba	St. Rita of Casia; St. Catalina of Siena; the Virgin of Carmen	bracelets in sets of five
Ibeyi	Sts. Cosmas and Damian; Sts. Crispin and Crispinian; Sts. Justa and Rufina	two drums, sets of bells, or maracas

By this time it should be evident that the orishas of Santería are as markedly different from the Catholic saints who stand for them as the origin patakis we looked at in this chapter are from the Judeo-Christian creation accounts. And yet these saints are among the caminos of the orishas. St. Barbara, whose sword may have reminded Yoruba slaves of Changó's ax, is one of his caminos; St. Francis with his rosary beads is a camino of Orúnla with his divination chain. The next chapter contains a brief *itá,* life and times, of the major orishas within

Santería. Some of the legends associated with their names will be recounted so that a deeper understanding of Santería can develop. If we can learn something about the character of the gods, and how they became associated with Catholic symbols, then we can better appreciate the complexities of Santería.

Chapter 3

The Orishas and Their Legends

In the last chapter we learned how the orishas came into being; we looked at them as a group and considered how their patakis or legends are viewed by followers of Santería. But who are the individual orishas? What are they like and what have they done? A pataki exists for each orisha, telling of its relationships with humans and with other orishas. Some of these legends have their origin in Africa; others come from the Cuban slave community; still others are synthesized stories from both hemispheres. Regardless of their origins, we remember that the stories of the orishas should never be taken literally. Whether a particular pataki "really happened" is not what is important. The purpose of these stories is to provide guidance and practical help for santeras and santeros in the here and now. Keeping this in mind, we now turn to the stories of the gods.

Obatalá: Lord of the Head, King of Purity

Obatalá was the first orisha created by Olodumare after the disastrous experience with Omo Oba. He is the most powerful orisha and is thus recognized as the head of the Yoruba pantheon. He fathered many of the orishas and is also considered the father of humanity in recognition of the fact that he created all human heads. As owner of all human heads, he is in charge of human thoughts and dreams. When the mind is troubled and confused, Obatalá provides serenity, and when times are difficult he can bring clarity. He is the patron of lawyers, writers, and physicians. He is associated with the color white, which indicates purity. Known as the King of the White Cloth, he is portrayed as a white-haired old man in white clothes; his devotees also often dress in white. He is praised with the names Ala ba la se (the one who clutches the center), Alamo rere (the one who handles the chosen clay), A-te-rene-k-aiye (the one who covers the extension of the land), Oba-ti-ala (the king who is dressed in white), and Oba-ti-o-nla (the great king). It is believed that Obatalá, who represents the highest level of existence, lives on the top of a mountain (see Table 8 on pp. 87-90).

Originally, the orishas had no power of their own. When they wanted to do anything, they had to petition Olodumare for ashé, which he dispensed only in quantities sufficient for that specific activity. Because only Obatalá knew where Olodumare lived (remember that soon after the creation he withdrew from the world), it was his duty to take these daily requests for ashé to him. In other words, if someone prayed to the love god Oshún for a mate, she in turn had to approach Obatalá and request the power to answer the request. Obatalá had to take the request to Olodumare, who would either grant or deny the request. Obatalá would then have to go back to Oshún to convey Olodumare's answer. With time, this arrangement became tiresome for Obatalá; he tired also of having all the orishas speak negatively about him when he was away petitioning Olodumare on their behalf, for they loved to accuse Obatalá of manipulating their requests in order to enhance his own powers.

So one day, Obatalá brought all of the orishas with him to Olodumare's home. "Olodumare, please release me from this duty of being messenger for all of the orishas!" he said. "Give each of them sufficient power to answer the prayers of humans on their own!" In hopes of at last getting some peace from his troublesome creations, Olodumare granted the request and dispensed a bit of his power to each orisha. To Obatalá he gave authority over all human heads, and thus he is to be turned to when clarity is desired.

Obatalá is known as the father of peace. Once, during a battle between the warring brothers Changó and Oggún, he appeared on the scene as a white dove hovering over the combatants. His presence brought an end (however temporary) to the brothers' feuding. For this reason the white dove is a symbol of Obatalá, and for this reason he is petitioned for peace when his fellow orishas act cruelly toward humans.

While Obatalá has been revealed through several Catholic saints, he is best known as Our Lady of Ransom. (As mentioned earlier, crossing between genders is common among the orishas. It is not unusual for male orishas to mask themselves behind female saints, to possess female bodies, and to be revealed through female paths — or for female orishas to do the opposite. For example, one legend states that for creation to be fertile, Obatalá became two separate entities, one male known as Oddudúa, and one female known as Yemmú — although as mentioned in the last chapter, some santeros and santeras consider Oddudúa to be the female aspect of Obatalá. Further, one of his symbols is the snail — an animal with both male and female sex organs.) In 1218, a wealthy man named Peter Nolasco gave away all his possessions and founded the Order of Our Lady of Ransom in Spain. At the time, Spain was under Moorish rule and many European Christians were toiling as slaves for the African Moors. Moved by a vision of the Virgin Mary, Nolasco began a religious order whose main purpose was to ransom these Christian slaves. Members of the Order took a vow to give all they had for the redemption of captive Christians, even to the point of assuming their place in captivity. It is ironic the descendants of these European slaves were to become slaveholders themselves, and that the saint who symbolized their redemption was to be adopted by their African captives.

Elegguá: Lord of the Crossroads

Elegguá is considered the youngest and cleverest of the orishas. It is believed that his worship originated in the Yoruba city of Ketu, Nigeria, although some oral traditions indicate an earlier home in the city of Òfà. His parentage is unclear: some claim he is the son of Oyá, but Oyá is the legal wife of Oggún and the mistress of Changó, and Elegguá may be the son of either. Others insist he is the son of Obatalá and Yemmú. Still others claim he was one of the first orishas created by Olofi (see Table 9 on pp. 91-93). Regardless, after Obatalá, Elegguá is the most powerful orisha, the divine enforcer and the first among the warriors.

His name in Yoruba literally means "messenger of the gods," and in this role he guards the paths of divine and human communication, using mice as his agents. Yet the divine messenger is a trickster who especially enjoys putting gods and humans alike in compromising positions. Like other tricksters in earth-based religions, he forces others to consider the spiritual consequences of their actions, forcing seekers to explore alternatives previously unexplored. His penchant for trickery is based on the pataki in which he saves Olodumare's life by eating the mice that threatened the almighty god. After punishing all of the orishas who had challenged him, the story goes, Olodumare turned to Elegguá and offered him whatever he wanted. Elegguá requested the privilege of doing as he pleased, whenever he wanted, without restrictions or limitations. In the absence of these restrictions he became able to see what is hidden to humans and gods alike, and thus he is the greatest judge among the orishas.

Some have suggested that Elegguá, the divine messenger, is the patron orisha of the Internet, the ultimate communication network (or series of paths). More commonly those about to take a long journey invoke him: by blowing tobacco smoke and spraying rum from their mouths onto the vehicle, they insure that their intended paths will remain open and free of obstacles. More broadly, he holds the keys to all human destinies, opening and closing doors that can lead to happiness or to disgrace. Because he is a master diviner who knows the past, present, and future without the need for oracles, Elegguá knows which path is best for everyone, making him the master of people's fates.

One legend claims that Elegguá was originally a human prince, son of King Oquiboru and Queen Anaqui. One day on a walk the young prince came across an amazing sight: a coconut that radiated light. Picking it up, he brought it home to show his parents. Sadly, when he arrived home, the coconut ceased to emanate light, causing his parents to doubt his story. Frustrated, the young Elegguá threw the coconut behind his door and soon forgot about it. Soon afterwards the young prince grew sick and died. Around the same time, his father's kingdom, which had been extremely prosperous, became impoverished. Alarmed by these negative events, King Oquiboru gathered his advisors together. After much consultation, they concluded that the cause of everything was the coconut thrown by the deceased Elegguá behind his door! When they went to investigate, they discovered the coconut was still there, neglected and teeming with parasites. They replaced the coconut with a stone, and soon prosperity returned to the kingdom. This is why Elegguá and the other orishas are manifested in stones, and why coconuts are a traditional offering to Elegguá.

Whenever the orishas are called upon, or whenever a sacrifice is made to one of them, Elegguá must first be consulted. A portion of every sacrifice must first be offered to him. This is because there was a time when Olodumare was sick and in bed. All the orishas were gathered around, and one by one they attempted to cure him. But they all failed. Suddenly Elegguá appeared and offered to try to bring about a healing. The other orishas were perturbed that one of the smallest and youngest among them would have the gall to try what they had failed to do. Yet Elegguá succeeded. To thank him Olodumare made him the first orisha to be honored in every ceremony, the intermediary between humans, orishas, and Olodumare. Unless Elegguá's name is invoked in all offerings, the petitions of the believer will never reach the ears of the orishas. And thus the one perceived to be last becomes first.

Even though practitioners of Santería do not believe in the existence of a deity who personifies evil, early Christian missionaries incorrectly linked Elegguá, due to his role as a trickster, to Satan as he is understood in the New Testament — an evil being who stands in opposition to God's ultimate salvific plan for humanity. In reality Elegguá, like all the other orishas, is beyond good or evil. A better comparison might be to Satan in the book of Job in the Hebrew Bible. In this book Satan is one of God's agents, responsible for testing the faith of believers. Like this Satan, Elegguá is not the embodiment of evil; rather, he works evil in the service of a higher power.

In Santería Elegguá is usually manifested as the Catholic saints Anthony of Padua, Benito the Holy Infant of Prague, or the Holy Child of Atocha. The latter is one of his most popular manifestations. During medieval times, when most of Spain was ruled by the Moors, the town of Atocha was invaded and many Christians living there were captured by the victorious Moors. These prisoners were being starved to death because the Moors prevented the adult villagers from bringing them food or water. One day a child appeared, dressed as a pilgrim and carrying a basket of food and a gourd of water. The prisoners were fed because the Moors allowed the child to bring food and water; yet the basket of food and the gourd of water never depleted. No one knew who the child was, so the Christians concluded that the child was Christ, disguised in order to trick the Moors.

Elegguá is also associated with Anthony of Padua, the thirteenth-century native of Lisbon. Although born to a wealthy and powerful family, and destined to become a great nobleman, he forsook his privilege to become a poor Franciscan. One of the most beloved of saints of the Catholic Church, he is usually portrayed bearing the Child Jesus in his arms while holding a lily. What these Catholic images have in common is the presence of a child. A connection to Elegguá can be made due to the orisha's fondness of children and his frequent disguise as a child.

Orúnla: The Lord of Divination

There is only one path for Orúnla, and only men are initiated into his mysteries. His worship is said to have originated in the holy city Ilé-Ifé, though some claim an older origin, Oke Igeti, while others insist his hometown is Ado. Tradition claims he was a human teacher who came to Ilé-Ifé, teaching its inhabitants new religious rituals, a system of ethical living, and a deeper, more mystical vision of the future. Toward his latter years, he developed and taught a new and more complex divination system, known as Ifá, and traveled throughout Africa sharing this newfound wisdom. Some Yoruba scholars even claim that he traveled as far as Palestine, where he became known as Melchizedek.[1] Whatever Orúnla's origins may have been, he has become the symbol of wisdom, the orisha who seeks to uncover what is hidden. Additionally, he is considered a gifted physician. Physically weak, he chose to be a diviner and herbalist rather than a warrior. His knowledge of the future and his understanding of illnesses combined make him the ideal counselor for humankind.

In the New World, Orúnla never physically possesses his priests, although in Africa his priests do at times become possessed. Rather, he communicates with his santeros through the more intellectual means

---

1. See, for example, Akin Fagbenro Beyioku, *Órúnmilàism: the Basis of Jesuism* (Lagos: Tika Tore Press, 1943).

of oracles, particularly the Table of Ifá and the divination chain that he developed, which is known as an opele. He is therefore referred to as the scribe of the orishas, for he "writes" the messages from the orishas that his priests communicate to others. Of course, the image of a scribe is not meant to imply servitude. Rather, it is a reference to his unsurpassed wisdom.

When Olodumare heard that Orúnla was developing a divination system, he began to mock the orisha. Only Olodumare, after all, can predict the future! But Orúnla's fame as a great diviner spread, and eventually Olodumare decided he would have to put a stop to such foolishness. He devised a plan: he would pretend to be dead, and when Orúnla appeared to pay his last respects, Olodumare would prove to all that the orisha's forecasting was inferior and untrustworthy. However, Eleggúa, who likes to hide behind doors and eavesdrop, overheard Olodumare's plans. He quickly warned his friend Orúnla of the trap being designed for him. So on the day when Orúnla was supposed to go and pay his last respects to the supposedly deceased Olodumare, he instead proclaimed that Olodumare was not dead but remained strong. He was playing dead to test Orúnla's abilities as a seer of truth. Impressed, Olodumare apologized and acquiesced to Orúnla powers, showering him with gifts.

Some in Santería maintain that Eleggúa taught Orúnla how to read the oracles. Regardless of whether this is the case, one thing is certain: the two orishas are inseparable friends. The story is told of when Orúnla wondered how many of his companions were true friends. He decided to hide himself, and have his wife declare his death. One by one his friends came to pay their last respects. But after offering their consolation, this group of friends informed the presumed widow of a supposed unpaid debt of Orúnla that was due to them. Some even claimed that some of Orúnla's personal possessions were items they had loaned him, and now they were requesting their return. When Eleggúa came to pay his last respects, Orúnla's supposed widow asked if anything was due him. Taken aback, Eleggúa insisted that if anyone was in debt, it was he — to the generosity and friendship of Orúnla. Hearing this, Orúnla revealed himself, and since then, the two have been the best of friends.

The Catholic manifestation of Orúnla is usually St. Francis of Assisi. Francis, an early-13th-century native of Assisi in Italy, was the son of a prosperous cloth merchant. He indulged in earthly pleasures until his renouncement of riches and conversion to Christ, after which he founded a religious order that would eventually bear his name, the Franciscans. These monks professed poverty and established monasteries near universities and other centers of learning. While it is difficult to find a substantive correlation between St. Francis and Orúnla, numerous images and statues of St. Francis clutching his rosary beads may have reminded the Yoruba of the divination chain used by those who belong to Orúnla's priesthood.

Changó: The Lord of Thunder

Oral tradition informs us that Changó was the name of the third king of the city of Oyo and fourth king of the Yoruba, known for his powers of divination, his bravery, his brawling, and his womanizing. His cruel tyrannical rule lasted seven violent years, until the royal council of Oyo, tired of his despotism yet fearful of his powers, conspired to dethrone him. According to one version of the story, the dejected King Changó withdrew to the forest, where he hanged himself. Another account states that as a mighty warrior, Changó united a loose federation into a kingdom. However, once the wars ended, the new king became bored, so one day he ordered his two brothers to fight a duel. The duel ended in the death of one of the brothers. Overcome with grief, Changó went into the forest and hanged himself. Regardless which tradition is accepted, he is the only orisha to have experienced death. His title, *Obakoso,* which means "the king did not hang," refers to the belief that he ascended into Heaven where he became an orisha — an orisha known for his libidinousness and his dispensation of vengeance on his enemies via thunderbolts. Thus he represents lightning, thunder, and electricity — even today I find myself murmuring "Que viva Changó (Long live Changó)" whenever I hear thunder crashing.

Changó's incurable womanizing also makes him the orisha of sexuality, specifically of male fertility. He encourages clandestine sexual adventures among his devotees. A kind of African Don Juan, he has always been able to seduce any woman he wants, and is credited with keeping forty-four wives sexually satisfied. He symbolizes the machismo most men deem necessary to triumph over enemies and obstacles.

Among Changó's enemies is his brother Oggún. Oggún, you will remember, was having an incestuous relationship with their mother Yemmú, and when Changó found out about it he swore revenge. He devised a plan whereby he would humiliate his brother by seducing his wife Oyá, the orisha of the cemetery. It mattered little to him that his legitimate wife was Obba, and that his mistress was the irresistible Oshún, the love goddess. Changó tricked Oyá, who happened to be his wife's sister, into coming to his palace at Oyo. At first she resisted his advances, but it was not long before she surrendered to him. The two made passionate love. Meanwhile, Oggún wondered what had happened to his wife. Hearing that she was with her brother-in-law in Oyo, he set out to fetch her.

When Oggún arrived at Changó's palace, he demanded his wife back. Changó reminded his brother of the shameful act he committed with their mother and declared his seduction of Oggún's wife justice. Of course, this only angered Oggún. Soon, the two brothers were locked in combat. They fought until it appeared as if Oggún was about to be defeated, when Oyá stepped in and brought an end to the battle. However, since that date, the two orishas, Changó and Oggún, remain mortal enemies. This ongoing enmity means that none of Changó's tools can be made of iron, for that metal belongs to Oggún. Even his emblem, the double-headed ax called *oshe,* is made of wood. Oggún left Changó's palace alone; Oyá remained as Chango's mistress. Although she is not as sensual as Oshún, she is a mighty warrior in her own right. When the couple fights, usually as a result of Changó's womanizing, their confrontations are fierce. Yet when she battles by Changó's side, the two together are able to accomplish anything.

Among the orishas, Changó is the most human, displaying all the complexities of human passion and emotion. For this reason he is much loved by the people. Yet despite consistently displaying a reckless and destructive use of power, Changó became the orisha of justice. This is due to the story of the gift given to him by the orisha symbolizing peace, Obatalá. One day, while Changó was contemplating how he might take vengeance on his brother Oggún, he was visited by Obatalá. Obatalá warned Changó that uncontrolled power was dangerous. Power requires direction so that it can be used for good. Having said this, Obatalá removed one of the beads of his white necklace and gave it to Changó to wear among the beads of his red necklace. With that bead, Obatalá conferred on the mighty warrior the wisdom to properly channel his power. Thus Changó can dispense justice rather than simply vengeance.

There are many paths to Changó, each manifested by a different saint (see Table 10 on pp. 94-95). Among these are St. Mark, St. Jerome, St. Elijah, St. Expeditus, and St. Bartholomew. However, Changó is most commonly identified with St. Barbara, a teenage girl believed to have lived during the third century in Nicomedia in Asia Minor during the reign of Emperor Maximinus Thrax. Her life is shrouded in contradictory stories; some Catholic scholars even question her existence. But most legends hold that Barbara was a princess who was imprisoned in a tower by her father Dioscorus because of her Christian faith. She stubbornly refused to renounce her faith or to marry one of her father's chieftains. Furious at her unwillingness to bend to his will, her father, in a fit of rage, drew his sword and beheaded her. Upon killing his virgin daughter, he was struck by a bolt of lightning that consumed his body, hence making St. Barbara the patron saint of lightning. Catholic statues of this saint usually have her wearing a crown and a red cloak with gold trimmings, symbolizing her royalty. In her right hand is the Holy Grail, the symbol of the faith she died for; in her left is a sword, the instrument that brought her death. At her feet is a small tower, symbolizing where she was imprisoned. To the believer in Santería, Changó, the orisha of thunder and lightning, has obviously manifested himself among Catholics as St. Barbara.

Ochosi: Lord of the Hunt

Ochosi, son of Yemayá, is a great hunter and a master in the art of magic; he can instruct an arrow as to where it must land. Before he became an orisha, legend holds, he was the historical king of Ketu, spending his days hunting. Because he spends much time in the forest, he has also learned much medical knowledge of the healing properties of herbs and plants. It is interesting to note that the worship of Ochosi has ceased in Nigeria, mostly due to the fact that the majority of the city's inhabitants where he ruled as god were deported as slaves to Cuba, where a large following developed.

One day Ochosi was approached by either Obatalá or Orúnla, no one remembers which, and hired to capture a quail for Olodumare. In no time, Ochosi, a skilled hunter, found a magnificent bird. He placed it in a cage, which he stowed in his hut for safekeeping. Having secured the bird, he returned to his hunting. But while he was away, his mother stopped by the hut to see Ochosi. She did not find him, but did come across the beautiful bird. She took it, assuming her son would not mind, fully intending to let him know the next time she saw him. When Ochosi returned home, he discovered the bird was missing. He flew into a rage. Taking his bow, he shot an arrow into the air, commanding that it find the heart of the thief. No sooner had he done this than he heard his mother shriek. Running to her house he discovered her dead, her heart pierced by the arrow. Overcome by grief, he swore never to hunt again and to commit himself to working for justice. He is still committed to helping hunters, but today many offerings are made to Ochosi by those who must appear before a judge. Ochosi rules over every legal case, judge, lawyer, and jailhouse.

Several paths exist for Ochosi, but they are elusive and obscure. His representations in Catholicism include St. Albert, St. Hubert, and St. James. But he is most commonly manifested as St. Norbert, born to a princely family at Xanten in 1080 C.E.. Norbert lived a worldly life at the German courts, converting to Christianity in 1115 CE after narrowly escaping death. He is best known for expounding the doctrine of Christ's physical presence in the Eucharist. Little connection can be made between him and the orisha Ochosi; a stronger link appears between the orisha and his manifestation in the life of St. Hubert. Hubert, a layman courtier of Pépin of Héristal at Nuestria in northwest France, lived during the eighth century. He was the grandson of Charibert, King of Toulouse, and the eldest son of Bertrand, Duke of Aquitaine. Hubert was passionately devoted to hunting. His conversion to the Christian faith occurred on Good Friday while he was hunting a stag. He saw a vision of a crucifix between the stag's antlers. Then he heard a voice warn him, "Hubert, unless you turn to the Lord, and lead a holy life, you shall quickly go down to hell." His association with the hunt led to his recognition as the patron of hunters and of those afflicted with rabies.

Oggún: Lord of Iron

Some say that Oggún was birthed from the bowels of the earth, making him the lord of all earth's minerals and metal ores. Others claim he is the son of Obatalá and Yemmú. Still others claim he was abandoned in the forest because he was the product of an extramarital affair; there he was discovered and reared by Elegg005. Today he resides in the depths of the earth and in the summits of the mountains — in fact, all mountains belong to him. As the lord of iron, Oggún exercises incredibly widespread influence. He is the patron of all things made with that metal and those who work with it, overseeing surgeons (who rely on scalpels), military personnel (who rely on war machines like tanks, ships, and airplanes), and police officers (who rely on guns and bullets). He rules over transportation because planes, automobiles, trains, and so on are all made of metal. (Whenever there is a train derailment, a plane crash, or an automobile collision, it is believed that Oggún caused the accident, thirsty for the blood of its victims.) Wars, too, are his to control. It is believed that he taught the earliest hunters how to gut animals with metal knives, and for this reason he is the first to be fed whenever a sacrifice is performed — in a sense, he is given the first taste of the offering. The carnage caused by wars, violent crimes, and transportation accidents has made Oggún a symbol of tragedy, pain, and loss; he is symbolized as a human-eating warrior. In life, he is believed to have been the first king of the Yoruba city of Iré in Nigeria, a city he received as a gift according to the following popular story.

When the orishas first descended to inhabit the earth, they were disappointed to find their path obstructed at every turn by a dense jungle. They despaired until Oggún stepped forward. He was able, he said, to cut a clear path through the shrubbery with his trusted machete. He did so, and as a reward for his labors he was given the city of Iré. Thus human beings have always relied on tools of metal to advance their civilization. The clearing of the road of obstacles may be a rigorous struggle, but it provides a clear path for those who follow.

To this day, Changó and Oggún are always feuding. Oggún, remember, was caught in incest with his mother. When Changó, his brother, found out about this, he was filled with hatred. Changó exacted revenge by seducing Oggún's wife Oyá, who found the handsome Changó more desirable than the homely Oggún. Filled with self-reproach, Oggún chose not to reclaim his wife, but rather to live as a hermit in the forest. Some say that his abdication plunged the world into war, and that as human beings began to fight more and more violently, the other orishas feared that the ensuing carnage would lead to the destruction of the world.

In another pataki, Oggún retreated to the forest dejected after his first defeat at the hands of Changó while battling over Oyá. No wars erupted, but neither was there peace, because in Oggún's absence civilization came to a standstill because humans could no longer work with iron. People began to struggle against one another for food, shelter, and the other necessities of life. The orishas got together and tried to persuade Oggún to leave the forest, but he would not. Not, at least, until the beautiful Oshún came to him alone and seduced him. She did not do so for the sake of humanity, however: her ulterior motive was to incite jealousy in her true beloved, Changó. So Oggún returned to civilization, but he did not make peace with his brother.

In another pataki, Oggún was married to Yemayá, orisha of the oceans. And all day long he worked at his iron forge. When he wasn't making iron, he was off making war. His wife, feeling neglected, begged him to stop his neverending labors so that he could rest with her. Oggún, patron of all workaholics, refused. Taking matters into her own hands, the slighted Yemayá allowed the ocean's waves to cover all the land. With no people and no land, Oggún could hardly work or fight a war! Shamed at being outwitted by a woman, Oggún left his wife and returned to the jungles to live a solitary life.

There are several saints that represent different paths of Oggún (see Table 11 on p. 96). He has worn the mask of St. Paul and St. James. Because of a pataki in which Changó tricks him out of his favorite ram, he has been connected with St. John the Baptist, who is depicted holding a lamb in many classical paintings. Since he is the orisha of war, he has been associated with the archangel Michael, who is said to have battled Satan. But most often he is St. Peter, one of the twelve disciples of Jesus. Peter is depicted by the Catholic Church with two crossed keys, and keys, made of metal, can also signify the lord of all metals.

Babalú-Ayé: Ruler over Illnesses

Babalú-Ayé originated in the African nation of Egun (known today as Benin). He was considered to be responsible for starting a smallpox epidemic. All who died from this dreaded scourge were believed to have been taken by "the king" — that is, by Babalú-Ayé. Victims' family members, furthermore, were required to offer thanks to this orisha for their survival; hence he became known as the one who kills and is thanked for it. He became known as the patron orisha of all diseases, especially of incurable ones, and today he is credited both for bringing about and for curing sickness. For many, he has become the guardian of those who are stricken with the AIDS virus.

When Olodumare decided to leave the world, a long time ago, he gathered together the orishas to divide his powers among them. To Oggún he gave authority over earth's metals; to Orúnla he dispensed the gift of divination; to Elegguá he offered power over pathways and doorways. And so on. When he came to Babalú-Ayé, he asked, "Babalú-Ayé, what gift shall I give to you?" Now, in his youth, Babalú-Ayé was an incorrigible womanizer, and in response to Olodumare's question he made the frivolous request that he wanted to become every woman's lover. Although disappointed with Babalú-Ayé's immaturity, Olodumare granted the request; but so that the young orisha did not lose all sense of discipline he added the stipulation that Babalú-Ayé was forbidden to touch a woman on Thursday during Easter week. Year after year he obeyed Olodumare's law — until the day he met the most beautiful woman he had ever seen during Easter week. By Thursday, they were engaged in a sexual relationship. When he woke up on Friday morning, he found his body covered with terrible sores. These made him repulsive to everyone, including the women to whom he wished to make love. Everywhere he went, people recoiled in horror and disgust. But Orúnla took pity on him. After consulting the oracles, he advised Babalú-Ayé to acquire two dogs and exile himself to the land of Dahomey, where he would be declared a king. Following Orúnla's instructions, he sadly left with two dogs. Along the way, Olodumare sent a purifying rain to soothe and cure the orisha. Thus restored to health, he was declared a king by those living in Dahomey.

A different pataki tells us that Babalú-Ayé died from the sores with which Olodumare afflicted him. But the women of the world, saddened by his death, begged Oshún to bring him back to life. Of course, she could not do this on her own. So she went to find Olodumare. She brought with her some sweet honey, and when she fed it to him, she aroused his passion, which had been dormant for eons. Olodumare requested more honey, but Oshún held back, telling him he would get no more until her request was granted. Caught up in feelings long forgotten, Olodumare granted Oshún's request to bring Babalú-Ayé back to life, but he did not cure his sores.

Still another legend has the lame Babalú-Ayé at a party thrown by Obatalá. Attempting to dance with the other orishas made Babalú-Ayé appear clumsy and uncoordinated. All of the orishas laughed at the spectacle. Infuriated by their disrespect, Babalú-Ayé unleashed all manner of epidemics and plagues. Although Obatalá was able to contain the diseases among the orishas, he was unable to fully contain them among humans, and so diseases entered the world. Obatalá, angered by Babalú-Ayé's impulsive action, banished him from the holy city of Ilé-Ifé. He relocated to Dahomey. After a while, lonely and seeing all the suffering he had caused, he began to regret what he had done. From that moment forward, he dedicated his life to nursing those afflicted by the diseases he unleashed during his fit of anger.

Santeras and santeros see the biblical character of Lazarus as the only Catholic manifestation of Babalú-Ayé. This is not the Lazarus who was the brother of Martha and Mary, whom Jesus is said to have raised from the dead; rather it is the Lazarus in one of Jesus' most famous parables. This story revolves around a poor beggar named Lazarus and a rich man outside whose gate he begs. Day after day poor Lazarus, starving and covered with sores like Babalú-Ayé, is ignored by the rich man. But when they both die, the rich man goes to hell while Lazarus goes to heaven. The story conveys the moral that the rich are responsible for the plight of the poor, and their neglect of the least among the people will be punished. During the Crusades of the Middle Ages, an order was established in Lazarus' name, and one of its duties was to care for lepers. To practitioners of Santería, the connection between him and the orisha who controls all diseases is clear.

Yemayá: Mother of the Fishes

If Obatalá symbolizes the seed of life, then Yemayá germinates that seed. She is the mother of all that exists: Mother of the World, mother of humanity, and mother of several of the orishas. Infertile women offer fertility rites to her in hopes of conceiving children. She is symbolized by the sea, for it is from the life-giving properties of water that all living things come into being. Most followers of Santería believe that Yemayá emerged from the orisha Olocun, the androgynous deity responsible for the worldwide flood that is part of Santería's creation story. In legends, she has been married to Babalú-Ayé, Aganyú, Orúnla, Inle, and Oggún; all these marriages symbolize the coming together of different forces of nature, the myriad sources of life.[2] Some even believe she had a sexual relationship with Olodumare as Olofi, and the product of their union was the sun, moon, planets, and stars. As the queen of the universe, her crown is the rainbow, visible whenever she returns to earth as rain. And when Yemayá first walked the earth, a fountain of water was born wherever her feet touched land, becoming the rivers, swamps, and creeks we see today. Nevertheless, her greatest gift to humanity is the seashells, which are used by the orishas to communicate with their children.

One of the most well-known legends about Yemayá concerns her adopted son Changó. As a young boy, Changó ran away from his parents Obatalá and Yemmú. He was discovered by Yemayá, who took him in and reared him as her own son. In time he became a man and went out into the world to seek his fortune. He traversed the earth, and as he

---

2. This is important, as it indicates a kind of scientific reasoning behind the myths. Yemayá's marriage to Aganyú, for example, represents the birth of life. She represents the sea, he the molten lava which comes from beneath the earth. Science tells us that when this hot lava is cooled by the ocean's waters, minerals form. Forms of bacteria soon develop on these minerals; they are considered to be the most basic forms of life.

did so he had numerous amorous relationships. Becoming an incurable womanizer, he began to spend most of his time at parties, dancing and seducing women. On the rare occasions when he wasn't making love, he was out making war. Many of the orishas surmised that his actions were the result of his anger toward his birth mother Yemmú, who he felt had abandoned and betrayed him all those years ago.

One day he was at a party when he noticed Yemayá. He was smitten with her mature beauty. In an instant he forgot her years as his stepmother and became intent on seducing her. Yemayá was not impressed, and knowing about the life of heavy drinking, brawling, and skirt chasing he had been living, she decided to teach him a lesson. She suggested that they leave the party and go to a place where they could be alone. Delighted at such an easy conquest, Changó followed Yemayá.

She led him to a boat on the edge of a lake, telling him that her home was on its far shore. Hesitantly Changó, who disliked water, climbed aboard. When the boat reached the middle of the ocean, Yemayá plunged into the sea and disappeared below the waves. Changó grew frightened, for he did not know how to swim or how to handle a boat. And then he noticed a gigantic wave approaching. The wall of water crashed down on the tiny vessel. Knocked off the craft, Changó found himself sinking to the ocean floor. Desperately he paddled to the surface and managed to pull himself back into the boat. It was then that he saw Yemayá approaching him, riding yet another wave. Changó beseeched her to help him. "I will help you," she replied, "under one condition: that you learn to respect your mother." He cried out, "My mother? But she abandoned and betrayed me when I was just a boy!" Then Yemayá reminded Changó that he had two mothers, one who birthed him and one who raised him. Then Changó recognized Yemayá and repented for the way he had treated her — and for the way he had been treating women in general. The anger and bitterness he held toward his birth mother Yemmú dissipated. To this day he loves to seduce women, but because of Yemayá he shows much more respect for them than before.

Several paths exist for Yemayá (see Table 12 on pp. 97-98). In Catholicism, she is recognized only as Our Lady of Regla, protector of sailors and patron saint of the Bay of La Habana in Cuba. In the middle of the seventeenth century this image of the black Madonna was brought from Spain; her skin color and her association with the sea make her a perfect mask for Yemayá.

Oshún: Goddess of Love

Oshún embodies sensuality and feminine beauty. She teaches that love is the foundation of a life of joy. She is the love which exists between two individuals, the chemistry that sparks sexual passion. She is irresistible to human and to orisha when she dances, rubbing her honey-dipped fingers across the lips of whomever she wishes to seduce. She has been romantically involved with Orúnla, Changó, and Oggún, and has had sexual interludes with Ochosi and Oko. Unfortunately, this means that outsiders often view her as simply promiscuous. But in Santería, eroticism is recognized and accepted as a powerful force. Her success in returning Oggún to humanity when he was in forest hiding, for example, indicates that sensuality is one of the civilizing forces of humanity. Furthermore, Oshún's many relationships allow her profound insight into the complexities and difficulties of interpersonal dynamics. For this reason, she is in the best position of all the orishas to help those who find themselves in conflict-laden relationships. Not only can she empathize, but she can also offer guidance.

She also symbolizes hope for those who find themselves living in exile. According to legend, she journeyed from Africa when her beloved African children were forced by slave traders to go to Cuba. She demanded an explanation from Yemayá, who admitted the orishas' powerlessness in preventing this catastrophe, but who was willing to straighten her hair and lighten her skin to the color of copper, so that all in the new land of Cuba might join together in worshiping her. Just as the Yoruba slaves found a source of support and comfort in Oshún when facing the difficulties of colonial Cuba, exiled Cubans today, who find themselves in the United States because of the Castro Revolution of 1959, discover the same support and comfort in Oshún's Catholic mask of La Virgen del Cobre. For this reason, she is considered one of the most beloved orishas of the Cuban culture, affectionately called *Cachita*.

Men from miles around would come to Oshún's house when she was young, begging her mother for Oshún's hand in marriage. No one knew the young orisha's name, but her beauty was renowned. Her mother turned them all away until one day, yearning for the hordes of would-be suitors to leave her alone, cried, "Enough! I will consent to a wedding to any man who can figure out the name of my daughter!" Among the men was the great diviner, Orúnla; he was confident the oracles would reveal to him the beautiful young orisha's name. But try as he might he could not get them to tell him, and he eventually asked his friend Elegguá the trickster to help him.

Elegguá hid by the door of Oshún's house. Days went by, but the mother was careful never to mention her daughter's name. One day, however, the old woman became exasperated when the girl spilled a mixture of herbs and water on the floor. "Oshún!" she cried. No sooner had she yelled this than Elegguá flew back to Orúnla. Orúnla marched triumphantly up to his beloved's mother and demanded to be wed to Oshún now that he knew her name.

So they were wed, but unfortunately their marriage did not remain happy for long. At a party one day, Oshún eyed Changó dancing. Taken by his passion, she seduced him; thus passion and sensual abandonment became joined. However, the libidinous Changó had more than one passion. Though Oshún fell in love, his heart remained with his mistress and fellow warrior Oyá. Once Oyá, enraged that Changó sometimes preferred the wild passions of Oshún, and aware of Changó's fear of death, brought skeletons home to serve as sentries. This prevented Changó from leaving Oyá's house. But when Oshún showed up and began flirting with the dead sentries, they forgot their duty, allowing Changó to escape with his beloved.

Oshún manifests herself in multiple paths (see Table 13 on pp. 99-100). In Catholicism she is Our Lady of Charity of El Cobre, a symbol of hope. The following story is told about her: around 1610 two Native American brothers, Juan and Rodrigo de Hoyos, along with a ten-year-old black slave boy named Juan Moreno, went rowing on Cuba's Nipe Bay in search of salt. At about 5:30 in the morning, after waiting out a fierce storm, they came upon a carved statue of the Virgin Mary floating on a piece of wood. Despite the rain and waves, the statue was completely dry. At her feet was inscribed, "I am the Virgin of Charity." In effect, she was the first Cuban rafter to be rescued at sea. Since then she has been dearly beloved by Cubans, and in 1926 she was officially declared their patron saint.

Oyá: Ruler of the Cemetery

Oyá is the orisha who rules over cemeteries and the wind. She is Changó's favorite concubine; together the two of them make fierce love and war. In many legends she is the youngest sister of Yemayá and Oshún.

Long, long ago, Oyá was the orisha whose domain was the sea, and Yemayá was the orisha whose domain was the cemetery. But Yemayá hated the cemetery, and one day when she overheard Oyá complaining about her watery domain, she sensed an opportunity to trick her sister into a trade. So Yemayá invited Oyá on a picnic. As they walked, Yemayá made sure to bring them past a cemetery. From afar, she pointed toward the sturdy land, bragging about the immensity of her domain. She greatly impressed Oyá, who was more than happy to exchange her seas for firm ground. Only after the switch was made did Oyá realize that the land she admired from afar was a cemetery. For this deception, Oyá has never forgiven Yemayá, and to this day, both must be kept separated.

Oyá is also a mighty warrior in her own right. One day, Changó was engaged in a losing battle. Surrounded, hungry, tired, and wounded, he knew it was only a matter of time before he would be captured and killed. The only possible refuge was at Oyá's house deep in the forest. When he arrived there, he begged for help. "If I could only escape my enemies' circle, Oyá, I could regain my strength and vanquish them, but I have no way to break through their lines!" Oyá had an idea. She shaved Changó, cut off her hair and made it into a wig for him to wear, and clothed him in one of her dresses (this could be the origin of Changó's sexual duality). Disguised, Changó was able to walk though the enemies' encampment undetected. Once safe, he rested and regained his strength. Soon he was ready once again for battle. He rode into the enemy's camp at full force. At the very same moment, Oyá appeared, swinging an ax, for she is the wife who is fiercer than her husband. Together they routed Changó's foes. Since then, the two have been inseparable war companions, and together the two of them are invincible. To this day, when the winds are strongly blowing, people know that lightning is not far behind.

Some say that Oyá is the owner of fire, and that she merely permits Changó to exercise power over it. For this reason she is mainly manifested within Catholicism as Our Lady of Candlemas, although she has also been identified with Saint Teresa and Our Lady of Mount Carmel. Candlemas Day, or the Feast of the Presentation of the Lord, is celebrated each year on the second of February, exactly forty days after Christmas. Throughout Spain, parades and feasts observe the anniversary of the day Mary and Joseph took the baby Jesus to the Temple in Jerusalem. The day is celebrated as the "feast of candles," a reference to the Catholic belief that Jesus is the light of the world. But in this fire followers of Santería see their orisha Oyá.

Osain: Lord of the Forest

The lord of the forest is Osain, believed to have sprung forth from the earth's depths like an herb. He is celibate, and is instantly recognizable because he has one eye in the center of his forehead, one arm, and one leg. One of his ears is uncharacteristically large and totally deaf; the other is small yet hypersensitive to sound, able to hear the fall of a leaf from miles away. Although considered a master hunter, Osain is lame, using a twisted tree branch to help him hop around. This twisted branch has become the symbol by which he is usually recognized.

There are many stories about how Osain lost half his sight and two of his limbs. Some say it happened in a confrontation with Changó after Osain made unwelcome advances toward Oyá. Oggún stepped in to help Osain; if he had not, the damage might have been much worse. Others believe that animosity existed between Osain and Orúnla, and that with the help of Changó, Orúnla prepared a spell that caused a bolt of lightning to strike the forest, setting it on fire and trapping Osain, causing his disfigurement. Still others claim that because of Osain's renown as a healer, others could not find work in that profession. One unemployed physician asked Osain to share some of his clients, but the orisha rebuffed him. Angered, the healer asked Elegguá to intervene. Always the trickster, Elegguá caused Osain's house to collapse, leaving Osain maimed. Still others insist he was simply born deformed. Regardless of which legend is accepted, there is agreement in

Santería that no spell will be able to work its magic without first enlisting the help of Osain, master herbalist.

For a long time there was animosity between Osain and Orúnla. Many point to the latter's decision to move into the forest as the start of their contentious relationship. Osain hated that the influx of visitors seeking Orúnla's divination skills constantly disrupted his privacy. Others insist that the enmity was born of Osain's pride, for he saw his skills as an herbalist as vastly superior to Orúnla's as a diviner. Normally a deep thinker whose actions are motivated by logic and reason, Osain's antisocial emotions once got the best of him. He challenged Orúnla to a duel. Orúnla's refusal led Osain to ambush the unsuspecting Orúnla, badly thrashing him, and leaving the orisha of divination half-conscious on the steps of his home. With time, the two orishas made peace, and today Osain prefers the company of Orúnla to that of any of the other orishas.

Within Catholicism, Osain is most recognized as Pope St. Sylvester I, who was head of the Church during the reign of the Emperor Constantine. In reality, little is known about Pope Sylvester, and the many legends surrounding his life — most of which have to do with lavish gifts being bestowed on the Church — shed no light on why he would be associated with the solitary, disfigured orisha of the forest.

Aganyú: Patron of Travelers

Aganyú, a powerful giant, is the patron of travelers. He is also the orisha who rules over volcanoes and their rivers of molten lava.

For a long time, Aganyú worked ferrying travelers across the river in his small boat. One day the orisha Yemmú, wife of Obatalá, secured his services (some legends say it was Yemayá). But once she disembarked on the far riverbank, she realized that she had left her money at home. Attracted to the huge, muscular Aganyú, Yemmú offered to have sex with him as payment. He consented, and some months later the product of their union was Changó (other legends claim Changó and Aganyú are brothers). Obatalá, of course, assumed that Changó was his son, for Yemmú never told him of her dalliance. Nevertheless, Aganyú, fearful of the most powerful orisha of all, kept his distance, avoiding both Yemmú and the young Changó. But no secret can be kept forever; as time went on, rumors began to circulate about Yemmú's indiscretion. When Obatalá discovered the truth about Yemmú's adultery, he forgave her. The child Changó also heard the rumors, but unlike Obatalá, he set out to confront Aganyú. When they met, Aganyú refused to recognize Changó as his son. But even as a child Changó was full of passion and intensity, and his persistence caused Aganyú to erupt in rage. Lava poured forth from his mouth, hurling Changó into the skies. He landed in the arms of Olodumare, unhurt by the lava because, as Aganyú's true son, he too was invulnerable to fire. Taken by the child's plight, Olodumare gave Yemayá custody of Changó, to rear as her own until he reached adulthood. This greatly pleased Yemayá, who had no sons of her own. It was many years later that Aganyú and Changó, father and son, made everlasting peace.

Aganyú is most commonly recognized as the Catholic Saint Christopher, who is considered the patron saint of travelers, automobiles, and of the city of La Habana in Cuba. In reality, all we know about Christopher is that he was martyred during the reign of the Roman Emperor Decius (249-251). However, several legends about him exist. In the most popular one, Christopher is preparing to cross a river when a child asks to be carried to the opposite bank. When Christopher places the child on his shoulders, he discovers that the child is almost too heavy to carry. He later discovers that the child is Jesus, and that his heaviness is the weight of the whole world, which Christ constantly bears. The early Yoruba in Cuba could not have failed to see the similarity between St. Christopher, who ferried Christ across the river, and the orisha Aganyú, who ferried Yemmú.

Oko: Lord of the Harvest

Oko is the orisha responsible for crop fertility. Although mainly a hunter, he became associated with farming after discovering the secrets needed to produce a bountiful harvest. These he discovered after being ousted from the city of Irawo, where in ancient times he was a chieftain, for contracting leprosy. Through experimentation with different types of herbs, he found a cure for his disease, and having cured himself he returned to Irawo to a hero's welcome. He taught his people just enough to plant crops for a maximum yield, but he continued to guard the secrets of agriculture closely, refusing to divulge them to anyone. In addition to presiding over agriculture, Oko is a prudent arbiter of disputes, especially between different orishas and between human women. He spends much of his time dealing with the numerous arguments that occur between Changó and his paramours. Some believe he is the husband of Olocun, a marriage symbolizing the union between earth and sea. Ironically, the orisha of fertile fields is believed to be impotent. For this reason he carries a staff, carved as a penis, whenever he is farming or hunting. It is said that anyone wanting children should worship and offer sacrifice to this staff. For this reason he is known as *Orisha l'okó* (God is a penis), a play on the name Orisha Oko.

Once Oggún wished to know the secrets of agriculture, for no matter how hard he tried, his own fields remained barren. Despondence at his failure began to affect his relationship with his wife Yemayá; he lost all interest in having sex with her. While Oggún was away at war, Yemayá began to visit the lord of the harvest, starved for affection and intent on discovering the secret to a bountiful harvest. Oko, who was celibate and somewhat naïve about women, was taken by the attention Yemayá bestowed upon him. Each day she would appear at his field to chat amiably for a little while before going on her way. With time, Oko began to look forward to his daily meeting with Yemayá.

One day Yemayá complained that she was feeling faint. "Is there anywhere I can go, Oko, to escape the oppressive heat of the sun?" Oko helped her to his hut, which was close by. Leaving her momentarily, he went to fetch her some water so that she could be refreshed. When he returned, she was lying in his bed. Concerned for her health, Oko approached her to see what he could do to restore her strength. And of course, Yemayá seduced him. After their tryst (which happened despite Oko's impotence), Oko dreamily began to disclose the secrets of the harvest. When Yemayá had gotten all the information she wanted, she quickly took her leave, never to return to Oko. When she got home she told her husband Oggún the secrets of the harvest, but refused to tell him how she came by them. Soon Oggún's harvest was as bountiful as Oko's, and the naïve orisha of agriculture never suspected a thing.

The Catholic mask for Oko is St. Isidore the Farmer. A native of Madrid who lived during the twelfth century, he spent most of his life working in the fields of an estate outside the city. One legend claims that when the lord of the estate came out to chastise Isidore for going to Mass and thus arriving late to work, he found angels plowing the fields alongside him. Married to Saint Mary de la Cabeza, the two maintained a life of sexual continence after their only child died in infancy. Like Oko, he is the patron of farmers, field hands, and beekeepers.

Ósun: Messenger of Obatalá

Ósun is one of the four warrior orishas, along with Elegguá, Oggún, and Ochosi. Originally, he was the messenger of Obatalá and Olofi, and today he watches over the heads of believers in Santería. He never lies down to rest, but always stands at attention.

When Ósun was a youth, he resided with Obatalá and Yemmú, along with their children Oggún, Ochosi, and Elegguá. Ósun had the responsibility of informing Obatalá of everything that occurred under his roof while he was away at work each day. It was during this time that Oggún commenced his infamous sexual relationship with his mother Yemmú. Elegguá, always vigilant, brought Oggún's incestuous activities to Ósun's attention. Ósun scolded Oggún for his immoral behavior, but he did not inform Obatalá what was happening when he was away.

Now Oggún, the strongest of the brothers, was responsible for distributing the household food. When he found out that Elegguá was spying on him, he refused to provide him with any nourishment, and instead gave Elegguá's portion to Ósun. Ósun would eat the extra food Oggún provided; then, being full, he would fall fast asleep. With the so-called "messenger" out of the way, Oggún would kick Elegguá out of the house in order to continue his activities with Yemmú. Frustrated, angry, and hungry, Elegguá informed Obatalá about what was occurring. When Obatalá went to investigate, he found things just as his son had said — and he noticed Ósun napping contentedly. Besides feeling infuriated by Oggún, he felt betrayed by his messenger Ósun, who was asleep on the job. So he relieved Ósun of his duties as messenger and instead bestowed the responsibility on Elegguá. Additionally, he decreed that from then on, before any other orisha ate, Elegguá must be fed. But in spite of Ósun's demotion, he was still permitted to be the guardian of believers' heads.

Ósun is represented as John the Baptist, cousin of Jesus, who lived in the wilderness as a messenger, proclaiming repentance and the coming of the messiah. In the biblical account, John the Baptist was arrested when Herod, ruler of Galilee, began having a sexual relationship with his brother's wife, Herodias. Like Ósun who scolded Oggún for improperly having sexual relationships with a family member, John the Baptist confronted Herod for his transgression. His boldness got him arrested and later beheaded at the request of Salome, Herodias's daughter, who pleased her uncle with a seductive dance.

Inle: The Androgynous Healer

Inle has only one path. He is seen as a cautious and calculating orisha who is inclined toward scientific methods. As an orisha, his domain is the water of the rivers; thus he is the patron of fishermen. He is also the patron of physicians because of his skill at healing human illnesses. He is among the sixteen most-worshiped orishas of Santería, yet he is not very popular within the religion. This may be due to his reputation for being unmanly, something we will see in the pataki below. In it, he seems to be a kind of kept man who will allow himself to be mutilated for the sake of a woman. His inability or unwillingness to stand up to her is not respected in a culture in which machismo is prevalent. This is further reinforced by Inle being described as a beautiful, androgynous youth. In light of these characteristics he has been named the protector of homosexuals.

Inle was a beautiful young man who made a living fishing. One day, the sea goddess Yemayá, impressed by his beauty, appeared to him. It was love at first sight. She invited him to her domain in the bottom of the sea, where they spent months making passionate love. During this time Yemayá showed Inle her enormous treasures and taught him many mysteries, including the art of divination. As time passed she started to tire of her young lover; however, she feared dismissing him, since he knew the secrets of her domain. Would he reveal her secrets to the other orishas? Would his acquired knowledge in divination minimize her own powers? Eventually she returned him to his home, but not before she had cut off his tongue. For this reason Inle is unable to speak during the reading of oracles, unless he speaks through Yemayá.

Probably because of his healing ability and his fisherman's skills Inle is manifested as the archangel Raphael. Raphael, whose name literally means "God has healed", is one of the seven beings who stand before the throne of God in the Septuagint book of Tobit. Little is known of him except that God sent him to earth to heal a man named Tobias of his blindness and deliver Sara, Tobias's daughter-in-law, from the clutches of the devil.

Obba: Patron of Neglected Wives

Obba makes her home in the lakes and lagoons of the world. The legitimate wife of Changó, she is the patron orisha of neglected wives.

Changó quickly tired of his wife Obba, for she lacked the sensual passion of his many mistresses. It wasn't long before Obba began to feel hurt by his neglect, seeing him run off to Oshún for sensual pleasure and to Oyá, Obba's sister, for companionship. His infidelities were often and obvious, but Obba refused to confront or to leave him. She believed that her duty as wife was to show respect and honor to her husband by never bringing an accusation against him regardless of how true it was or how much she was hurt.

Still, one day Obba approached Oshún (others say it was Oyá) for advice on how she too could incite such passion in Changó, but Oshún tricked her. "Cut off one of your ears," she said, "and add it as an ingredient to Changó's favorite meal. That will make him desire you." That evening, Obba followed Oshún's advice. After Changó finished eating his meal, he noticed the bandage on the side of Obba's head. Just as Oshún had hoped, when Changó discovered what she had done, he was repulsed and swore never again to engage in intercourse with Obba. Thus she empathizes with and watches over wives who are neglected by their husbands.

Obba has been equated with St. Rita of Cascia, patron of impossible cases and considered by some Catholics to be the ideal role model for married women. As a young woman she wished to enter the Augustinian order, but her parents insisted that she marry. Respecting the desires of her parents, she married a brute of a man, spending eighteen years of her life in absolute dread of her husband. When he was killed in a brawl, he repented on his deathbed due to her prayers. After his death, Rita entered a convent, where she devoted herself to contemplating Christ's sufferings. One day in the year 1441, she felt a sharp pain in her head while saying her prayers. A thorn from the crucifix she had been contemplating had imbedded itself in her forehead. The wound was so offensive that she went into seclusion for the remainder of her days. The similarities between Obba and St. Rita cannot be missed. Both have wounds on their heads, but more importantly, both women serve a patriarchal society by providing an ideal model for women who must suffer silently when married to brawling and womanizing husbands.

The Ibeyi: The Heavenly Twins

The Ibeyi are the twin children of Changó and Oyá (though some say Oshún is really their mother, and in many patakis they are raised, like their father, by Yemayá). They serve as messengers of Changó (see Figure 2 on p. 85). Eternal children, all the orishas treasure them for their innocence, exuberance, and joy. As twins they represent life's duality, and as children they protect all who are young, watching especially over children who are sick. They make their home in the palm tree. There are seven paths to Ibeyi, each with different gender combinations and names. As male twins, they are Taewo and Kainde, Ibbo and Iwe, or Alawa Akuario and Eddeu. As female twins, they are Olori and Oroina, or Ayaba and Alba. As male and female twins, they are Araba and Ainá, or Adden and Alabba.

Though the Ibeyi are just children, they are important because of the time they saved the life of Obatalá. It is said that Obatalá's enemies set out to kill him by bribing his cook to poison him. Overhearing the plot — the enemies were not paying attention to the little orishas nearby — the Ibeyi warned Obatalá of the impending danger and revealed to him

Figure 2. The image on the left is Changó, dressed in red and wearing his beads. In front of him are his two children the Ibeyi (the twins), who protect children and bring good luck. To the right is a female representation of the male orisha Obatalá, who created humanity and is considered the head of the Yoruba pantheon. Photo taken by author at *la casa de los orishas* (House of the Orishas) in La Habana, Cuba.

85

the identities of the enemies who had devised the plot. In thanks for their loyalty, Obatalá increased the stature of the young twins within the faith.

In Catholicism the Ibeyi are most commonly linked with the martyrs Cosmas and Damian. These saints of the third century were twin Arab brothers martyred during the reign of the Emperor Diocletian. They were physicians who practiced their profession without charging their patients.

Additional Orishas

These are the most commonly worshiped orishas in Santería, but they are just the beginning of the Yoruba pantheon. Among the rest are Ajé Chaluga, the orisha of health, luck, and fortune; Oraniyán, the creator of land; Oké, guardian of the mountains; Oroiña, the source of universal fire and the focal point of solar energy; Oggué, patron of the herds, specifically animals with horns; Dadá, orisha of gardens and the newly born; Oyé, a giant orisha of storms; Ochumare, the orisha of the rainbow; and Yewá, who is in charge of transporting the bodies of the dead to Oyá.

Table 8. Paths of Obatalá

Path	Name	Description
1	Abany	Lives in the water and protects the blind; signified by model tin boats
2	Achó	A warrior who directs the wind of rhythm and stimulates dancing; signified as St. Joseph of the Mountain
3	Agguidai	Messenger in charge of human petitions
4	Aguiniyán	Governs the relationship between the orishas and the world
5	Alabalache	Represents the oracles, guides the seashells, and knows the past, the present, and the future
6	Alagüemma	Owner of the Ceiba and the chameleon, who is friendly and protective, signified as St. Lucy and/or the Sacred Heart of Jesus
7	Airanike	Warrior on horseback; symbolized by the rainbow
8	Ana Suaré	Represents suffering and anger
9	Ayagguná	Violent aspect of the peaceful Obatalá; wages a fearless and aggressive war against evil; dresses elegantly; rides a white horse while wielding a machete; rules gunpowder and is signified by Jesus at the age of 33
10	Ayaluá	Serves as the exterminator who lives in the air above the sea, the abode of unknown secrets
11	Aycalambó	Represented as a drunk covered with shells
12	Ayenolú	Wears a multi-colored handkerchief and incites calm

Path	Name	Description
13	Bibí Nike	A cyclops who battles for the things that are difficult
14	Edegú	King of the earth
15	Efún Yobí	Although his past role is unknown, he was worshiped in Africa and is signified as St. Joseph of the Mountain
16	Ekundire	With a sword in one hand, he rides a tiger
17	Elefuro	Protector of oil
18	Eururu	Serves as a counselor of the young
19	Eyenike	An old warrior who serves as town guardian
20	Eyuaró	Unmoving and unchangeable, embodying consent
21	Igbá Ibó	Old, wrinkled, white-haired man who represents the divine thoughts of the Supreme Being, signified by the eye of Divine Providence; hides from human view, for to gaze upon him is to go blind
22	Obá Lufón	Taught humans how to speak, how to have sex, how to weave with needles, and carpentry; signified as the sun in the guise of Jesus of Nazareth; protector of mothers
23	Obá Moró	An old man of suffering who instructs the young about the sacrifices required to reach one's goals; signified as Jesus' crown of thorns
24	Obalabi	Female who is in charge of announcements
25	Obanlá	An old woman who wears a crown and carries a silver cane, she is the one who lights one's path; signified as the sun with sixteen rays

Path	Name	Description
26	Obón	Owner of the mysteries of Egypt who is in charge of departing souls and is found close to the head of those who are dying
27	Obrala	A youth who rides a wooden snail and lives near a peregun plant
28	Ocha Griñán	An old peaceful warrior who serves as Olofi's messenger; signified as the crucified Christ
29	Ocha Orulú	King of metals
30	Ochalufón	Gave humans the capacity for speech and uses bees as his messengers
31	Ogán	A guardian who dwells near pots
32	Okeilú	Provides housing to the homeless
33	Oloyú Okuni	Ruler of human eyes
34	Olufón	Old and calm, he protects speech and loves being in the light
35	Ondó	A virgin who lives by the rocky seashore, protecting arriving boats
36	Orischa Iwin	Patron of potters; protector of palace doors
37	Orisha Ayé	Female mystic born in the sea; signified as a large seashell
38	Orishanlá	Trembling old woman with a large hand; protects against tricks; needs to be covered with a white sheet; signified by St. Anne, mother of the Virgin Mary
39	Orisha Yeyé	A beautiful woman who protects femininity and tempts men; owns monkeys, carries a bow and arrow, and lives in desert air

Path	Name	Description
40	Oshereilbo	Both male and female; covered in parrot feathers and shells
41	Oyé Ladé	A hunter
42	Oyú Alueko	A diviner
43	Talabí	A female who likes to pretend to be deaf and represents indifference; protects children and is associated with St. Rita of Cascia
44	Yekú-Yekú	Male or female elder who represents humility, patience, and health; signified as the Holy Trinity
45	Yemmú	The primordial mother; signified by the Immaculate Conception

Table 9: Paths of Elegguá

Path	Name	Description
1	Abailé	Serves as messenger, intermediary, and cleanser; responsible for moving things from one place to another
2	Achí Kuelú	Represents the spirit of the land or gnomes who guard the earth's minerals (especially gold); manifested as an old, small man living in tunnels; born in Ojuani and eats doves
3	Afrodí	A friend of Ifá who can be summoned only by men; inhabits ploughed land
4	Agbalonké	Serves as guide for the souls of the deceased; manifested as a strong man who punishes with fire those who bother him
5	Agbanukué	Guardian of homes who can strike his enemies with blindness; protects the babalawo, serving as his security
6	Agbarikokó	Guardian of the secrets that are discoverable by humans
7	Agberú	Wife of Echu, who is in charge of receiving sacrifices
8	Agbó Bará	Represents tricksters and spies
9	Agbobarmelekí	Stimulates erections in men; manifests himself in the act of masturbation
10	Ageló	Takes the form of an alligator, guarding the home of Orúnla
11	Agganiká	He is dangerous, vengeful, and in constant conflict
12	Aggó Meyó	Guards against tricks

Path	Name	Description
13	Agogó	Regulates the passing of hours
14	Agogoro	Can be found in garbage heaps and other places of waste
15	Agongó Ogó	Uses a big stick to attack or defend from enemies
16	Agongó Oló Oñá	Owner of the crossroads
17	Agosolé	Prevents tricks and lies
18	Akaderé	Lives among homes and protects them
19	Akeré Mewé	Guards the secrets of gold
20	Akéru	The messenger that fetches and carries
21	Alá Akomako	Likes to hide things and prefers offerings that have been stolen; punishes with fire
22	Alaarú	Is in charge of doors
23	Alá Ayiki	A gluttonous child who is addicted to the liquor *aguardiente*
24	Alagwanna	Lives in the forest, representing misfortune, causing accidents and death at the crossroads
25	Alá Lu Banché	Lord of every action of both gods and mortals
26	Añiki	Mother of all children of Elegguá
27	Aroni	A one-armed, one-legged midget healer, familiar with Osain's herbal secrets; prone to violence
28	Barakikeño	Manifested as a mischievous and troublesome child, he is the smallest of all the Elegguás

Path	Name	Description
29	Beleke	A young jealous child who guards the home and masters the secrets of the herbs; signified as the Holy Infant of Atocha
30	Bi	A warrior who lives on street corners and causes accidents
31	Laroye	Lives behind doors in clay vessels, loves to eat candy, is spoiled, and is signified by St. Anthony of Padua
32	Makó	Protector of thieves; enjoys hiding things
33	Mikke	Enjoys hiding things
34	Ocuboro	A king with power over life and death
35	Ogguanilebbe	A constant companion of Oggún
36	Onibode	Guards the doors of both houses and cities

Table 10: Paths of Changó

Path	Name	Description
1	Addima Addima	Also known as Olufina Kake; an orphan child who is signified as the apostle Bartholomew
2	Alafi Alafi	King of kings, Lord of lords, the great teacher and profound thinker, ruler of Oyo
3	Alaye O Eluguekon	Receives power and ashé from Osain; wields a double-edged ax
4	Bakoso U Obakoso	Festive and full of life's zeal, he constructs his home in the palm tree where he sits on his throne; signified by a very black, handsome man who loves to dance
5	Ebbora	Represents the one who sits on the raw, explosive energy of gunpowder
6	Eyee	A fierce, fire-breathing warrior who casts thunderbolts and wields a machete, manifesting an extremely powerful presence that strikes his enemies with fear
7	Gaufu	Signified with the sun
8	Jakuta	A dangerous path that uses stones and thunderbolts in battle; signified by the solar divinity
9	Lubbe Bara Lubbe	Was the most gifted diviner prior to Orúnla, deals with required actions to ensure a proper past, present, and future
10	Lubbeo	The one who sits on his throne in the palm tree
11	Oban Yoko	Represents a mature, tranquil orisha who contemplates the mysteries of the cosmos and participates in irenic and fraternal actions

Path	Name	Description
12	Obaya	Represents the moment the fourth king of Oyo was deified, hence honoring the "king who did not hang himself"; also known as Obba Oso or Obba Koso
13	Obbadimeyi	A twice-crowned king
14	Obbalube	The absolute and unquestionable king whose will is strictly obeyed; also represents the interaction which occurs with Oyá, his concubine
15	Obbaña	The king of the drums
16	Obbara	Represents the poor who are scorned but hope for a better future; Olofi has gifted him with several pumpkins filled with gold
17	Obbarra Koso	The king of Ara Koso in all his majesty
18	Olofin Dada	Owner of treasures, whose path is very old
19	Olufina	Represents fraternity, being a close friend of Oggún; resides in the ceiba, which he owns
20	Omanguerille	A warrior of action who battles through the use of his mind, theorizing and organizing warfare, even if these plans are never implemented

Table II: Paths of Oggún

Path	Name	Description
1	Achibirike	Signified by the archangel Michael
2	Alilúo	Signified by St. Gabriel
3	Arere	Signified by St. Peter and St. Paul
4	Bi	Causes all sorts of accidents
5	Dei	Represents the farmer
6	Kubú	Represents murderers
7	Meyi	Represents a split personality, one of which is violent and bloodthirsty and the other is gentle and hardworking
8	Nili	Signified by St. John the Baptist
9	Ora	One of the secret names of Oggún
10	Toyé	Represents the one who works with metals

Table 12: Paths of Yemayá

Path	Name	Description
1	Achaba	She is Orúnla's wife, wise but dangerous, skilled in magic
2	Acuaro	She loves dancing but does not practice magic
3	Akuará	Sister of Oshún, she loves to dance, and protects the sick; arises from the confluence of two rivers, living in fresh water
4	Akuté	A fearsome and severe warrior with a sharp knife hanging from her waist, yet afraid of dogs; skillful as a dancer
5	Asusú	Serves as the messenger of Olocun and is present in dirty and turbid waters, specifically the waters of lavatories and sewage; keeps company with the dead, is very serious, and slow to answer her children
6	Awoyó	The perfect woman of honor who is loving and wise; the oldest and highest manifestation of this orisha, defending against evil; wears a rainbow for her crown and seven skirts when in battle for her children
7	Konlá	Divinity of the sea foams, living entangled in seaweed; the protector of navigators
8	Mayalewo	Powerful in magic, she is involved in a relationship with Oggún; lives in lakes, lagoons, or natural springs in wooded areas
9	Okuti	An unforgiving and harsh warrior who battles besides her husband, Oggún, with a knife hanging from her waist; abides by the coast's breakers, and owns the coral reefs and mother-of-pearl; loves to dance with a snake on her arm; communicates with her children via mice

Path	Name	Description
10	Yembó	This manifestation is responsible for teaching Changó how to be a man; very sensual, but not promiscuous

Table 13: Paths of Oshún

Path	Name	Description
1	Akuaro	A hard worker who does charitable work and loves to dance; destroys evil spells and heals the sick; lives between the river and the sea and is enthused by music
2	Alolodi	Orúnla's lover who sits at the river's bottom with the fishes, a half moon, and a star; like him a gifted diviner; deaf, called by a copper bell, dislikes dancing; a conscientious home-maker who loves embroidering; identified with waterfalls
3	Aña	Owns the Batáa drums, is powerful in magic, and identifies with the swamps
4	Awé	Works with the dead, is full of sorrow, and keeps herself untidy
5	Dokó	Wife of Oko and patron of sexual acts
6	Edé	The perfect hostess, she loves elegant social functions; known for being judicious
7	Fumiké	She loves children, providing fertility to barren women
8	Funké	A wise woman who teaches
9	Kayode	Loves to dance and be at parties
10	Kolé	Lives on muddy streams; wears a faded yellow dress and eats only what a vulture brings her; despite her poverty a powerful sorcerer
11	Moro/Kari	A beautiful, coquettish, perfumed young woman who loves parties, scandalous love affairs, and admiring herself in mirrors
12	Sekesé	She is extremely serious

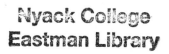

Path	Name	Description
13	Yumu	Lives where the river meets the sea; knits fishing nets from the river's depth; dislikes parties; deaf so that her followers must ring a large bell in order to be heard; leaves the river only to battle beside Oggún or to dig graves

Chapter 4   The Rituals

To many in the United States' Euroamerican culture, Santería is perceived as a dangerous cult, an occult religion composed largely of sorcery and magic. Consider, for example, these remarks by Alden Tarte, a Miami lawyer who in 1987 represented a group of homeowners who wanted to shut down a Santería worship center in their neighborhood: "Santería is not a religion. It is a throwback to dark ages. It is a cannibalistic, voodoo-like sect which attracts the worst elements of society, people who mutilate animals in a crude and most inhumane manner."[1]

The French philosopher Pierre Bourdieu contends that "sorcery" and "magic" are names imposed upon the religions of those existing on the margins of society in order to disqualify them. Those who do this naming, of course, use the legitimating term "religion" to refer to their own brand of sorcery and magic.[2] For many within mainstream American society, Santería fits clearly into the former category. Yet all religions have rituals and procedures that appear normal to those within the faith but strange and foreign to those outside it. To the oppressed and marginalized who are in danger of losing their identity to that of a larger mainstream culture, mainstream religious expressions like Christianity may appear exotic if not downright threatening. Much de-

1. George Volsky, "Religion from Cuba Stirs Row in Miami," *The New York Times,* June 29, 1987.

2. Pierre Bourdieu, "Genesis and Structure of the Religious Field," *Comparative Social Research,* Vol. 13 (1991): 12.

pends on the social upbringing and geographic location of the one gazing at the other's religion.

While many if not most religions can be understood in terms of their doctrines, Santería, having no central creed, has to be understood in terms of its rituals. It is a religion based on orthopraxis (right actions), not orthodoxy (right doctrine). This emphasis on rituals shows that the religion is more than simply an abstract set of beliefs and teachings; in a profound sense, it ties believers to a particular social order, giving meaning and purpose to their lives, as well as justifying the overall faith community and its role within the society at large. The purpose of this chapter is to review the religious practices of Santería's devotees. Although rituals that take place in Miami, for example, will vary greatly from those that take place in New York, or Los Angeles, or La Habana, I will try to focus here on the aspects that are basic to all of them. As we do so, we must be careful to avoid the temptation of exoticizing or romanticizing Santería. Our exploration must be respectfully conducted, realizing that for those who practice them, these rituals embody their relationship with the Divine. Our journey begins where most of Santería's rituals take place: the house-temple.

The Ilé

As the reputation of a santero or a santera grows within their community in response to the knowledge and power they possess, more and more individuals will seek them out for spiritual guidance. Eventually, a *casa de santos* (house of saints), known as an *ilé*, will be formed.[3] The ilé serves as a kind of house church, as followers of Santería do not construct opulent temples or churches for the orishas (see Figure 3 on p. 103). Most ilés are simply basements or bedrooms converted to house the believer's sacred objects. Shrines are built to the different orishas (yet it is interesting to note that no shrine is constructed for or to the supreme being, Olodumare, nor are images of him fashioned) and a space for worship, called an *igbodu*, is created.

---

3. The definition of the word *ilé* is interestingly ambiguous, similar in some ways to the Christian term *church*. It can mean the entire earth (as the home of the orishas) as well as the individual, local spiritual community.

Figure 3. Jesus Bello meditates with other worshipers at the Church of the Lukumí Babalú Ayé in Hialeah, Florida, a city on the outskirts of Miami. Over one hundred devotees worshiped the orishas for over two hours on this 4th day of June in 1987. Devotees are typically dressed in white, which symbolizes purity, and wear the beads that correspond to their orishas. Photo courtesy of the Historical Museum of Southern Florida.

Visiting an ilé is in many ways similar to visiting a doctor's office in a poor neighborhood. Imagine the following scene: individuals waiting to see the santero sit around the living room, the television tuned to some Latin American soap opera. Bored children entertain themselves as best they can with a few mismatched toys as they wait for their parents' turn to enter the room containing the saints. Adults chat with one another, quietly singing the praises of their priest's knowledge or potency. When new visitors arrive, ceremonial greetings, including the

103

bumping of elbows or hips, are exchanged, hugs are given, and African words are muttered. Everyone in the room has come to the santero because they have a problem: a woman has a child who is sick and the doctors are unable to produce a cure; a man's wife is being unfaithful; a man is in danger of losing his job; the pending court case of a woman's son looks unfavorable. They have come because on previous occasions they followed the directions of the santero — offered a sacrifice, took an herbal bath, or lit a candle at church — and their problem was solved. Some of the people in the room are devout Catholics, or Protestants, who faithfully attend church on Sundays but visit the santero whenever they have a problem. The santero is fine with this arrangement, as are those waiting their turn in his living room. Only the Christian clerics seem to have a problem with it.

The faithful sitting around any santera's or santero's living room, waiting to consult the orishas, see themselves as being in touch with the real spiritual world while still maintaining their membership within their respective Christian communities. Indeed, they see what they do at the ilé and what they do at church as complementary. Carlos Cardoza-Orlandi, a Christian minister and scholar, relates the story of a Dominican family in New York City who were members of the Protestant church where he was pastor. Their child became gravely ill. They took the child to a doctor; they also asked their congregation for prayers. Additionally, unbeknownst to the pastor, they visited a santero. With time, the child regained its health. When Cardoza-Orlandi discovered that this family had also visited a santero, he asked the father whose miracle had cured the child: Was it the orisha? Or was it Jesus Christ? The father, puzzled by the question, replied that it was God who cured the child. It was the pastor's problem to decide whether the Christians' prayers or the santero's rituals were responsible.[4]

Each ilé, or casa de Santería, is comprised of those who occasionally seek the help or guidance of the orishas, as well as men and women who are in the process of becoming priests. The head of the home church is called the *padrino* or *madrina,* the Spanish words for godfather and godmother. Other santeras and santeros who belong to a par-

---

4. Carlos Cardoza-Orlandi, "Drum Beats of Resistance and Liberation: Afro-Caribbean Religions, the Struggle for Life, and the Christian Theologian," *Journal of Hispanic/Latino Theology,* Vol. 3, No. 1 (1995): 56.

ticular ilé are assigned a hierarchal order based on seniority — a seniority determined not by age but rather by length of consecration to the priesthood. For this reason, it is common to see individuals in their sixties paying homage to children five or six years of age. Those who are children of Obatalá carry great prestige within any ilé for they are able to be the mouthpiece of any orisha.

Although each ilé is in practice quite autonomous, it is not uncommon for many ilés to be loosely linked together. Each is under the spiritual direction and guidance of one padrino, who in turn is under the authority of his spiritual elder (another padrino). The ultimate authority in Santería exists in the *Ooni*. The Ooni is the spiritual head of the Yoruba of Nigeria and of all who worship the orishas in the Americas. Historically the Ooni was a linear descendant of one of the original families responsible for founding the Yoruba nation. But even though an authoritative figure is recognized in Santería, his powers are greatly limited, for all of these different ilés are only loosely connected, with power and authority highly decentralized. The lack of centralization allows ilés to practice their rituals and develop their cosmological worldviews differently to suit their members' needs.

All individual santeras and santeros are consecrated, recognized as extensions of the supreme spiritual source, Olodumare. As such, their primary purpose in life is to serve as mediators between mortals and the orishas. Toward this end they officiate during ceremonies and rituals, divine individuals' destinies, annul evil spells, and serve as diagnosticians and healers. They are entrusted with the responsibility of keeping ashé active. They are recognized as *ahijados* (godsons) or *ahijadas* (goddaughters) of their padrinos and madrinas, and brothers and sisters of all who are in the faith. Just as parents teach their children how to live, mature, survive, and succeed in life, so are padrinos and madrinas obligated to teach their ahijados and ahijadas how to live and conduct their lives. With two specific orishas serving as parents to the believer, and two humans serving as padrino and madrina, a ritual family relationship based on mutual trust is established, not through blood, but through initiation. A sacred trust is established that must never be violated.

Whether male or female, those seeking to be inducted into the faith are known by the term *iyawó* (literally "bride"). Iyawós receive spiritual guidance from their padrinos and madrinas, turning to them for all their spiritual needs. With time, as they gain a deeper understanding of the mysteries of the orishas, they too can become padrinos or madrinas and "birth" their own ahijados and ahijadas.

While santeras and santeros serve as priests of the religion on a day-to-day basis, there are times when they are confronted by a particularly difficult case, one which requires the expertise and ashé of a high priest. In such times they usually turn to a *babalawo,* which means "father of mystery" (*baba* literally means father while *awo* refers to the secrets revealed in divination). Babalawos are male high priests who are able to perform certain duties that are beyond the ability of santeros and santeras. For example, they are the ones who are usually responsible for animal sacrifices and are the only ones who can read the oracles of Ifa. Babalawos' role in the faith is ambiguous, however; despite their powers, they are prohibited from conducting the ordination rituals for santeros and santeras. And the need for their skills has begun to dwindle as more and more santeros and santeras have chosen to specialize in the sacrifice of animals or to conduct the more advanced forms of divination.

Every ceremony and ritual has a *derecho* (literally "right") or fee that belongs to the orisha, not to the santera or santero. The derecho is determined by the orisha, and must be paid before the ritual is performed. It is expected that the derecho will be used to purchase ritual paraphernalia such as candles, offerings, or items of appeasement for the orishas. For a santera or santero to use a derecho for personal gain would be to invite the wrath of the orisha. It is believed that anyone who dared to commit this sacrilege would dearly pay for the offense by having the orisha's vengeance fall upon their entire life.

Entering the Faith

There are several roles available in Santería. Each offers a different level of protection, power, and knowledge to the devotee. As the believer progresses through the different levels of the faith, they move from a religious expression which relies mostly on the Catholic influences of the religion toward greater reliance on its African elements. For the neophyte beginning their spiritual journey, the orishas are seen through the lens of Catholicism. But as they move toward the final ordination process of "making saint," they discard the Catholic saint masks and focus primarily on the orishas. One reason those only casually familiar with it believe that the practitioners of Santería are confusing religious imageries is that they usually have contact or do interviews with those who are beginning the spiritual journey and therefore rely more on the Catholic symbols. Because most santeros and santeras are leery of discussing their faith with outsiders and because of the secretive nature of the religion, a complete picture of the religion is usually lacking.

We will now move through the four major entry rituals in the order of the least to the most significant, although it should be remembered that one could stop the process at any one of these rituals and still remain an active believer. They are: (1) obtaining the beaded necklaces; (2) receiving the Elegguá; (3) receiving the warriors; (4) making saint. Believers may differ on the order of importance of the first three rituals; however, all will agree that the most important ordination to be conducted is making saint. Once the first three rituals are completed, the devotee is considered half way to making saint.

Elekes

The first step toward entrance into the faith is the acquisition of beaded necklaces known as *elekes* (in Spanish, *collares* — see Figure 4 on p. 110). Although on the surface this sounds like a simple task, it is in fact the first of many complex rituals the iyawó will undergo in the journey toward becoming a priest of Santería.

The colors and patterns of the beads on the elekes will be those of the orisha that serves as the iyawo's ruling head and "guardian angel," and so the first thing that must be done is to determine who that orisha is. This must be done by a babalawo, in a divination ritual known as *bajar a Orúnla* (to bring down Orúnla). Cowrie shells are consulted in the presence of at least five other babalawos. If the shells are unclear as to who is the ruling orisha, or if two orishas are competing for the same head, then Obatalá is chosen to be the guardian orisha because he is the owner of all heads. The babalawo tells the iyawó who the orisha is, but he may not give the elekes.

Once it is determined who are the iyawó's orishas, necklaces are made by the madrina. Each orisha owns a particular eleke with specific colors and shapes (see Table 14 on pp. 108-9). Variations in color combi-

Table 14: Elekes of the Orishas

Orisha	Description of Eleke
Obatalá	White beads or a repeated design of twenty-one white beads followed by a coral bead
Elegguá	Three red beads alternated with three black beads
Orúnla	Alternating green and yellow beads
Changó	Six red beads alternated with six white beads or add to this design a red bead alternated with a white bead six times
Ochosi	Green beads or alternating green and brown beads or alternating blue and amber beads
Oggún	Seven brown beads alternated with three black beads or seven green beads alternated with seven black beads followed by a green bead and a black bead seven times
Babalú-Ayé	White beads with a blue strip
Yemayá	Seven white or crystal beads alternated with seven blue beads follow one white and one blue bead; pattern is repeated seven times

nations are determined by the particular path of the orisha. The necklaces are strung with cotton string, then washed in herbal water, then "baptized" by washing them in a special mixture called an *omiero*, consisting of blood from sacrifices offered during the ceremony and juices extracted from herbs that are sacred to the orishas, along with (but not limited to) water (from rain, rivers, or seas), honey, aguardiente, powdered eggshell, corojo, and cocoa butter. The orisha Osain, ruler of all herbs, is believed to be embodied in the omiero; hence the process of creating it is also known as "making Osain." The cotton string with which the eleke is strung absorbs the ashé from the omiero.

The primary purpose of the elekes is to protect the wearer, which they are believed to do for as long as they are worn. They are removed

Orisha	Description of Eleke
Oshún	Yellow or gold beads
Oyá	Nine white beads alternated with nine black beads or alternating red and brown beads with white and black stripes
Osain	One white bead alternated with nine red beads followed by eight yellow beads; some insist he has no necklace
Ósun	Has no beads
Aganyú	Blue beads with brown stripes
Oko	Lilac beads or alternated blue and pink beads
Inle	Alternating ultramarine and coral beads or dark green beads
Obba	Pink and yellow beads or purple and lilac beads
Ibeyi	Same as those of Changó and Yemayá

for bathing, participating in sexual activities, sleeping, and, for women, during menstruation. If they break, it indicates either impending death for the wearer or a serious problem with the orisha whom the necklace represents. When this happens, the wearer should immediately contact the madrina to discover what is wrong, and what must be done to rectify the problem.

Initially the iyawó is given four to six elekes, known as *el fundamento* (Spanish for "the foundation"), representing the following orishas: Elegguá, Obatalá, Oshún, Yemayá, Changó, and Oyá. Usually Elegguá's is the first necklace given, for it is he who opens the doors to every Santería ritual. This is usually followed with that of Obatalá, the Lord of the Head. With time, the iyawó can select two additional neck-

Figure 4. Elekes and other paraphernalia associated with Santería are sold at a botánica, a store that caters to the needs of the faith community. Note especially the Christian crosses next to the elekes. Photo taken by the author.

laces, choosing from among Oggún, Babalú-Ayé, and Aganyú. Along with the elekes, a variety of other shells, plants, or seeds may be worn or carried by the believer to provide good fortune or to ward off evil. These amulets, called *resguardos,* are worn as medallions around the neck or carried in a pocket or purse.

Making Elegguá

In the previous chapter we met Elegguá, who is one of the warrior orishas and is responsible for determining the destinies of humans. As Lord of the Crossroads, it is he who opens the doors of opportunities for people, and so it should come as no surprise that he is essential to converts' initiation into Santería. Again the babalawo is consulted, and using seashells he divines the iyawó's past, present, and future. Then, based on what he learns, he chooses materials that will be made to construct a graven image of Elegguá (see Figure 5 on p. 111). The initiate is instructed to pick up three stones along a path, usually in a forest or near a body of water. Through the divination the babalawo then determines which of the three stones will serve as the foundation upon which the image will be constructed.

A head is then sculpted, usually out of clay or cement. Cowrie shells are used to make eyes, ears, and mouth. When finished, this figure is not thought of as a representation of Elegguá, but in fact is considered to be the orisha. He is placed on the floor, at times inside a small house or cabinet, as close as possible to the front door of the believer's house so that he can protect the house from evil spiritual forces. If an enemy is causing trouble, the possessor of Elegguá can write that person's name down on a strip of unlined paper and place it under the image. Doing this ensures that the person named will be suppressed by Elegguá, making them impotent in their attempts to inflict harm. Periodically blood from a sacrifice must be sprinkled on Elegguá to strengthen his ashé, and from time to time he should be

Figure 5. The head of Elegguá, formed out of a stone. Eyes, ears, and a mouth are shaped by cowrie shells. Elegguá is placed on the floor, at times inside a small house or cabinet, and as close to the front door as possible so that he can protect the house from evil spiritual forces. Photo courtesy of Santería priest Nelson Hernández.

given his favorite offerings: rum, cigars, coconut, toasted corn, smoked fish, opossum meat, or candy. To neglect him can lead to closed doors and lost opportunities.

Receiving the Warriors

Guerreros, the Spanish word for warriors, is used to refer to the warrior orishas: Elegguá, Lord of the Crossroads; Oggún, Lord of Iron; Ochosi, Lord of the Hunt; and Ósun, Messenger of Obatalá. After Elegguá is made, the other warriors are acquired to protect the believer from danger and to do battle with enemies both spiritual and physical. Just as the iyawó received the elekes from their madrina, so they receive from their babalawo the objects that are associated with the warrior orishas: iron tools for Oggún, an iron bow and arrow for Ochosi, and an iron chalice surmounted by a little rooster for Ósun (see Figure 6 on p. 112). If this iron chalice ever tips over, it indicates that danger is near. While the elekes protect from danger, the guerreros attack any enemies who attempt to do harm.

Asiento

The most important, the most secret, and the most elaborate ritual in Santería is the *asiento,* "ascending the throne," the ceremony through which the iyawó becomes "born again" into the faith, becoming once and for all the child of the orisha determined to be their parent. Prior to the ritual, the individual is considered impure and is therefore required to "die" to their old self. The ritual is a process of purification and divination whereby the convert becomes like a newborn, even to the point of having to be bathed and fed like a baby. They are taught the secrets and rites of their god, they learn how to speak through the oracles, and they are "resurrected" to a new life in which they can unite their consciousness with their god. From the moment of the asiento, the convert begins a new life of deeper growth within the faith.

The rituals of receiving the necklaces, making Elegguá, and obtaining the guerreros are essential in eventually becoming a santero or a santera. Performing them is usually considered *medio asiento* (half the asiento). But to become a priest or priestess of Santería requires a ceremony known as *hacer el santo,* literally "to make the saint," also known

Figure 6. Images on the right are Elegguás, while to the left are iron chalices for the orisha Ósun. These talismans of the guerreros (warriors) are for sale at a botánica. Photo taken by the author.

as "making orisha" to those who hold to the more Africanized form. The purpose of this ritual is to condition the person's mind and body so that all of the supernatural powers of their orisha can be invested on the one being ordained, allowing him or her literally to become the orisha. This ceremony, which requires at least sixteen santeros or santeras as witnesses, is also known as an asiento. Asiento, the Spanish word for seat, refers to the way in which an orisha "mounts" the one being ordained. To be mounted by an orisha means to be spiritually possessed.

Mainstream American culture tends to think of possession in terms of Hollywood films like *The Exorcist* and *The Believers* — in other words, with negative, if not downright demonic, connotations. But for believers in Santería, to be possessed by an orisha is a great honor. Indeed, it is a responsibility, for it is only through possession that the orishas can manifest themselves to the faith community. It is important to note that even though the orishas may even at this point be identified with Catholic saints, it is the orisha (for example, Changó) who possesses the devotee, not the saint (for example, St. Barbara). Only trained spiritual leaders are properly prepared to serve as conduits for the orishas. When an orisha possesses a person, that individual is said to be mounted, and is referred to as a horse, due to the way in which they are controlled by the orisha riding them. The *ori* (head) of the one possessed becomes a living manifestation of the orisha. Their individual consciousness recedes and the personality traits of the orisha take them over. At this point, anything said by the person is considered to be a direct revelation from the orisha.

During possession, gender lines can blur as male orishas spiritually possess female bodies and vice versa. When I was young, I would often witness brawny men who were possessed by Oshún begin to display seductive feminine characteristics, while dainty women possessed by Oggún would become belligerent intimidators. When Changó possesses one of his children, the one mounted is able to eat fire or place their hand in fire without being burned. For this reason, lit cigarettes must be extinguished, lest the person possessed by Changó attempt to swallow them whole. To be spiritually mounted is considered a great honor to the one being possessed. Their body, after all, is what enables an orisha to commune with mortals. While mounted, the possessed person can predict the future, uncover what is hidden, provide advice, see activities occurring elsewhere, or do anything else capricious gods feel like doing. The orishas, clearly, are not distant, abstract deities; those at the asiento can see, talk to, hear, hug, worship, and consult these gods face-to-face. But being face-to-face with a god can be dangerous, and the possession can sometimes become violent, endangering the person being ridden by the orisha. When this occurs, other members of the ilé attempt to restore calm by blowing into the eyes and ears of the possessed individual, while rubbing cocoa or corojo butter on their feet or hands. Those who are possessed seldom recall what they said or did while mounted by the orisha.

Each asiento differs according to which orisha becomes the parent of the iyawó. The iyawó does not choose an orisha; rather, one of the orishas chooses the iyawó. The neophyte becomes the child of a particular orisha, who in turn is recognized as their parent. Originally, all the inhabitants of an African city-state would worship the same orisha, but the imposition of slavery changed that. Now a devotee can have a relationship with all of the orishas even though only one can be "asentado," seated, on them. Indeed, the iyawó can be initiated into only one path of one orisha, for each path contains its own unique regulations and taboos. The orisha into whose mysteries the iyawó is initiated becomes known as that person's *dueño de la cabeza* (owner of the head) or *santo de cabecera* (the head's saint). To most believers, only Obatalá, Elegguá, Changó, Ochosi, Oggún, Yemayá, Oshún, and Oyá can become the owners of an ori, head, although some santera/os insist that Babalú-Ayé can also. These orishas are considered the foundation of Santería. Even though only one orisha can own a head, a second becomes the second parent.

The iyawó is also said to be inhabited by an *eleda,* a guardian angel who resides atop their head. Some in Santería assert that the eleda and the orisha who owns the head are the same entity; others insist the eleda is the spirit of a dead person; others do not claim to know its identity. Whichever the case may be, all agree that the eleda corresponds to the human mind. It is described as the center of energy within the human head, the seat of intuition often said to be located above the bridge of the nose. Among the first steps in the ordination process is the *registro de entrada* (literally "entry exam"), a rite that determines the identity of the iyawó's eleda and is conducted about a week prior to the asiento.

The eleda must never be ignored lest it abandon the individual and leave them susceptible to evil influences. All it takes is some fruit, candy, a lit candle, or a glass of water with some honey to catch the attention of an eleda that is not kept properly fed. As long as the eleda is diverted, the person is vulnerable to all manners of spiritual attacks. A hungry eleda could even cause an accident to the head of the person whom it is supposedly guarding so that it can feed on the spilled blood. The best and most common way of keeping an eleda content is through a process known as a *rogar la cabeza* (literally "to beg or pray the head"), in which the person's head is "fed" with liquid, usually the milk of a coconut. This process spiritually fortifies the individual, providing clear vision and a tranquil mind. This ritual can be used either as a curing rite or, as in the case of ordination, as a preparation for other rituals.

The process of ordination introduces the iyawó to the rituals and mysteries of their ruling orisha. Part of oral tradition of Santería, these secrets span back centuries, having been passed down from one generation to the next. The iyawó receives them from his or her padrino, like initiates in centuries past, except that African names and verses that were once transmitted verbally are now meticulously handwritten by the iyawó, transferring this oral tradition into a *libreta*, or notebook. It is claimed that the libretas contain cures for nearly every illness with which individuals can be afflicted.

Traditionally, preparation for ordination into Santería has taken as long as three years. But within the United States the process has been pared down so that it takes as few as three months for men and just a matter of weeks for women. The ceremony itself has been reduced to seven days. It is still a lengthy process because the iyawó must learn the secrets of the herbs by which diseases and illnesses can be cured and evil diverted. The cost of ordination, as determined by the orisha, can be as much as $5,000; although, as in any religion, there are unscrupulous practitioners, some of whom have been known to charge as much as $45,000.

Prior to the ordination of a priest, a reading that reveals the destiny of the iyawó is performed. This particular divination, known as the *itá*, discloses the life, times, and the ultimate destiny of the individual, specifically their lifelong responsibilities as a priest. It also reveals the taboos the person must observe and the path of the orisha that should be received during the asiento.

Following the itá, the initiate's head is prepared to serve as the seat of the orisha. Among some today, as was widely practiced in the past, the head is shaved and marked with red, yellow, and green circles. A small incision is made on the scalp, into which a pasty substance containing the orisha's secrets is inserted. In this way the orisha's ashé becomes forever part of the person, allowing the new priest to serve as a mouthpiece for their orisha in rituals. The preparation time usually begins with five days of isolation and concludes with a three-day feast, attended by others who have made saint, at which the iyawó is formally presented to the community. During the asiento, the iyawó is given a new African name to symbolize their new life of service. In effect, they are reborn. The highlight of the feast is when the iyawó sits on a ceremonial throne called an *apotí* (or in Spanish, *trono*) and is literally crowned and dressed in the regalia of their orisha.

During this feast, the iyawó is usually possessed by their orisha for the first time, although this is becoming more rare in the United States. If it does happen, a guinea hen's head is severed and its blood is offered to the iyawó to drink. Great care is taken when summoning the ruling orisha to possess the iyawó, because if the wrong orisha is called to mount the iyawó, the orisha who is slighted might well withdraw all future protection as well as arouse the anger of the orisha that was mistakenly summoned. The end result would be a string of bad luck that would take many offerings and cleansings to reverse. The end of the possession indicates that the iyawó is married to the orisha. Following it, the iyawó sits on the apotí and surveys all the sacrificial offerings made, sampling some of the blood from each.

After the ceremony, the iyawó stays for a given number of days with the sponsors of the ceremony, during which time the iyawó is washed in an omiero consisting of blood from the sacrifices offered during the ceremony and juices extracted from herbs that are sacred to the orishas. The omiero is made by several santeros and santeras, who sit around a pail singing songs to the orishas. As they sing, they extract juices from the plants and herbs associated with the orisha about whom they are singing. Traditionally as many as 121 different plants were used in creating the omiero; but due to the difficulty of obtaining wild plants and herbs in concrete jungles like New York City, only a fraction of that number are used nowadays.

During the iyawó's possible seven days of seclusion, he or she drinks three tablespoons of the omiero every morning and eats a very restricted diet. They return home when the week comes to an end, only to return within three months for a cleansing. After six months another cleansing takes place, and the sacred stones of the foundational orishas and the *caracoles* (seashells) needed for divination are presented to them. To have these sacred stones means that the initiate can now work with these particular orishas. At this point the iyawó is at last considered a santera or a santero, with all the powers and responsibilities that entails.

Traditionally, the iyawó was required to observe celibacy for a year following their ordination in light of their new "marriage" to an orisha, but most ilés have relaxed this rule, merely prohibiting sexual contact for a few days. Iyawós must also wear white for up to a year during their ordination, and may be forbidden to shake hands, listen to (or tell) dirty jokes, visit anyone in a hospital, or enter a cemetery. This ensures that malignant spirits do not interfere with the iyawó's development. Throughout this year, the iyawó is properly trained in the basics of the religion. They learn how to attend to the orishas with rituals, prayers, offerings, and songs. And they memorize their itá and learn the arts of divination and communication with the dead.

Bembes

Santería is a dance religion. The *bembe* is a festival of drumming and dancing performed for the orishas (see Figure 7 on p. 119). Through a set of three sacred ritual drums known as *batáa* the messages of worshipers reach the orishas and the orishas respond to their devotees. The drums are consecrated to the orisha Osain and are believed to be the home of a spirit called Aña — hence they, too, must be fed through sacrifice and can be the recipients of prayers.[5] They must always be treated with respect: dancers must never turn their backs on them while dancing, and women may never play them.

The centrality of drumming to the Yoruba religion may be traced

---

5. The batáa, consecrated to Osain, is composed of three drums, known as the *iyá*, *itótele*, and *ocóncolo*. The iyá is the largest of the three drums, sometimes surrounded by little bells. The itótele is the medium-sized drum, and the ocóncolo is the smallest.

Figure 7. Bembes, the drum and dance festivals performed in honor of the orishas, have become a tourist attraction for mainstream Western consumption. Such bembes are routinely performed on the streets of La Habana.
Photo taken by the author.

back to a legend that tells of a time when the Yoruba people were at war with their neighbors, the Congolese. The Yoruba approached Orúnla for guidance, and he instructed them to make three drums and to play them prior to battle. The Congolese, who loved to dance, heard the drums from afar and could not resist the urge to throw a party. Before long they had made themselves completely drunk, making it easy for the Yoruba to vanquish their enemies.

Today bembes are generally given to honor, thank, supplicate, or repay an orisha. The rhythm of the drums invites the orishas to come and possess the dancers, bridging the gap between the physical and the spiritual worlds. Dancers are stirred by it into a collective trance, their dance postures reflecting the physical or personality traits of the orisha to whom the bembe is dedicated. For example, the dance for the trickster Elegguá is full of buffoonery. That of the disabled Babalú-Ayé is slow and lumbering. Oggún's is bellicose. If performed well, the

119

dance steps enhance the ability of the orisha to enter the dancer's body. If performed poorly, however, they may well offend the orisha, who will then stay away from the bembe.

It is said that only those who were mounted by their orisha, who have gone through the asiento ritual, are able to be physically possessed. All other possessions are considered theatrical. If the possessed person can provide clairvoyant counsel, providing information and facts it would be impossible for them to know otherwise, then it can be assumed that they have legitimately been possessed by the orisha. If the possessed person is a non-initiate, chances are that a dead spirit is possessing them; such individuals can be removed from the bembe and coaxed back to their senses.

It is not unusual for insults — for example, crying out that Changó is a weakling — to be made to reticent orishas in an attempt to coax them to a bembe. The idea is that if the orisha is not drawn by the beating drums, he or she may at least be offended and come down to challenge the mockers. Of course, the moment the orisha makes his or her appearance, the celebrants quickly soothe him or her through flattery. Whether lured by insults or by dancing, the orisha could either be in a good or a bad mood, and this will impact the outcome of the bembe. If in a good mood, the orisha will join in the festivities, laughing, dancing, and generously purifying all those in attendance. In some ilés, if there are birds present intended for sacrifices, the orisha might bite off their heads and sprinkle the ashé-filled blood upon the participants. On the other hand, an orisha in a dark mood will quickly sober the proceedings. The bembe will slip into uncomfortable silence as the orisha scolds those who have offended them. In either case, the orisha speaks through the one being mounted, sometimes offering advice or prophecy.

Now and again, in some bembes, it is possible for an orisha to possess more than one person at a time. Or an orisha may be present at more than one bembe simultaneously; after all, no single human body can contain an entire orisha. Like the forces of nature, the orisha is not restricted to just one geographic location. Sometimes, too, more than one orisha joins a single bembe. When this occurs, they treat one another according to the relationships portrayed in the patakis. For example, if a santera is mounted by Obba and a santero is possessed by Oshún, the two may find themselves sparring as they reenact the pataki in which Oshún attempts to trick and humiliate Obba. (Although Obba seldom takes possession of her children, when she does, her dance is usually done with participants holding their right ears.) More dangerous is when both Changó and Oggún appear. Their violent feud can easily erupt during the bembe, bringing harm to one or both of the individuals being possessed.

Ebbós

The food offerings, herbal baths, animal sacrifices, and so on requested by the orishas through divination are known collectively as *ebbós*. These ceremonies are meant to resolve whatever problem the individual consulting the orishas faces. It is never enough simply to ask an orisha for a blessing; the believer must also provide their own tribute. Ebbós should not be thought of as bribes; rather, they are meant to solidify the bond between devotee and orisha, and, more practically, to ensure that the latter will be able to provide the former with sufficient ashé to meet their need. It is important to remember that while everything receives ashé at birth, that ashé can be strengthened by the orishas. For example, when a candle is lit, the burning fire and melting wax produce a great deal of ashé, which can be consumed by the orisha and then used to help his or her petitioner. Each orisha is lord of certain days, and ebbós performed on these days are especially helpful (see Table 15 on p. 122). There are nine basic types of ebbós:

(1) Food offerings are made routinely, and they are meant to nourish the talismans (such as the head of Eleggúa we discussed earlier in this chapter) that house the orisha's ashé. Each orisha has its own favorite kinds of food, some of which are taboo to all but that orisha. For example, Oshún keeps all her magic herbs and sacred objects inside a pumpkin; thus for a child of Oshún to eat a pumpkin would be to show her disrespect (see Table 16 on pp. 124-25).

(2) Thanksgiving offerings are made in response to good fortune bestowed by an orisha or to the successful resolution of a problem about which the orisha was consulted. Such offerings could be as simple as placing the orisha's favorite fruit before it, or as elaborate as preparing a large feast and feeding the blood of the animals eaten to the orisha.

Table 15: Days and Numbers of the Orishas

Orisha	Day	Feast Date	Number
Obatalá	Sunday, Thursday, 8th day of each month	September 24	8
Elegguá	Monday, 3rd day of each month	January 1, June 13, or November 2	3, 21
Orúnla	Every day, especially Thursday or Sunday	October 4	16
Changó	Saturday, Friday, 4th day of each month	December 4	4, 6
Ochosi	Monday, Tuesday, Wednesday, 4th day of each month	December 4	3, 7
Oggún	Tuesday, Wednesday, 4th day of each month	June 29	7
Babalú-Ayé	Sunday, Wednesday, Friday	December 17	13, 17
Yemayá	Friday, Saturday	September 7	7
Oshún	Saturday	September 8	5
Oyá	Wednesday, Friday	February 2	9
Osain	Friday, Sunday	January 17 or December 31	6, 7
Ósun	Thursday	June 24	8, 16, 24
Aganyú	Wednesday, 16th day of each month	July 25	9
Inle	Friday	October 24	24
Obba	Friday	February 2 or November 25	none
Ibeyi	Sunday	September 27	2

(3) Votive offerings are meant to win the goodwill of an orisha. The ashé expended strengthens the orisha who can then, in return, grant the worshiper's desires.

(4) Propitiatory offerings are intended to appease angry orishas. Most often orishas become angry because of neglect. When it is determined that a propitiatory offering will require blood sacrifice, the animal killed will generally not be eaten afterwards.

(5) Substitutionary offerings are those in which a sacrificial animal symbolically takes the place of an endangered human life. For example, a santero may brush a devotee's body with a live dove so that the bird will absorb the negative energies clinging to the person. Afterwards the creature will be released to take away these energies, or killed but not eaten.

(6) Preventative offerings are precautionary ones intended to ward off attack. Although they are offered for the same reason as propitiatory ones, they are offered before the orisha demands them.

(7) Initiatory offerings are those made during an ordination ceremony. As in thanksgiving offerings, numerous animals may be sacrificed, with most of the blood going to the orisha and the carcasses prepared for participants to feast on.

(8) Foundational offerings are usually conducted at the building of homes, start of new business ventures, and so on. They are meant to confer the orishas' blessing on the new endeavor and prevent anything from thwarting it.

(9) Sanctification offerings are used to set apart the candles, herbs, and other paraphernalia of the faith, consecrating them as holy.

Burning candles and burning certain plants (such as tobacco, in the form of cigars) can release a great deal of ashé, but the greatest concentration of this spiritual energy is found in blood, for blood contains the life and soul of a creature. Most often, animals are sacrificed at events that mark milestones in individuals' lives — ordinations, weddings, births, deaths — and in offerings dealing with cleansing, thanksgiving, consecration, and healing.

Animal Sacrifices

While certain other religious groups also offer animal sacrifices, most people within the United States associate them exclusively with

Table 16: Foods of the Orishas

Orisha	Preferred Foods and Offerings	Preferred Sacrificial Animals
Obatalá	meringues, cotton, sweet soursop, yams, white doves, coconuts, cocoa butter, rice pudding	female goats, pigeons, white canaries, white chickens, white doves
Elegguá	rum, cigars, coconut, toasted corn, toys, smoked fish, opossum, candy, yams, mouse traps, whistles, guns	roosters, opossums, goats, monkeys, sheep, oxen, deer, bulls, turtles
Orúnla	red snapper, plums, white wine, yam puree, black hens, coconuts	occasionally a dark chicken or goat; usually does not require sacrifices
Changó	apples, rams, corn meal, okra, cactus fruit, red wine, corojo butter, bananas	roosters, sheep, goats, pigs, bulls, oxen, rabbits, deer, turtles, quails; in case of a powerful curse, horses
Ochosi	smoked fish, yams, pigeons, mangoes, corojo butter, roosters, toasted corn	doves, guinea hens, deer, red roosters, sheep, goats, pigs
Oggún	pigeons, rum, yams, cigars, sapodillas, smoked fish, roosters, green plantains, toy cars, toy trains, toy planes, toy weapons	roosters, black dogs, young bulls
Babalú-Ayé	toasted corn, beans, tobacco, rum, coconut water, pigeons	doves, hens, gelded goats, snakes, wild pigs, roosters, quails

Orisha	Preferred Foods and Offerings	Preferred Sacrificial Animals
Yemayá	banana chips, black-eyed peas, cane molasses, watermelon	ducks, turtles, goats, lambs, roosters, rams, fish
Oshún	honey, pumpkin, rum, cakes, jewelry, spinach with shrimp, white wine	yellow hens, female goats, sheep, female pigs, female calves, female rabbits
Oyá	eggplant, hens, star apples, female goats	black hens, black doves
Osain	sap from trees and herbs, tobacco smoke, seeds, flowers, grain, rum	turtles, turkeys, quails, owls, goats, red roosters, monkeys, guinea
Ósun	none	white doves
Aganyú	green plantains	roosters, guinea hens, goats, bulls
Oko	goats, corn wine, yams	monkeys, red roosters
Inle	fish, oranges, sweet potatoes, rum cakes, almond oil	white fish, white roosters, white doves
Obba	doves	doves, chickens, goats
Ibeyi	Candy, cookies, cakes, toys, fruits, yellow rice	pigeons, guinea hens, baby chicks

Santería. Even within Santería, however, there are many rules governing animal sacrifice; they are certainly not performed constantly or in-
discriminately. Before any offering is made, it must be determined by
means of divination whether the animal is acceptable to the orisha,
and if so, what parts of the animal are to be offered. Ordained santeros
and santeras are permitted to sacrifice birds, but only babalawos who
have undergone a secret ordination called the Knife of Oggún may sacrifice four-legged animals, slicing open their jugular veins and catching
the blood in the orishas' tureens.

Some animal sacrifices may be prepared and eaten following the
offering, such as those offered during an ordination. Consuming a sacrifice provides members of the faith community with an opportunity
to commune with one another and with their deities. A common bond
develops among those who share a meal, and the sacrifice to the orisha
ritualizes the bond, making it sacred.

Other sacrifices, like those involved in a ritual cleansing, must
not be consumed. In such sacrifices, it is believed that the devotee's
negative energy is transferred onto the animal; thus, to eat the animal
would be to take that energy back into the body. Rather, the carcass of
the corrupted animal must be left in the open, where it can decay and
return to the earth from which it came. These uneaten sacrifices are
usually left near a location where the orisha to whom they were made
resides: by a railway (made of iron) for Oggún; in the cemetery for Oyá;
at a fork in a road for Elegguá. In Miami, many of whose large Cuban
population are practitioners of Santería, it is common to find the remains of dead animals on the banks of the Miami River, a clear indication that an ebbó was made to Oshún. And every morning civil ser-
vants at the Dade County Courthouse must dispose of the numerous
dead animals, burning candles, and food items left on the building
steps as pleas to Ochosi for assistance.

According to legend, human sacrifices were once a part of the
Yoruba religion. A pataki tells us that the King of Benin was directed by
a diviner to offer a human sacrifice lest his daughter Poroye, who was
traveling, lose her way. The king refused. Soon after, Poroye found herself wandering through a dense forest, becoming with each passing
minute more and more uncertain of her location. Approaching a deep
pit, she heard cries for help. At the bottom of the pit was the orisha
Orúnla, who had fallen in and been trapped there for seven days.

Poroye helped Orúnla out of the pit, and in return the orisha promised to grant any request she desired. Being childless, she asked him to have sexual intercourse with her so that she could be a mother. Orúnla consented, and nine months after their fateful meeting Poroye gave birth to a daughter, whom she named Olomo.

Some time passed when Orúnla decided to make a human sacrifice to his ancestral guardian. He ordered that a slave be obtained. The girl Olomo was chosen for the sacrifice; unbeknownst to him, she had grown up in disgrace because her father was unknown. Shortly before the offering, the orisha heard the child chanting to herself, "I am Poroye's daughter, and if I had a father, I would not be offered as a sacrifice." Alarmed, Orúnla asked the girl why she had no father, and the girl replied that her mother had helped her father out of a pit, afterwards they had had relations, and then they had parted ways. Moved, Orúnla confessed that he was Olomo's father. He substituted a goat for the girl, and decreed that from that day forward, no one would offer human beings as sacrifices to the orishas.

Other Sacrifices and Spells

While the media like to publicize accounts of sacrificed animals turning up in courtrooms, graveyards, and the like, sacrificial rituals are becoming, according to santero Ernesto Pichardo, more and more rare in Santería. Only perhaps two per cent of the cases he is involved in require the use of an animal sacrifice.[6] More common are *despojos,* ritual herbal baths meant to cleanse individuals or buildings of impurity. To the chagrin of many santeros and santeras, some companies have begun to mass-produce bottles of water for despojos, each including the herbs necessary for popular requests such as luck, fortune, and love.

Devotees of Santería may also cast spells in order to achieve their desired ends. For those who face trial, for example, a special powder is made to solicit Ochosi's help. The person who must stand before a judge is required to scatter the powder discreetly in the courtroom where they are being tried, rubbing whatever remains on their forehead. It is claimed that those who use this powder will either win their

6. Steven G. Vegh, "Santería Worship May Be Behind Animal Killings: Macabre Evidence Found in Norfolk Beach," *The Virginian-Pilot,* November 8, 2001.

case or be released from custody. Unfortunately, in response to the anthrax attacks that followed the terrorist attacks of September 11, 2001,
strange powders have become subject to a great deal of scrutiny in
American courtrooms. Recently in the chambers of Miami Circuit
Judge Kevin Emas, a white powder was discovered. The area was quickly
cordoned off as courthouse officials prepared to contact hazardous
material crews to deal with the threat. But as the call was about to be
placed, a woman stepped forward and told a bailiff that she was responsible for the white powder. At first she claimed that her children
had put baby powder in her pockets and that she had simply removed
it. However, when summoned before the bench, she confessed that the
powder was *polvo de la justicia* (justice powder), which she spread in
keeping with her Santería beliefs so that her sister, who was being ar-
raigned before Judge Emas on armed robbery charges, would be released.[7] A similar situation occurred in Union City, New Jersey, which is
also home to a large Cuban population. There, Municipal Judge Joseph
Falbo offered a reward of $1,000 to anyone providing information lead-
ing to the arrest and conviction of the person or persons responsible
for leaving eight chicken heads, grains of feed corn, broken glass, and
an unlit candle behind his courtroom bench — an offering discovered
when a court clerk unwittingly stepped into the bloody mess.[8]

Of course, spells are just as useful outside the courtroom. If a
woman wishes to seduce a man, she can take seven earthworms, some
of her menstrual blood, a dash of her feces, hair from her head and pu-
bic hair, and place them in the sun to dry. When they are dried, she can
grind them into a fine powder and place the powder in the man's food
or drink. Once he has ingested, followers of Santería believe, he will
submit to her. Another way a woman can ensnare a lover is by placing
cooking oil into a pot and adding a few drops of ink, mercury, and
seven peppercorns. She must then remove all of her clothes and stand
before her Elegguá. There, she must tie a ribbon around her waist, and
while tying seven knots in the ribbon say, "By the seven words that
Christ said on the cross. With two, I look at you. With three, I see you.

7. Juan Carlos Rodriguez, "It's Not Anthrax, Your Honor, It's Just A Santería Ritual," *Palm Beach Daily Business Review*, December 3, 2001.

8. Matt Ackermann, Henry Gottlieb, Michael Booth, and Heather MacGregor,
"Fowl Play," *New Jersey Law Journal*, Vol. CLIV, No. 2, Index 93, October 12, 1998.

With the Father, the Son, and the Holy Ghost, let [the man] come and be at my feet."

When these spells are cast against other individuals, some basic questions concerning the ability of humans to determine their own fate or destiny are raised. Do humans have free will? Are their fates determined by the gods? Or are they in the hands of the one casting the spell? If the spells work, as santeros and santeras claim they do, do we then conclude that humans can fall under the control of any individual who has the esoteric knowledge necessary to dominate them? After all, ebbós can be conducted with good or with bad intentions, and in the above cases it is irrelevant whether the person standing trial is guilty, or if the man being seduced loves the woman who desires him. It is unimportant if, in the above two cases, the man loves the one casting the spell. All that matters is how proficient the individual is in the art of sorcery.

Adura

The Yoruba word for prayer is *adura*. As in many other world religions, prayer in Santería is a way of communicating personally with the Divine, offering praise and supplication, and receiving the power to grow and to transform spiritually. Because each orisha is associated with one specific sphere of nature, it makes sense for the believer to approach the orisha who will likely have the most power over their situation — a prayer for healing from sickness would be addressed to Babalú-Ayé, for example, rather than to Oshún.

Although prayers can be spontaneous, fervent requests uttered in any language, a multitude of prayers in the Lucumí language (a Latinized form of the Yoruba language) exists for the many rituals associated with the faith. While an animal is being sacrificed, while an omiero is being prepared, while an oracle is being read — in short, when any ritual is being conducted, a prayer is recited. Many are directed toward a particular orisha. For example, a formal prayer to Eleggguá for good fortune is: "Owner of all four corners, head of the paths, my Father, remove evil so I can walk with much health, without illness, without loss, without revolution, without death. In the name of all the children of the house, I give you thanks, my Father Eleggguá." A prayer to cleanse one's house while pouring water at the front door is: "I let fall three small portions of fresh water at my door. My house fresh, my head fresh, my heart fresh, my grace or mandate fresh, my children fresh, all that come to my house fresh. Everything, diviner of immortality, my Father."

Ewe

The most important ingredients in any ritual, even more important than sacrificial animals, are herbs. In Santería, every plant is alive, complete with personality (some cooperative; some shy; still others volatile!) and temperament, and is guarded by a spiritual entity and infused with ashé. These herbs and trees communicate to humanity their healing properties; however, few humans know how to listen properly to the forces of nature. Through an acute ability to find harmony with nature and to discern the ashé of each living thing, and with a competent knowledge of the medicinal properties of plants, roots, waters, trees, and flowers, collectively called *ewe*, santeros and santeras are able to concoct herbal remedies capable of curing any illness. Thanks to the ewe, humans have the potential to live lives that are healthy and abundant. For this reason every santero and santera is an herbalist, a diagnostician, and a healer, knowledgeable about everything that resides in the forest.

The orisha who is lord of the forest is Osain. Legend has it that Inle once ruled the forest, but he ceded control of it to Osain after the latter proved he was the better herbalist. Osain, however, was a jealous ruler; he kept all the ewe of the forest in a large gourd, which he hung from a tree branch. Every time an orisha needed an herb to cast a spell, he or she had to first approach Osain and ask for it. But Osain was miserly with his ewe. One day Changó needed just a small amount of ewe for a spell he was concocting; Osain refused to give them. Frustrated, Changó complained to Oyá. In response, she began to fan her skirt, creating an enormous gale. The wind toppled the gourd, sending it crashing to the ground and spilling all its contents in different directions. All the orishas rushed into the forest to pick up the ewe, which they then divided among themselves. They permitted Osain to remain lord of the forest, but only on the condition that from that time forward he willingly share his ewe.

Because each herb belongs to at least one orisha, permission must be obtained before any herb is used. Thanks must be given, too; since Santería holds all nature in reverence, a prayer is offered asking for the right to take the life of the plant. Once permission is granted, the herb can be used to develop a medicine, cast a spell, or whatever the santera or santero intends. We saw previously how an omiero, an elixir composed of anywhere between 21 and 121 herbs, was used in some of Santería's ordination rituals, but these are certainly not the only uses for an omiero. Possible uses are endless. For example, if a person suffers from severe headaches, migraines, or mental illnesses, an omiero can be concocted using herbs that are under the auspices of Obatalá; or if a couple are infertile, an omiero can be made for them with herbs that are sacred to Yemayá, who is in charge of motherhood. Other omieros can be used to obtain luck, to become sexually potent, to obtain legal justice, to succeed in business, to attract a lover. In short, there exists a recipe for just about any objective a santero or santera might wish to accomplish through the use of the ewe's ashé.

Most santeros and santeras are experts in the field of herbal remedies to illness. Furthermore, visiting one to be treated for an ailment does not preclude the use of modern medical procedures. It is not uncommon for a santera or santero to determine, based on the oracles, that an individual requires both their own skills as well as those of a physician or surgeon. The trouble with modern medicine is not that it is ineffective, but that it tends to focus on treating physical symptoms, to the exclusion of spiritual ones. Followers of Santería recognize that any quest for harmony within the body requires both a spiritual and a physical treatment. Thus they do not view the medical doctor as a threat, but as an ally whose skills, along with their own, can restore health, wholeness, and harmony to the body.

When we consider that what we call modern medicine often consists of pills developed from the ingredients of plants, Santería's use of herbal elixirs to cure illnesses makes sense. Furthermore, as herbal supplements are becoming more and more popular in mainstream American culture, modern medical tests are confirming what santeros and santeras have been doing for years. For example, anise is an herb that belongs to the orisha Oshún. Practitioners of Santería claim that consuming anise as a tea calms upset stomachs. Medical experts have determined that anise stimulates the body to secrete fluids necessary for the normalization of the digestion process (see Table 17 on p. 132).

Table 17: Medicinal Properties of Some Plants and Herbs

Herb or Plant	Latin Name	Santería's Claim	Medical Claim
Anise Seed	Pimpinella	Calms upset stomachs	Stimulates body to secrete fluids that normalize digestion
Chamomile	Chamomilla recutita	Calms stomach; mild sedative; effective vaginal or intestinal wash	Calms irritable bowel syndrome; helps morning sickness; calmative for stress, attention deficit disorder, insomnia; treats irregular premenstrual syndrome in women
Cinnamon	Cinnamomum cassia	Alleviates intestinal problems	Relieves intestinal gas to suppress flatulence by restraining chemicals that cause inflammation
Elecampane	Inula helenium	Cures bronchitis	Used as a long-term treatment for respiratory diseases like bronchitis
Rosemary	Rosmarinus officinalis	Eases childbirth pain; treats bronchitis, headaches, and rheumatism	Treats Alzheimer's Disease, circulatory problems, eczema, rheumatic disorders, menstrual cramps, irritable bowel syndrome
Sarsaparilla	Smilax	Treats syphilis; alleviates nervous disorders	Treats sexually transmitted diseases, skin conditions, and gout; but not nervous disorders
Witch Hazel	Hamamelis virginiana	Astringent; mosquito repellent; roots cure colic; reduces tumors	Astringent; relieves itching of insects; no apparent effect on colic or tumors

Remedies prepared for non-medical purposes are more question-able scientifically. For example, one preparation meant to attract the love of another person involves swallowing a few kernels of hard, dry corn. Once the corn has passed through the digestive tract, it is removed from the feces and washed, toasted, and ground into a fine powder. This powder is slipped into the drink of the intended lover, and it is believed to be efficacious in making the drinker fall in love. Sometimes the ingredients have merely a symbolic value; other times the ewe has no apparent connection to the effect it is intended to produce. For example, if police officers come to search an individual's home, hanging crabgrass at the four corners of the house is supposed to effectively disorient them. And washing one's eyes with bog onion is meant to promote clairvoyance.

How does one obtain fresh herbs and plants during the winter if one lives in the northern cities of the United States? Houseplants will not do; only wild ewe contains the ashé necessary for spells. Wherever there is any substantial concentration of Hispanics, there are religious stores called *botánicas*. Although no precedents exist for such stores in Cuba or Africa, they have proliferated in the United States, in part of necessity and in part due to the commercialization of the religion within a capitalist economic environment. Botánicas cater to practitioners of Santería by providing them with traditional herbs, plants, roots — most shipped from Florida, Latin America, and the Caribbean — and religious merchandise like statues of the saints, candles, beads, and so forth (see Figure 8 on p. 134).

Sacred Trees

Certain trees are also considered sacred, particularly the ceiba and the royal palm. The former is thought of as the home of the orishas, who perch on its high branches. So sacred is it that the devotee of Santería must request permission before crossing its shadow; if they do not, the tree may become offended — and when angry, it may prevent its medicinal secrets from being used effectively by the offender. In its massiveness it represents the great power of the Creator, and for this reason neither lightning strikes it nor floods engulf it. Many ebbós are left at the foot of a ceiba or are buried in its shadow. The royal palm, on the other hand, is believed to be the cosmic tree of life, symbolizing

Figure 8. Because herbs, plants, and roots needed for the sacrifices, offerings, and spells of the religion are at times hard to come by, botánicas routinely stock and sell them to the faith community. Photo taken by the author.

the beginning of created reality. It is believed to be the home of Changó, which explains why it is always the victim of lightning. When a palm tree is struck by lightning, it is said that Changó is coming home.

Otanes

Stones, known as *otanes,* are also crucial to the rituals of Santería. Without them, the santero or santera would be impotent. According to legend, when the orishas left their community of Ilé-Ifé, what remained were stones resonating with their ashé. Today these stones can be found scattered among ordinary rocks, and by "listening" carefully the devotee of Santería can discern which stones are alive with an orisha's presence. Not surprisingly, these special stones are likely to be found near each orisha's habitat: one can expect to find Ochosi's stones in the forest, Yemayá's by the seashore, and Oshún's on a riverbank. Wherever they are found, they will fill believers with the sudden urge to pick them up and take them home. Indeed, keeping their otanes safe and with them was so important that when the Yoruba were deported to Cuba as slaves, they would swallow them in order to ensure the orishas' presence at their new destination.

Otanes are not merely symbols, but are believed to contain the very real presence of the orishas. When a santero or santera finds one, they are required to treat it like a living entity. They must feed it with blood at least once each year, refresh it in herbal baths, and house it in a special tureen known as a *sopera.* Soperas are generally large, lidded ceramic soup tureens decorated fancifully in the colors of the orishas whose stones they house: white for Obatalá, white with blue for Yemayá, and so forth. There are some exceptions: the stone of Oggún, for example, is kept in an iron cauldron; that of Changó resides in a wooden vessel called a *batea;* Olocun's is kept in water inside a blue earthenware urn. To pray before a sopera is to petition the orisha whose presence is in the stone it contains. Usually, soperas are kept in cabinets known as *canastilleros* in a room of the house or apartment set aside for them (see Figure 9 on p. 136). All santeros and santeras receive soperas for Obatalá, Changó, Yemayá, and Oshún when they are ordained; many possess more.

Figure 9. During the asiento rituals, a trono (throne) is set up for the orisha. Before this trono are food offerings consisting of fruits, cakes, and favorite dishes of the orisha, who is housed in the soperas elevated above the offerings as though sitting on a throne. Also before the trono are candles and a basket with monetary offerings to be used for the purchase of future offerings. The orishas consume the ashé of these offerings which empowers them to help their followers. Photo taken by Santería priest Nelson Hernández.

Magic

From an anthropological perspective, magic such as we have discussed in this chapter can be understood as a nonscientific belief system held by an individual or by a group of people who believe that the utterance of an incantation or the concoction of an elixir can bring about certain desired events through supernatural powers. Failure of these events to occur is blamed neither on the incantation nor on the elixir, but rather on the individual who must have deviated from the prescribed formula.

Sir James George Frazer, in his classic 1890 study *The Golden Bough*, classified magic as either imitative or contagious. Imitative (or homeopathic) magic is based on belief in the law of similarity, which maintains that "like produces like, or that an effect resembles its cause."[9] The magician believes that he or she can produce any desired effect merely by imitating it. This form of magic usually involves the magician producing a facsimile of the object he or she wishes to affect; to act upon the likeness, then, is to act upon the object itself. A common example of humiliating, dominating, or otherwise bringing harm on a person, for instance, begins with obtaining a coconut, then naming it after the person one wishes to influence. The one working the spell then kicks the coconut around the house, recognizing that it is not the coconut itself being kicked, but the victim for whom it is named. What the coconut experiences is an imitation of what is then expected to happen to the victim.

Contagious magic, by contrast, is based on the law of contagion, which contends that "things which have once been in contact with each other continue to act on each other at a distance after the physical contact has been severed."[10] The magician in this case believes that whatever is done to a material object that was once connected to a person will be able to affect that person from afar. For example, if harm is desired to befall a person, the individual casting the spell must obtain something personal that belongs to the victim — discarded nail clippings, some hair, or bodily fluid (ideally semen) would serve perfectly. Personal clothing, too — particularly undergarments — would work as

9. James George Frazer, *The Golden Bough: A Study in Magic and Religion* (New York: Macmillan, 1951), 12.

10. Frazer, *The Golden Bough*, 12.

well. Using one or more of these items, an ebbó can be offered requesting a specific outcome. For example, the object might be placed in a miniature coffin and buried in the cemetery as an offering to Oyá, the owner of the cemetery, as the magician all the while wills a similar outcome for the intended victim.

Imitative magic and contagious magic may be combined for maximum potency. The well-known imitative practice of creating a wax doll in the image of the intended victim is made even more effective by employing contagious magic as well — by clothing the doll in scraps of the victim's clothing, for example, or putting a lock of their hair on the doll's head. Whatever is done to the doll is believed to happen to the victim.

Conclusion

From the rituals we discussed in this chapter, we can see that Santería is a very earth-based religion. Stones, plants, water, and blood are the four essential components to the ceremonies and spells that are at its core. Thus it makes sense that believers in the faith are less concerned with orthodoxy, a set of correct beliefs and doctrines, than with orthopraxis, right actions. A final set of natural objects — seashells — are also important, and it is to them that we will turn in the next chapter.

Chapter 5   Oracles

In the worldview of Santería, the physical and the spiritual worlds influence and affect each other. There is no rigid dichotomy. A physical illness may be the result of a spiritual misalignment; just as easily a spiritual predicament may be the outcome of incorrect or neglected actions. In either case, Santería attempts to reestablish the proper balance between the physical and the spiritual as well as between "good" and "evil," thus restoring the believer to a state of wholeness. But how does one know which area in life is out of balance? Through the process of divination.

The roots of divination reach back to the creation story. According to patakis, Olodumare created the universe in such a way that the spiritual and the physical reflected one another. The orishas knew how to discern this order, and before they departed earth for their heavenly abode they taught human beings how to divine it as well, through the use of divination instruments like shells and coconuts. These are the same instruments used today for divination.

The purpose of divination is not merely to foretell future events, though it often involves that. Rather, it is intended to inquire into the harmony, or the lack thereof, between individuals and the spiritual world, between "good" and "evil." The ultimate question of anyone who consults the oracles is, "Am I in balance with my destiny?" If the answer to that question is no, then divination can provide remedies, restoring good health, fortune, or love. While Santería teaches that individuals' destinies are essentially fixed, negotiated between the ori and

Olodumare, their actions are not predetermined. Men and women may live in alignment with their destinies, or they may ignore or rail against them and thus never reach their fullest potential. Consulting the orishas via divination is the best way for individuals to ensure that they are continually living in harmony.

Anyone may arrange a meeting with a santero or santera to consult the orishas, even those who do not practice the faith. Followers of Santería are not interested in proselytizing. Because ashé is universal, there is no real need for a conversion, and the orishas stand ready to help anyone who approaches them. Unlike many Western religious traditions, which emphasize the need for correct doctrine, Santería's immediate concern is with the problems faced by individuals. Once these problems are resolved, then the mysteries of the faith may be revealed little by little to interested seekers.

Divination, whatever form it takes, is not intended to be an exact science. Much depends on the experience, knowledge, and ashé of the santero or santera who serves as interpreter of the orishas. Indeed, since the orishas can never be wrong, if an oracle turns out to be incorrect it is assumed that there was an error on the part of the interpreter: the diviner conducted the ritual improperly, or forgot some crucial piece of information, and so forth. Whatever the case, the oracles of Santería are not disproved; the seeker is best advised to seek out a more knowledgeable and qualified diviner.

Several divination systems exist by which seekers can consult the orishas. It is not this book's goal to provide a step-by-step description of how to conduct them; rather, we will simply provide a brief overview with the intent of better understanding them, not duplicating them.[1] The two oldest and most authentic are the *regla de ocha* and the *regla de Ifá*. These two rites are largely unchanged from their African roots. The latter is considered the more precise and authoritative of the two, and can be conducted only by babalawos. We will also look briefly at a Chinese system of numerology, many aspects of which were appropriated by practitioners of Santería in nineteenth-century Cuba.

1. Although considered secret, there are several published books on Santería's divination rituals that can serve as "how-to" guides for the novice, notably T. Medina and E. Hernández, *El camino de Osha* (Caracas: Editorial Panapo de Venezuela, 1995); E. Cortez, *Manual del oriate: secretos del oriate de la religión Yoruba* (New York: Vilaragus, 1980); Carlos Elizondo's *Manual del italero de la religion lucumí* (n.p., n.d.).

Four Coconut Pieces

The coconut is in Santería an object of adoration, containing healing, cleansing, and divination properties. In Yoruba, the name *obi* refers both to the coconut (which is more prevalent in the Western Hemisphere) and to the kola nut (which is more readily available in Africa). Because the Yoruba people were unable to find kola nuts in Cuba, they simply substituted the coconut for it. There is also an orisha called Obi who is identified with the coconut. Legend has it that Obi was the favorite of Olofi, creator of the orishas. Obi was renowned for his sincerity, which so impressed Olofi that he made him pure white and gave him a place atop the highest palm tree. Unfortunately, Obi's elevation led to vanity. One day he asked his comrade Elegguá to invite all their friends to a party; Elegguá, indignant at Obi's changed character, filled the guest list with poor, ragged people. When Obi saw his house full of indigents he was incensed and threw everyone out. Elegguá quickly informed Olofi what had transpired. Olofi decided to test Obi by transforming himself into a beggar. In disguise he went to visit Obi, only to be turned away with obvious disdain. But Obi's disdain turned to fear as Olofi revealed his true identity, and though the orisha begged for forgiveness Olofi was unmoved. "Henceforth you will fall from the palm tree and roll in the dirt," he declared. "Your beauty will now be hidden. Furthermore, you will be the one through whom anyone, rich or poor, may communicate with the orishas." Thus the coconut became brown on the outside and white on the inside, and thus it is used in divination rituals.

An individual need not be a full santero or santera in order to *dar coco al santo* (literally, "give the coconut to the saint"). Anyone who has made Elegguá may use the coconuts, for Santería teaches that the coconut cannot lie in his presence. Furthermore, any orisha can be consulted via the coconuts. Thus it is the most universal divination system in the faith. Unlike other divination systems, which rely on the interpretations of experts, the coconut is questioned directly and responds directly. It is by far the simplest and most elementary form of divination. It is employed in every ordination ceremony to inquire whether the orishas are satisfied with the offerings made to them. In everyday life it is usually used to discover what offerings a particular orisha may be requesting, whether an error was made during a ritual, or whether an orisha is satisfied with an offering.

To use the coconut, it is first split open, then quartered into four pieces of approximately two inches each. The seeker then conducts a short ritual to sanctify the coconut pieces with water and prayer. Then the pieces are checked for sturdiness, for to break a coconut while casting it portends ill fortune. Any orisha or egun (though most consult Elegguá) may then be asked a brief, direct question, phrased so that the answer will be yes or no. After the question is asked, the coconut pieces are cast on the floor. Some land with the inner white pulpy side facing upward; others land with the brown outer shell facing upward. Depending how the four pieces land, one of five possible direct answers will be given, for the coconut can speak only five words.

If all the sides facing upward are white, it is called *alafia* and it signifies a tentative yes. The coconuts are then cast again to confirm this. If it is repeated on the second cast, or if *itagua* or *eyife* (both of which we will look at in a moment) is cast instead, then the answer to the question is definitely yes. Itagua occurs when three of the pieces are white and one is brown; it means that the answer is yes but that the ceremony must be repeated because of an error in the divination procedure. Eyife occurs when two of the pieces are white and two are brown, and it signifies a definite yes — usually accompanied by many blessings from the orishas. If three of the pieces facing upward are brown and one is white, then the coconut is saying *ocana-sode*, which means no and that the questioner can expect something evil to occur. The final possibility, for all the sides facing upward to be brown, is called *oyekun*, and it also means no — and that death and destruction may well occur if action is not taken soon! Ocana-sode and oyekun require immediate consultation with a santero or santera to determine how the individual can be restored to harmony with their destiny and with the orishas (see Table 18 on p. 143). Additionally, if one coconut piece lands on top of another, the questioner can expect a positive turn of events. But if one falls on its side, impending death is predicted and the individual should again consult with a santero or santera as quickly as possible.

Sixteen Cowrie Shells

The casting of cowrie shells is thought to be the most important divination system within Santería. Through it the future can be predicted,

---

Table 18: Interpreting the Coconuts

O O O O

Alafia means a tentative yes, but the coconuts should be cast again to be sure. If on the second cast the pattern is alafia, itagua, or eyife, then the answer is yes. If, however, on the second cast the answer is ocana-sode or oyekun, then the answer is no.

O O O ●

Itagua means yes, but the coconuts must again be cast because an error was made during the divination procedure. By recasting the coconuts and asking yes/no questions as to what part of the procedure was done wrong, the questioner can correct the error, then proceed with the original line of questioning.

O O ● ●

Eyife means a positive yes.
There is no need to cast the coconuts again.

O ● ● ●

Ocana-sode means no.

● ● ● ●

Oyekun means no, and warns of tragedy.

---

the past understood, and opportunities in the present seized. It requires the skills of a priest; those santeros and santeras who are highly regarded by the faith community for their skill in reading the shells are called *italero* (see Figure 10 on p. 144). The cowrie shells used in divination are the "mouths" of the orishas. They are sometimes referred to as *diloggún,* which is the Yoruba word for sixteen. Each orisha has its own shells, which are usually kept in the tureens where the otanes are

Figure 10. This 1978 photo shows Santería priest Ramon Martinez casting cowrie shells during a consultation. Photo courtesy of the Historical Museum of Southern Florida.

housed. While some priests have eighteen shells for each orisha and others have twenty-one, all agree that just sixteen are used in divination. The shells are cast onto a small carpet or straw mat, where some land with their opening facing up and others land with it facing down.

The process of casting the shells begins with prayers, ebbós, and sacrifices meant to strengthen the orishas and to persuade them to speak through the shells. Throughout, the priest being consulted holds certain items in his or her hands: a small rock (called *ota*), a long, small, white shell (called *ayé*), a guacalote seed (called *erí-aguona*), and a ball of husk (called *efún*). These are used to determine whether the answer the shells give is yes or no, which is dependent on which hand is holding which item. Prior to casting the shells, the santero or santera raps on the floor three times, three being the sacred number of Elegguá.

The first questions asked attempt to uncover any obstacles that might prevent a fruitful reading of the shells. For example, is it beneficial to do a reading? Are the dead favorably inclined toward the questioner? Is their favorable disposition firm? If the answers to these and similar questions are yes, the reading can continue; if not, additional votive offerings may be required. Through yes and no questions, the cause for the negative response can be pinpointed. Is an orisha upset? If so, how can they be pacified? What ebbó will appease them? Is a dead spirit responsible for the negative response? Usually, the obstacle can be overcome, but the orishas on occasion will indicate that they want nothing to do with the questioner, at which time the santera or santero cannot continue.

If the initial questions are answered affirmatively, or if any additional ebbós that had to be made are accepted by the orishas, then the santera or santero can continue by casting the shells again. This time, the number of shells that land with the opening facing upward corresponds to a particular *odu*, that is, to a set of specific legends, proverbs, verses, and sacrifices (see Table 19 on pp. 146-47). If between one and twelve shells fall with their openings facing upward, the santera or santero can proceed to interpret the odu. If more than that do so, however, a babalawo must be called in to read them. In either case, the shells will later be cast again, and the second throw will narrow the focus of the first one. Thus there are 256 possible combinations (16 odu × 16 sub-messages), and, in addition, some odu (5, 6, 7, 9, and 11, known as the minor odu) require the shells to be cast yet again for confirmation.

Table 19: The Odu

Openings Facing Up	Name	Oracle Proverb	Orisha(s) Speaking
1	Ocanasorde	With one, the world was created. If there is nothing good, there is nothing bad.	Obatalá, Elegguá, Changó, Egun, Oggún, Aganyú
2	Eyioco	An arrow between brothers. Your brother is your enemy.	Obatalá, Elegguá, Changó, Ochosi, Oggún, Ibeyi, Orúnla, Ósun
3	Oggundá	Arguments cause tragedies.	Olodumare, Obatalá, Elegguá, Ochosi, Oggún, Yemayá
4	Eyorosun	No one knows what is at the bottom of the ocean.	Obatalá, Orúnla, Changó, Ochosi, Ibeyi, Olocun, Yemayá
5	Oche	Blood flows through veins.	Olodumare, Obatalá, Elegguá, Orúnla, Oyá, Oshún
6	Obbara	From lies the truth is born. The king does not lie.	Elegguá, Orúnla, Changó, Oshún, Ochosi
7	Oddi	Where the grave is dug, there the burial is made for the first time.	Obatalá, Elegguá, Oggún, Yemayá, Oshún, Inle
8	Eyeunle	The body is ruled by the head. Only one king rules the people.	All the orishas

Openings Facing Up	Name	Oracle Proverb	Orisha(s) Speaking
9	Ossa	One's best friend is one's worst enemy.	Obatalá, Oggún, Oshún, Oyá, Obatalá, Aganyú, Oké
10	Ofun-Mafun	Where the curse was born.	Elegguá, Oshún, Oyá, Oggún, Ochosi
11	Ojuani	Bailing water cannot be done with a basket.	Elegguá, Oshún, Oyá, Oggún, Ochosi
12	Eyila	Where there is war, warriors do not sleep.	Changó
13*	Metanla	Where the illness is born. Sick blood.	Obatalá, Oshún, Oyá, Babalú-Ayé
14*	Merinla	Family that fails to get along. Envy exists.	Los Guerreros
15*	Marunla	What moves you, paralyzes you. Dead blood.	Obatalá, Elegguá, Oshún, Oyá
16*	Meridiloggún	You entered this world to become wise, if you hear counsels.	Olofi

*These must be read and interpreted by a babalawo.

The odu are intended to express truths outside the limitations of any one culture or situation, depending on the priest's ashé, experience, and knowledge for their interpretation.

Each odu is quite complex, usually beginning with the recitation of a proverb, followed by a prayer or a song. Some require the santero or santera to take a specific action. For example, the first odu (the one that applies if only one shell falls with its opening facing upward) requires a phrase and a prayer to be spoken. The second odu entails that the priest stand up, spin around once, and sit down again prior to continuing; the eleventh and twelfth call for immersing the cowrie shells in water and then casting the water away. Each odu is also associated with several orishas who may speak through it, several events that may occur after it, several ebbós that should be given in conjunction with it, and several legends that will relate to the situation of the person seeking consultation.

Say that in the first throw, nine shells fall with their openings facing upward. Nine indicates that Obatalá, Oggún, Oshún, Oyá, Aganyú, and Oké, or any combination of them, are speaking. It also means that the applicable proverb is, "One's best friend is one's worst enemy." This oracle can be unpacked in many ways. Some of the possible interpretations are: (1) If you are married, the relationship is about to end; if planning to marry, beware, for someone wants the relationship to end. (2) Stop feeling anger; calm down, for anger prevents you from thinking clearly. (3) Move to a new home. (4) Consult a physician and do not let sick people spend the night. The ebbós suggested when a nine is rolled are (1) making an offering to Oggún; (2) saying a prayer to Obatalá; (3) feeding any other orisha the seeker has been neglecting.

Also, at least one story is attached to the odu — a tale which, again, can be interpreted in different ways so as to be relevant to the seeker's situation. In the case of the ninth odu, the seeker is told the legend of the three obstacles Obatalá faced on his journey to visit his son Changó, king of Alafia. The first obstacle came in the form of Elegguá, the trickster, disguised as an old man having difficulty carrying a tray. Obatalá approached, wanting to help, but as he did so he dirtied his clothes, forcing the orisha home to change. Starting out again, he encountered a frightened boy stranded on a tray in the middle of a pit of mud. He reached out to help the child, but as he did so he fell into the mud, forcing him home again to change his clothes. Setting out a third time, he journeyed successfully to the land of Alafia. Seeing Changó's white horse, he approached it — only to be arrested by soldiers suspecting him to be a horse thief!

Say the second throw produces a thirteen. A thirteen following a nine indicates the proverb, "Under the bed is a hidden enemy." This axiom narrows the focus of the nine, allowing the santera or santero to tailor the oracle to the particular situation of the seeker. It should go without saying that the above interpretation of 9-13 is extremely simplified; because so much depends on the needs of the seeker, we can provide only a broad overview of this kind of divination.

Ifá

One day when I was thirteen years old, my mother and I went to visit a babalawo who lived in the Bronx, one whose reputation was well known. My mother needed advice regarding some decisions she would soon need to make. The babalawo lived in a dingy apartment building in an economically depressed part of town. Though I was a teenager, I remember feeling apprehensive about the visit. After we left, I asked my mother what the babalawo had said while she was consulting privately with him. She started to laugh. He was obviously a fake, she said, for he predicted that within three years she would give birth to her second child, a son. Imagine, a woman in her mid-forties having a second child after over a decade! We never returned to that babalawo, but if we had, he would have had the last laugh. Within two years, shortly after my fifteenth birthday, my mother gave birth to my baby brother. Coincidence? Not to believers in Santería. This babalawo, they would claim, simply revealed my mother's destiny so that she could decide what course of action she should take to lead her toward greater harmony. If it wasn't a coincidence, how then did the babalawo peer into her future? By reading Ifá.

Unlike the santero or santera, the babalawo divines the future by means of a system known as the Ifá. This divination system is associated with a series of odu whose complexity makes Ifá the most prestigious of Santería's oracles. Nowhere else in the faith is the purity of the old African traditions better maintained than in the divination system of Ifá. Hence babalawos rightly claim a purer tradition. But because of its complexity, and because in the Americas only men are permitted to learn its secrets, it is much less popular than divination via cowrie shells. Although homosexuals have historically been excluded from the priesthood, such restrictions are beginning to be relaxed. Only babalawos of the orisha Orúnla, considered the first babalawo, can divine through Ifá. Santería teaches that Orúnla was the only orisha present when each ori negotiated with Olodumare for its destiny; hence he is charged with speaking through Ifá to guide human beings in fulfilling their destinies. When properly trained, the priest of Orúnla has access to all past, present, and future events, and to the mysteries and secrets of each individual.

The patriarchal nature of Ifá is perpetuated by a pataki involving Orúnla and Yemayá. The former, legend has it, was recognized by all the orishas as the greatest diviner among them due to his mastery of the diloggún. But one day, during a period when he and Yemayá were involved in a romantic relationship, he went away on a trip. While he was gone, Yemayá discovered the secrets of her lover's divination skills and promptly went into business for herself. In no time she was a better diviner than Orúnla. When Orúnla returned and discovered that his trust had been violated, he ended the relationship and devised a new system of divination that only his priest could read. Further, he declared that only men could be his priests, ensuring that women would never again have access to his secrets. Since then, babalawos have stopped reading the cowrie shells, and women have been excluded from learning the secrets of Ifá.[2]

The ceremony of ordination into Ifá is known as *la mano de Orúnla* (the hand of Orúnla) or the abofaca. The individual who becomes a babalawo is forbidden to curse or to swear; he is also required to bathe daily and to always present himself publicly wearing dignified clothing. Following a rigid system of rules and regulations, he attempts to learn the secrets of Ifá, which he then vows never to reveal to outsiders. Usually over a decade of study is spent learning the mysteries; easily a whole lifetime could be spent memorizing all the Ifá. The babalawo

2. Yet on at least two occasions in the remote past, women ruled as Ooni, the spiritual head of the Yoruba. And in her book *Santería: The Religion* (New York: Harmony, 1989), Migene González-Wippler recounts the story of a Jewish woman, Patri Dhaifa, in New York City who, although she was ostracized soon after, successfully became a babalawo in 1985. See especially 110-120. (Some claim that this incident never occurred, but was told to González-Wippler simply to shroud the truth from outsiders.)

must always approach his responsibilities with trepidation, never using his skills in anger or for vengeance or personal gain, recognizing that even a small error on his part could bring harm, perhaps even death, to his client.

The Table of Ifá

Legend has it that the Table of Ifá originally belonged to Changó, who failed to appreciate the gift because of his overwhelming interest in partying. Originally, Orúnla's gift was dance, about which he could not care less. While Orúnla's passions lay in divination, Changó's interests were in frolicking. With time, it occurred to them to exchange their gifts. Since then, no one can out-dance Changó, and no one is a greater diviner than Orúnla. Neither orisha ever regretted the trade.

Because Orúnla is the only orisha to have witnessed every person receiving his or her destiny from Olodumare, only he is able to reveal the secrets that every person's future holds. The babalawo's job is to consult Orúnla to determine whether his client is aligned with his or her destiny. The client need not tell the babalawo the nature of his or her problem; Ifá can be trusted to diagnose the client's problem correctly. In fact, the wise client takes pain to conceal the reason for the consultation, lest the babalawo be tempted to lie or to fake verses that seem to bear on his client's situation. (That dishonest babalawos exist is verified both by clients and by other babalawos.) If Orúnla reveals that the client is indeed in harmony with his or her destiny, then the consultation need not continue; all is well. But if disharmony is present, Ifá will help determine the root of the problem causing the disharmony.

After the client whispers his or her fears to the derecho (the fee that is due for the consultation), the babalawo takes sixteen kola nuts with his left hand and withdraws the bulk of them with his right, leaving behind one or two nuts. (Some babalawos use kola nuts; others use palm nuts; still others use cowrie shells, although babalawos using cowrie shells is rare.) Through the random fall of the nuts upon a round or rectangular wooden tray between six and eighteen inches in diameter, the babalawo can discern the exact destiny of anyone seeking his counsel, using a binary pattern signified by drawing one or two lines on the tray. If one nut remains in his left hand, he draws two lines; if two remain, he marks one. By repeating the process eight times, he

Table 20: Ifá's Patterns

Ogbe	Oyeku	Iwori	Odi
I	I I	I I	I
I	I I	I	I I
I	I I	I	I I
I	I I	I I	I

Irosun	Owonrin	Obara	Okanran
I	I I	I	I I
I	I I	I I	I I
I I	I	I I	I I
I I	I	I I	I

Ogunda	Osa	Ika	Oturopon
I	I I	I I	I I
I	I	I	I I
I	I	I I	I
I I	I	I I	I I

Otura	Irete	Ose	Ofun
I	I	I	I I
I I	I	I I	I
I	I I	I	I I
I	I	I I	I

produces one of sixteen basic binary patterns (see Table 20 above). This entire process is then repeated. Thus the diviner creates eight marks — each mark consisting of either a single or a double line — placed in groups of four. These are marked on the tray and read from right to left. One of a possible 256 patterns (16 × 16) is produced, and it is the babalawo's job then to arrive at the corresponding odu and then interpret it. Orúnla taught this method of communication with Olodumare to his sixteen sons, who in turn passed it down, generation by generation, to today's babalawos.

Since each odu has sixteen verses, we may calculate at very least

4,096 possible interpretations that may be arrived at from the casting of kola seeds. Yet 4,096 is a conservative estimate, for the number sixteen is seen by some babalawos as a symbolic number signifying completion. Other babalawos claim that a single odu can have over 100 verses! Regardless as to how many exist, these verses are the core of Ifá, and no babalawo can be considered competent until he has memorized at least a thousand of them. For this reason, these priests are held in deep respect by others. Each odu contains both a prediction and a required sacrifice, and while each one is different, many also contain myths, information about the origins of the odu, and specific ways in which the mythical stories are to be applied. Usually the latter information commences with the words, "Ifá says," clearly indicating what is necessary for resolving the client's problem. But much of the other information is so archaic and shrouded in mystery that even the babalawo cannot be certain of its deeper meaning.

The odu itself can be cryptic, forcing the babalawo to rely on his experience, his knowledge of patakis, and, of course, his own ashé. Santería teaches that every problem a person could possibly face has an analogous counterpart in creation; thus each odu is manifested and can be interpreted on countless different levels. In Ifá, odu are the very foundation of existence, touching on aspects of religion and spirituality, history and legend, and science and medicine. Using the Table of Ifá, the babalawo can help his client to see these patterns and to live in harmony with them — or, of course, the client may choose to reject them and move further and further from his or her destiny.

Opele

Another way of reading Ifá involves using a chain known as *opele*. The chain is about fifty inches long, interrupted with eight concave shell pieces, round pieces of leather, or pieces of coconut, all of which can land with either the convex or concave side facing upward when the opele is cast. The babalawo holds the chain in the middle and casts it with his right hand. For each shell or other item on the chain, if the concave side is facing upward, a single mark is made on the Table of Ifá, and if the convex side faces upward, then a double mark is made. As with the casting of kola nuts on the Table of Ifá, these series of marks will refer the babalawo to a particular odu.

Using the chain allows the babalawo to arrive at the same markings and corresponding odu more quickly than he would by casting the nuts on the Table of Ifá; one single cast of the chain is equivalent to eight separate manipulations of the nuts. Regardless of whether one uses the opele or the Table of Ifá, the divination system is identical, making use of the same figures and their related odu. Usually, the opele is employed for day-to-day consultations, while the Table is reserved for more extensive divination readings.

Chinese Numerology

The opening of China to European penetration in the 1840s created a new source of potential slave labor for the Caribbean. In 1847 the first two hundred Asians were brought to Cuba; this trickle became a flood of 140,000 over the next two decades, surging in 1939 to over 300,000. Per the terms of an 1817 treaty (Chinese laborers were first taken to Trinidad in 1806), they were not to be regarded as slaves; however, the distinction between slave and indentured servant was one of name only. Although they usually arrived in Cuba with an eight-year labor contract, their procurement was similar to that of African slaves. And because they possessed no economic value to their masters after eight years, they tended to be treated even worse than slaves were. True, at the end of their contracts, laborers could in theory become tenant farmers or pay for return passage to China. But few lived long enough to exercise either option — an estimated 75 percent died during their years of servitude.[3]

Those who survived and remained in Cuba became part of the culture there, enriching it with elements of their own. One contribution the Chinese made to Cuban culture was a gambling game known as the hanging bag. In this game, a dealer wrote a number on a slip of paper and stuck it in a bag which was strung to the ceiling. He or she then gave a clue based on a system in which each number between one and one hundred corresponded to a different object (see Table 21 on pp. 155-56). Those who correctly guessed the number won a portion of all the bets collected.

3. Gonzalo de Quesada, *The Chinese and Cuban Independence* (Leipzig: Breitkopf & Hartel, 1925), 4-6.

Table 21: Chinese Numerology

1. Horse or Head		39. Small Snake or Rabbit
2. Butterfly		40. Priest
3. Sailor		41. Lizard
4. Cat or Mouth		42. Duck
5. Nun		43. Scorpion
6. Turtle or Tortoise		44. Leather or Year
7. Seashell, Snail, or Feces		45. Shark or President
8. Corpse or Death		46. Smoke or Bus
9. Elephant		47. Bird or Homosexual
10. Whale or Big Fish		48. Roach
11. Rooster		49. Drunk
12. Madonna or Whore		50. Police
13. Peacock or Pimp		51. Soldier
14. Striped Cat or Tiger		52. Bicycle
15. Dog		53. Electric Light
16. Bull		54. Hen or Flower
17. Moon		55. Crab
18. Small Fish		56. Candy or Queen
19. Worm		57. Bed or Telegram
20. Cat		58. Photograph
21. Snake		59. Phonograph
22. Frog		60. Dark Sun or Clown
23. Steam or Steam Ship		61. Big Horse
24. Dove		62. Marriage
25. Gemstone		63. Murderer
26. Eel		64. Gunshot
27. Wasp		65. Food or Jail
28. Goat or Anus or Vagina		66. Horn or Divorce
29. Mouse		67. Stabbing
30. Shrimp or Penis		68. Cemetery
31. Deer		69. Well
32. Hog		70. Coconut
33. Vulture		71. River
34. Monkey		72. Ox
35. Spider		73. Park or Suitcase
36. Pipe		74. Kite
37. Witch or Witchcraft		75. Tie or Movie
38. Macaw or Crab		76. Dancer

77. Flag	89. Torrent or Lottery
78. Coffin or Bishop	90. Old Man
79. Train	91. Old Shoe or Streetcar
80. Doctor	92. Balloon or Plane
81. Theater	93. Revolution or Ring
82. Lion or Mother	94. Machete
83. Tragedy	95. War
84. Blood or Tailor	96. Shoe
85. Mirror or Spain	97. Mosquito
86. Convent or Scissor	98. Piano
87. Banana or New York	99. Saw
88. Glasses	100. Hotel or Toilet

While this system of numerology is not part of any of Santería's official divination systems, it is widely used by many who worship the orishas. If an individual has a dream about a particular person, animal, or object in the system, they may consider it a communiqué from the spiritual world. They might then bet on the numbers corresponding to the subject of the dream in the lottery, the horses, or *la bolita* (an illegal form of gambling popular among older Hispanics). Say, for example, that a woman had a dream about riding a horse that was being chased by a priest and a nun riding a bull. She would then want to bet on the numbers 1, 5, 16, and 40, for those are the numbers corresponding to the horse, nun, bull, and priest respectively.

Conclusion

Santería's oracles are not to be used lightly — to predict who will win the next Super Bowl, for example. Rather, they are used to address the problems faced by individual seekers. By peering into individuals' assigned destinies, diviners can determine whether a seeker's present path will lead to their fullest potential. If not, the orishas will guide the seeker so as to align their life with their destiny. While it is entirely up to the seeker to either follow or disregard the oracles' recommendations, failure to do so will lead to a life filled with misfortune. Obedience, on the other hand, will lead to a life of peace and harmony.

Chapter 6   Historical Roots

Memories can be deceiving. Sometimes events are dis-membered so that they can be re-membered differently. Most of us prefer to remember events that make us look good in our own eyes, forgetting those humbling moments that reveal our shortcomings and failures. If history is a collection of memories, then it is the positive memories accepted and constructed by a particular group, with negative memories conveniently discarded. More often than not, those with power and privilege impose their recollections on those with no voice to recount their stories. Yet in spite of such "official" histories, the collective experience of the oppressed can persist, forging a people's determination to survive and providing insight as to how a people see and understand themselves. Recounting these marginalized stories can also provide clues as to how people construct and understand their religious worldview. Unfortunately, we at times approach the study of history by reducing it to charts of dates and events. While such time lines are useful and necessary, they usually ignore the dynamic, often conflicting processes through which a people's belief develops. Although a timeline is provided at the end of this chapter, our focus here will remain on the process through which the oppressed found voice in the worship of the orishas as they migrated from Africa to Cuba, and then from Cuba to the United States.

    Throughout this book, I have defined the African roots of Santería as being Yoruba. While this may be broadly true, it would be a mistake to assume that Yoruba is the only African culture to have influenced the religion. Before exploring the religion's Yoruba roots more closely, it is important to note that the term "African" designates a mélange of cultures and peoples, though it has become to some extent a homogeneous term signifying the mixture of different peoples, traditions, and cultures. The famed Cuban scholar Fernando Ortiz provided a brief ethnological sketch of ninety-nine different African nations that were represented in Cuba by the start of the twentieth century.[1] The definition as African of black Haitians, Bahamians, Jamaicans and other islanders who traveled to Cuba in past centuries seeking work made the definition of African even murkier. While the cultures of these non-Yoruba people may not have survived, in many instances, some of their religious traditions, beliefs, and rites were absorbed by the Yoruba and reinterpreted in the formation of Santería.

Birth of the Yoruba People

Many anthropologists claim that Africa was the birthplace of human life. As we saw in the second chapter, Santería's beliefs hold that the city of Ilé-Ife was where creation began. As you recall, Obatalá, the chief orisha of the Yoruba pantheon, hung down from heaven on a golden chain. He spilled loose soil stored in a snail's shell upon the watery earth. Once the soil touched the water, he let loose a five-toed chicken that immediately started to dig. Wherever this soil was dispensed, solid ground appeared. After a while, enough solid ground existed that Obatalá let go of the golden chain and descended to earth. The spot where he landed became the city of Ilé-Ife.

This is the most popular rendition of the story, but there exists an older Yoruba version of it. While the methodology of how Ilé-Ife and the earth came to be remains basically the same, in this story it is not Obatalá who is responsible for the creative process, but his younger brother Oddudúa. While Obatalá was commissioned to create the earth, he was distracted on his way to his task. He noticed other gods partying by heaven's gate. When they invited Obatalá to join them, the great orisha accepted, soon becoming drunk on too much palm wine,

---

1. Fernando Ortiz, *Los negros esclavos* (La Habana: Editorial de ciencias sociales, 1975), 40-56.

causing him to fall asleep. Now Oddudúa heard Olodumare's instructions to Obatalá, so when he saw his older brother asleep, he took the material and set out to create the earth. It was he, then, who placed a handful of earth in a palm nut which he scattered on the watery surface while hanging from a golden chain, then set loose a five-toed cockerel to spread the ground.

Once Obatalá awoke from his drunken stupor and saw what his younger brother had done, he forswore drinking for himself and for all his children. Nonetheless, he went to earth to claim it for himself, for after all, Olodumare had given him the instructions on earth's creation. Besides, he was the older brother. Oddudúa, on the other hand, felt that Obatalá had by his negligence forfeited any rights to the earth. Soon, both brothers were quarreling and the other orishas started taking sides. Olodumare at last intervened, bringing the fighting to an end. He decreed that Obatalá would become the creator of humanity, bestowing upon him the power to mold human bodies, while Oddudúa, who did create the earth, would get to rule it, becoming its first king in Ife.

In addition to this creation story, there is a second myth about the foundation of Ilé-Ife that concerns Oddudúa. This story appears to have roots that are more political than religious. In this legend, Oddudúa — possibly a historical figure — was a prince in Mecca, son of the king Lamurudu.[2] As the region embraced Islam, Oddudúa refused to forsake the worship of the gods. Forced to flee Mecca, Oddudúa wandered the earth for a long time, finally settling at Ilé-Ife. Thus it is he who brought the religion of the orishas there. Prolific in life, he had seven children and many grandchildren who spread throughout the region, each starting their own kingdom. All the Yoruba kings, as well as those of other area kingdoms like Benin and Oyo, trace their lineage to Oddudúa. In the two stories concerning the foundation of Ilé-Ife and the birth of the Yoruba, Oddudúa plays a pivotal role. He is credited with establishing both the area's political and religious structures.

---

2. Other traditions and sources claim that Oddudúa migrated from Upper Egypt (Memphis), based on the similarities which exist between Egyptian and Ife sculpture.

On Being a Yoruba

The Yoruba settled along the northwestern shore of the continent of Africa, in an area that today is southern Nigeria, probably migrating to this area from the east, from either Mecca during the rise of Islam, or the Upper Nile region during the ascent of Christianity. By 1000 CE, small city-states began to develop along the coast between the rivers Mono and Niger. Three major Yoruba kingdoms developed in this region, Benin, Dahomey, and Oyo, each playing an important role in the affairs of the others, and all three playing a major role in the slave trade to Cuba. The kings of these areas had a father-child relationship with their subjects. The state was understood as a type of extended family, with the kings acting like brothers. These regions interacted with each other in familiar fashion. They all traced their lineage to the creator of the earth, Oddudúa, whose cosmic work began in Ilé-Ife, a major city in the southwest region. Here the orishas made their home, humans were created, and the first city to cradle civilization was founded. The ruler of Ife is the Ooni, who was, and continues to be, chosen from among the original families who founded the city. Today, scholars believe that sacred Yoruba culture developed at Ife during the twelfth century.

Ife became the capital of a loose confederation of city-states. Originally, this confederation was composed of sixteen regions, each with its own specialized religious function contributing to the harmony and well-being of the entire culture. The Yoruba constituted several ethnic groups, the Egba, Ife, Ijebu, and Ketu. These peoples organized themselves as urbanized theocratic city-states, ruled by kings, called *oba*. Like the Ooni in Ife, the oba were chosen from among the families believed to have first settled in the region. The Yoruba were among the most urban of the African people. Later Portuguese, British, and Dutch explorers would describe its cities, specifically Benin, as containing immense streets with immaculate houses. They were impressed by the overall wealth of the metropolis, complete with courtyards, galleries, and palaces. These Africans were not the ignorant savages usually depicted; rather, they were members of a society which established property holdings, conducted long-distance trade, and established different associations of commerce with business dealing deep within the African continent. The only disadvantage faced by Africans was that European culture was technologically superior in producing weapons of destruction.

In the mid-1400s Europeans began stealing Africans for forced labor. To the Yoruba mindset, these white people were akin to bogeymen; they could only wonder about the type of culture that would produce such savagery, causing great disharmony among the followers of the creator of all, Olodumare. What kind of land do these Europeans come from, where do they take Africans, and what has become of those who have disappeared? Those who were sold into slavery found out, as they were taken across the ocean to Cuba and to Brazil.[3]

This pattern was established in the late fifteenth century, when the Moors' 700-year rule of Spain came to an end. Once the cross vanquished the crescent in the Iberian peninsula, Portuguese sailors began to explore Africa's west coast in search of gold and abandoned Moorish trade routes. By 1448, with the Catholic Church's blessing, they brought the first African slave to Europe. For Spain to develop into an empire, Isabella, "the Last Crusader," queen of Castile, and King Ferdinand of Aragon needed to discover new trading routes to India, safe from hostile Islamic forces. Hence Christopher Columbus sailed westward in 1492. Rather than his discovering a new trade route to India, native populations in what would eventually be called the Caribbean discovered the lost sailors. Although they offered the strangers hospitality, within a generation the indigenous population was decimated by the newcomers. The islands they called home, and especially Cuba, were believed to have precious metals awaiting extraction. Because gold and silver from the so-called "New World" flooded Spain, the African coast ceased to be an important source of precious metals, and became instead a source of human labor to replace the vanishing indigenous population of the Caribbean. Hence the start of the slave route which brought Africans to Cuba, along with their traditions, customs, and gods. By the mid-sixteenth century, the British and Dutch had taken over these trade routes and provided slave labor to the Spanish colonies established throughout the Americas.

The demand for sugar in the late seventeenth century triggered a

---

3. Gold Coast Fanti-Ashanti people were mainly brought to British territories, i.e. the eastern United States, Jamaica, Bahamas, and Guiana, while Dahomey people were mainly brought to French territories, i.e. the French Antilles, Haiti, Louisiana, and Dutch Guiana. Diana González Kirby and Sara María Sánchez, "Santería: From Africa to Miami via Cuba: Five Hundred Years of Worship," *Historical Association of Southern Florida*, Vol. 48 (1988): 41.

demographic revolution in the West Indies as more and more Africans were brought to the Caribbean to work the emerging sugar plantations. It is conservatively estimated that nine to ten million slaves crossed the Atlantic; of this number, 6.3 million slaves are estimated to have been transported from West Africa, and of these, an estimated 23 percent came from the Slave Coast (western Nigeria, Benin, and Togo) while 42 percent came from the Niger Delta and the Cameroons. For about three quarters of a million to 1.3 million slaves (7 to 10 percent of the total), Cuba was their destination. There they worked 18-hour days, six days a week. Life expectancy for a slave after arriving in Cuba was usually seven years. Slave deaths exceeded births, which necessitated new acquisitions. It was considered more cost effective to work a slave to death and purchase a new one than to expend the resources needed for adequate slave health care.

The establishment of the Atlantic slave trade had more profound consequences for the Yoruba than simply the stealing of young Africans. Their homeland suffered the ravages of political unrest, chiefly caused by the slave trade, as kingdoms rose against kingdoms for the purpose of acquiring humans to sell to the European slavers. Benin, Lagos, Bonny, and Calabar became chief centers of the slave trade. The formerly stable kingdom of Benin was badly shaken by the rise and subsequent decline of the Oyo kingdom; in addition, civil wars broke out as royal houses struggled within themselves for supremacy. Contrary to allegations made by the propaganda disseminated among Europeans, the Yoruba were not ignoble savages captured in the slavers' nets, but rather part of an advanced culture of patricians and priests deemed to have been disloyal to the ascendancy of new rulers. The vicissitudes of monarchic power struggles resulted in those opposing the new hegemony becoming enslaved and expatriated. Captives of war were also routinely enslaved. Also, in times of drought, villages sold inhabitants whom they could not support for basic provisions. Under such an arrangement, both the slave traders and the victorious monarchic powers profited from the trade relationship.

Placed in chains, the captured Africans boarded ships that must have seemed like huge canoes. They were packed and tied deep in the belly of these ships, where the darkness engulfed them and the air remained stale. Wooden platforms were constructed with little space between slaves so that the maximum number of bodies could be packed.

With little room to move, they would arrive at their destination bruised and scraped from lying upon wooden planks for the entire journey. This is what happened to nearly all the men. Few of the young women were chained to the ship, however. The few times the men were allowed on deck, in leg shackles, to relieve the debilitating effects of cramped quarters, they would discover where the young maidens of their people were kept. They were allowed the "freedom" to roam the deck — that is, they were exploited by the sexual appetite of the crew. For amusement, the crew, through the use of whips and cat-o'-nine-tails, persuaded the Africans to dance. Refusal was met with flogging or the use of torture devices like thumbscrews and iron collars.

Down below, as they were chained in small compartments, the stench of vomit and feces would burn the captives' lungs. Cries to Changó, Obatalá, and Yemayá could be heard, but no deliverance ever came. Mostly men were chained throughout the ship, the oldest and weakest quickly dying. Early in the Atlantic slave trade, about 15 to 20 percent of the cargo perished. By the eighteenth century, this number was reduced to 5 to 10 percent; however, by the nineteenth century, as Britain attempted to curtail the slave trade, the mortality rate again increased to about 15 to 20 percent. In the captives' own eyes, those who died were the lucky ones, for they could now be reincarnated in Africa.

For those who lived, they could only ponder their fate. Rumors would circulate as to what awaited them. Many correctly guessed that they would be slaves in a new land, though others feared that these white people were cannibals intent on eating them, while others wondered if they would be offered up as sacrifices to the captors' gods. After several days they would reemerge from the belly of the ship, only to discover a land that, while resembling their home, was still vastly different. As they left the boat, one white man, a church official, would sit on an elaborate chair, wearing regal colors, sprinkling water and mumbling words the Africans simply could not possibly comprehend.

The consequences of the slave trade on Africa are incalculable. Obviously it stifled the development of the continent as a considerable number of young, able-bodied men and women were forced to work in developing European colonies. This forced migration eradicated many villages, while leaving other towns inhabited with old men and women. As different African ethnic groups competed with each other to supply Africans to the European traders, wars soon broke out, bringing more devastation to the area. At times, these wars broke out within the ethnic group, as was the case in the Yoruba civil wars. Additionally, the emphases on profiting in the export of Africans diverted attention from developing agriculture and industry. When the slave trade collapsed, European powers — most notably Great Britain — were able to step in and colonize these African kingdoms, further contributing to the underdevelopment of the region, as raw material needed for industry was appropriated.

For those Africans destined for slavery, tragically torn from their ordered religious life, there was no time to ponder philosophically the spiritual response to the calamity they faced. *Is the white people's god more powerful than the orishas? After all, the black person, not the white one, is the slave.* Although their gods were in this strange new land since 1517 when the first slave ship carrying human cargo disembarked on the island of Cuba, it was not until the nineteenth century that the slaves brought to the island firmly established the orisha religious traditions. These new slaves were compelled to adjust their belief system to the immediate challenges presented by their new social location. The trauma of being uprooted and having to adjust to the challenges and struggles of a new environment ensured that their religious beliefs would not stay intact. It is inevitable that the radically different social order faced in Cuba created profound consequences in how they understood and worshiped the orishas of their homeland. Although the same gods of their homeland were being worshiped, in a manner faithful to the traditions of the ancestors, simultaneously the faith adapted to the new subjugated situation in which Africans found themselves. This transition created the nascent state from where Santería would eventually emerge, where the Yoruba ethos survived by manifesting itself through Spanish Catholicism.

To take one example of adaptation, in Africa, Oyá was the god of the Niger River. Once the slaves arrived in Cuba, they were unable to find a river that reminded them of the majesty of the familiar river left behind. With time, Oyá was seen less as a river god and more as one of cemeteries, wind, and thunderbolts. Likewise, upon arriving in Cuba, the Africans found it difficult to find kola nuts with which to consult the oracles. So they simply substituted the coconut for the kola nut. Both the function of the orishas and the procedures of the rituals were changed to face the new environment.

Santería was also able to come into being because of the complete failure of the Catholic Church to be a guide, voice, and refuge for the multitudes suffering the harsh reality of slavery. After the unfamiliar, context-free ritual of baptism that took place upon disembarking from the slave ship, religious instruction was basically nonexistent. Priests were concentrated in the wealthier urban centers, particularly in La Habana. Because slaves were concentrated in the rural agricultural areas, years and decades would pass without them — or their masters for that matter — coming into contact with a priest. When they did, the encounter was often reduced to prayer instruction, in which the slaves were taught how to pronounce a few words they did not understand so that they could recite by rote a prayer to the master's god. In some cases, a poor priest (not usually among the church's brightest and best) would be hired by the sugar mill to attend to the spiritual needs of the slaves. Loyalty to the employer who was paying them, rather than to the teachings of Jesus, led many to concentrate their teachings on biblical passages that exhorted slaves to work hard (as if unto the Lord), not steal, and surely not rebel. As the years progressed, the influence of the church in the agricultural rural areas declined as clerics continued to find the urban centers more profitable. A spiritual vacuum developed — a vacuum which Santería would eventually fill.

Preserving the Faith

Catholic Cuba was more conducive to preserving the faith of the orishas than was the Protestant United States. Unlike the United States, which relied on breeding their slaves, it was more cost-effective for Cubans to import replacements for those slaves worked to death. Additionally, a greater number of slaves were made available to Cuba during the nineteenth century, due mostly to the Owu and Egba civil wars and the final 1840 conquest of Oyo by the Fulani, who were members of the Muslim faith. This latter forced migration of Africans to Cuba ensured a better opportunity to preserve the orisha traditions. As late as the 1930s former slaves known as *negros de nación* (African-born slaves) were still alive, remembering the religious rituals and customs of their birthplace, and transmitting that knowledge to the next generation. Hence the African culture did not diminish as rapidly as it did in the States, where the African heritage was more and more diluted and lost with each ensuing generation of slaves under Anglo rule.

The last official ship bringing African slaves to the island docked in Cuba in 1865, although the practice unofficially continued for a few years thereafter. So it should not be surprising that at the close of the slave trade, one third of the Cuban population were of African descent, of which about 75 percent were African-born, many still practicing the religious traditions of their African homeland.[4] In contrast, at the close of the American Civil War in 1865, the existing four million U.S. slaves were ten times the total number of slaves imported from abroad. The 427,000 slaves imported to former British colonies (including the 28,000 brought to French and Spanish Louisiana) represented 4.5 percent of all Africans imported to the Americas. Cuba alone, on the other hand, took in more slaves than the U.S. after 1808.[5]

Aside from these variations in slave importation patterns, there also existed differences in how slavery was structured within the U.S. plantation — differences that stifled the growth of African traditional religions in Anglo America. Because slaveholders in the American South required fewer slaves on their plantations than did those in the Caribbean, slaves had smaller support systems for continuing their religious practices and beliefs and less influence in disseminating their beliefs to the overall slave community. These smaller slave plantations perpetuated the loss of the traditional African belief system through the process of "breaking in" African-born slaves. U.S. Protestant slave masters sought the elimination of all aspects of Africanism, which they deemed to be primitive, if not satanic. Speaking an African language, playing the drums, or worshiping the orishas became capital offenses. Even gathering as a congregation for worship, or any other activity, was illegal unless supervised by white people. Furthermore, African-born slaves were generally looked down upon by the U.S.-born slaves, who saw the African-born as savages. Social pressure was thus exerted to get the African-born to learn and accept the new customs and existing norms. With the passing of each successive generation of U.S.-born

4. Philip D. Curtin and Jan Vansina, "Sources of the Nineteenth Century Atlantic Slave Trade," *Journal of African History* 5 (1964): 185-208; and Hugh Thomas, *Cuba: The Pursuit of Freedom* (New York: Harper & Row, 1971), 170.

5. Albert J. Raboteau, *Slave Religion: The "Invisible Institution" in the Antebellum South* (Oxford: Oxford University Press, 1978), 90.

slaves, the preservation and transmission of their original religion became less likely, causing a spiritual vacuum that eventually was filled by Christianity (specifically Protestantism), which became a bond insuring social cohesion among slaves.

In Cuba, the continuation of the worship of the orishas became that bond. Ironically, as some of the traditions and rituals were forgotten among the Yoruba in Africa, they were preserved among the slave communities in Cuba. This preservation was also due to how Catholic slavery in the Caribbean differed from Protestant slavery in Anglo North America. While both institutions were uncivilized and brutal, nuances did exist between the two systems. Slavery in a civil society influenced by Catholicism in theory guaranteed certain human rights. Because marriage was a sacrament of the church, family members could not be sold as they could among Protestants. Additionally, under Catholic rule, a slave could own private property, and was able to purchase his or her freedom or the freedom of others. Of course, before the reader concludes that Catholic slavery was much more humane than Protestant slavery, it is important to note that such safeguards were routinely ignored, especially outside the city, where the church lacked a presence. In fact, the treatment of slaves under Catholic rule proved in other respects to be more life-threatening.

The Cabildos

This island called Cuba was once free of Europeans. It was the start of the colonial venture that directly led to the decimation of the native population. The dwindling of the indigenous population facilitated Europeans settling on the island. Migrating from all different regions of the Iberian Peninsula, they spoke different languages and maintained different cultural idiosyncrasies. To ease the difficulty of transition, these groups created social clubs along racial and linguistic lines to serve as mutual aid societies. These societies resembled the civil associations that were not uncommon in the homeland, especially in Andalusia and Seville. They were started in the 1200s in medieval Spain as religious *hermandades* (fraternities), serving as guilds whose members, belonging to similar occupations, celebrated the feasts of the particular saint that served as patron of the group and provided each other with medical and financial support in times of need. Although these groups were mainly composed of whites, occasionally there were all-black fraternities composed of African slaves living in Spain.

When slaves began to be imported to the island of Cuba, both the slave masters and the church encouraged them to form their own social clubs, called *cabildos*. These cabildos, like their European counterparts, were also created along ethnic and linguistic lines; but the whites hoped that dividing the slaves into smaller groups to which they would be loyal would prevent them from uniting in rebellion. The cabildo also served a religious function, and as such can be seen as a forerunner to today's house-temples. As a mutual aid society it provided assistance to the sick; worked to improve its members' social, political, and economic status; purchased the freedom of its members; and provided burials for its dead from the funds collected through membership fees, donations, and inheritance (it was common for slaves to leave their meager earthly possessions to these societies). As important was the preservation of the rituals and beliefs of cabildos members' culture. Although a sanctioned institutional structure under the direction of the diocesan priest was created to facilitate the conversion of Africans to Christianity by providing them the opportunity to express their cultural traditions and customs within Catholicism, in reality, slaves and former slaves, at least to a limited degree, preserved their native languages, performed their rituals, and consulted the orishas. Ironically, the church believed that the cabildos provided easy access to the group for the church's evangelization ventures. But in truth, these cabildos created a space where the religious traditions of Africa could be preserved, and passed down to ensuing generations. Unbeknown to the Catholic authorities that organized the cabildos, they provided a social structure crucial to the survival of Yoruba religious beliefs and rituals.

Additionally, Catholicism's approach to conversion was less intense than that of Protestants in the United States. Baptism into the Catholic Church was dependent on memorizing a few simple prayers and learning some ritual protocols; Protestants, on the other hand, usually demanded some form of conversion experience. The Catholics also encouraged slaves to participate in the elaborate festivals to the saints. These saints' festivals, similar in structure to those venerating ancestors in Africa, were soon appropriated to help keep their traditions alive. Slaves were allowed to congregate in order to plan the festival and venerate the saint's holiday.

Nevertheless, as the Catholic churches' political power diminished, and as the slave trade was coming to an end, the Spanish colonial government became suspicious of the cabildos. After two wars for independence, in which a disproportionately large number of blacks fought, Spain feared that the cabildos were a source for insurrection. By 1884, the Good Government Law was passed, forbidding all cabildos from meeting or organizing festivals. By 1910, all black organizations were outlawed on the island by the new U.S.-backed Republic which feared a possible race war.

Besides the cabildos, the Yoruba traditions survived in societies of marooned or runaway slaves. These Africans who escaped the plantations formed societies in mountainous regions (especially in the eastern part of the island) and dense forests. Known as *cimarrones,* these runaway slaves, as early as the 1520s, created communities free from European supervision or subjugation. These "free" areas provided runaway slaves with the opportunity to continue their religious practices and rituals. However, given that they consisted of Africans from different parts of the continent, they found it necessary to modify customs and traditions for the sake of the community's unity.

Spanish Catholicism

The Yoruba slaves found themselves on an island where the dominant religion was Catholicism, but this was not the traditional Catholicism advocated by the official church; rather, it was a folk Catholicism practiced primarily by members of the lower economic classes. Throughout Spanish culture, two manifestations of Catholicism existed. The first was a very formal, hierarchical devotion that attracted primarily those in the upper economic classes. The second emphasized not holy sacraments, but rather personages, specifically the Virgin Mary, Jesus, and the saints. While the official church maintained a clear distinction between veneration (appropriate to the saints) and worship (reserved for God alone), this distinction was mostly lost on church members, who established annual festivals to honor these figures based on the elaborate miracle stories developed concerning their lives.

The essence of this popular Catholicism was forged during centuries of struggling against the Muslim enemies of the "true" faith. After seven centuries of Muslim rule, Spain's holy obligation rested in wresting the land from the hands of the "infidels," and once again establishing a Spain that was "Christian." Consequently, like the Jews, Muslims faced a choice: convert, die, or leave. This seven-hundred-year-old struggle to reclaim the land fused and confused nationalism with Catholicism. To be Spanish, by definition, meant to be Christian. In fact, to say, *"Hablo cristiano"* (I speak Christian) was a common way of saying, "I speak Spanish." This crusading worldview was transplanted to the islands of the Caribbean during the foundation of New Spain. Jesus' Great Commission to baptize all nations was understood literally by the Spanish monarchs, legitimizing Spanish sovereignty.

In addition, the Catholicism imported to Cuba was a pre-Reformation Catholicism. It emerged from a time prior to the Protestant Reformation of Martin Luther, a time when the Catholic Church enjoyed the power and privilege of being the sole interpreter of reality. Within this reality, Spanish folklore and mythology shaped and formed how Christianity was understood by the masses. Yet it was also a Catholicism undergoing its own reformation. Long before Luther nailed his theses on the church doors at Wittenberg, beginning what has become known as the Protestant Reformation, Isabella, queen of Castile, championed the reformation of the Catholic Church. With Archbishop Francisco Jiménez de Cisneros of Toledo, they introduced sweeping reforms to Spain's monasteries and convents, strove to enhance theological scholarship by encouraging the printing of books, founded the University of Alcalá, and published the Complutensian Polyglot, a multilingual edition of the Bible.

Even though Cuba was Catholic in theory, it was hardly Catholic in practice. Throughout its history, both under colonial rule and during the Republic years of the first half of the twentieth century, the cultural milieu there allowed most Cubans to refer to themselves as Catholics even if they seldom attended church or partook in its sacraments. One could dabble in the rituals of the orishas or consult Spiritists and still consider oneself Catholic. Generally speaking, Cuban spirituality easily moved between different religious expressions. According to a study done by the Catholic Church of Cuba in 1954, prior to Castro's Revolution, one out of every four Catholics occasionally consulted a santera or a santero.[6] Even today when Cubans reject Santería and insist solely on their Christianity, they still observe the adage, "*Tenemos que respetar los Santos* (We have to respect the Saints)."

According to Cuban historian Calixto Masó y Vazquez, the religious feelings of the Cuban population during the early twentieth century, "always prompted some attention to religious problems, being neither atheist nor fanatical; "nonetheless their religiosity, above all else the practice of their religious duty, almost bordered on indifference."[7] Adding to the dislocation between the Catholic Church and the masses, the rural areas, throughout Cuba's history, had little by way of official representation of the Catholic faith. La Habana developed at the expense of the economically declining countryside. The rural areas had almost no schools or churches. Years would pass between church masses and the administration of the sacraments. More than ninety percent of the area lacked electricity, milk, fish, meat, or bread. Illiteracy in rural areas was four times that of urban areas. The few times a priest would appear, he would usually preach against the political interests of those Cubans born on the island. The vast majority of clergy were conservative Spaniards politically aligned with Spain, especially during the wars for independence. They failed to connect with the masses because they normally served the pro-Spain privileged elite of La Habana.

Moreover, these rural areas lacked any semblance of medical facilities. Hence, when whites (whether slaveholders or peasants) needed medical attention, their desperation to heal a loved one led them to summon a Catholic priest, a difficult if not impossible task to accomplish, as well as an African healer. Seeking spiritual guidance from divergent religions began not to be limited to issues concerning health. Problems concerning relationships, financial survival, and simple well-being led isolated whites throughout rural Cuba, who possessed only an elementary understanding of Christianity, to turn to the orishas for additional guidance and assistance.

6. Agrupación Católica Universitaria, *Encuesta Nacional sobre el Sentimiento Religioso del Pueblo de Cuba* (La Habana: Buró de Información y Propaganda de la ACU, 1954), 37. For more statistics on slave imports and prices, see Hubert H. S. Aimes, *A History of Slavery in Cuba: 1511-1868* (New York: Octagon, 1967), 267-69.

7. Calixto C. Masó y Vazquez, *Historia de Cuba: la lucha de un pueblo por cumplir su destino histórico y su vocación de libertad* (Miami: Ediciones Universal, 1998), 467.

Participation in two dissimilar religious expressions is hardly unique to the Cuban experience. Throughout the Americas, the widespread phenomenon of cultural groups simultaneously participating in two diverse, if not contradictory religious systems, exists. Christianity, when embraced under the context of colonialism or slavery, usually creates a new space wherein the indigenous beliefs of the marginalized group resist annihilation. A unique hybrid developed as the religious traditions of Yoruba slaves took root on Caribbean soil. In this environment, a new religious expression, indigenous to the Cuban experience, began to form — an expression rooted in Christianity and the Yoruba reverence for the orishas. As this new religious understanding took shape, a third ingredient was added, Spiritism.

Kardecism

The third major component of Santería is Spiritism, also known as Kardecism, which originally was not considered a religious movement, but rather a positive science, combining scientism, progressive ideology, Christian morality, and mysticism. It became popular among disenfranchised Catholics because of its anti-clerical views and its criticism toward institutionalized Christianity. Originating in France, it was founded by an engineer named Hippolyte Rivail, who wrote under the pseudonym Allan Kardec. The movement first became popular in Europe, spreading later to Latin America, making its appearance around 1856.

Rivail attempted to use observation and experimentation in order to document the existence of the spiritual world and allow humans to access it for their benefit. As his movement grew in popularity throughout the Western Hemisphere, it generally took the form of small groups of mediums that assisted individuals in communicating with the spirits of the dead — the spirits known as egun in Santería. In these meetings, a group would gather around a table, where a medium would fall into a trance and bridge the gap between the physical world and the spirit world. The denizens of the latter could then communicate with the participants in the seance, advising them on how to move closer to enlightenment. Practitioners, as often as not, found in the spirits' counsel a connection to their pre-Christian past, to practices historically repressed by the official church — elements of Spanish folk religion, herbalism, African religious practices, and Amerindian healing practices.

While the middle and upper economic classes were first attracted to this movement because of its claims to be scientific, urban groups of lesser power and privilege turned to a less intellectualized form of Spiritism for help and guidance with the struggles of daily life. In the Spanish Caribbean, specifically in Cuba and Puerto Rico, which were still under Spain's colonial yoke, freedom fighters began to find in Spiritism an alternative to the Catholic Church, which they perceived to be in league with the Spanish monarchy. With the suppression of political organizations that challenged the colonizer's authority, Spiritism served as a political space for liberal ideas to flourish. The discontented discovered a progressive ideology that they perceived as advocating science, modernity, and democracy. Among the lower economic classes and rural poor, who considered themselves Catholic even though they seldom visited a church or a priest, the practice of Spiritism did not appear to conflict with their religious beliefs.

The importance of Spiritism in Santería is in large part due to the demise of ancestor worship among the Cuban African slaves. Ancestor worship was historically conducted within a particular extended family. Slavery, however, destroyed the family unit, making it impossible to continue the veneration of the ancestors. Fragmented family members were unable to come together to carry out the necessary rituals. The introduction of Spiritism to Cuba reintroduced ancestor worship to the African slaves, albeit with new, European flavors. Even so, the Cuban manifestation of Spiritism differed from its European counterparts. Mediums, during their trances, often channeled spirit guides who were Africans who died during their enslavement. Some of these guides were even from the indigenous natives of the island, the Taínos. For this reason, there is usually a statue of a Native American or of *el negrito José* (the little black man José) somewhere in the santero's or santera's home. Like Santería, Spiritism focuses on the needs of the devotees, specifically in areas of love, work, and health, attempting to deal proactively with the immediate concerns of the person seeking help.

With time, Santería became dependent on several of the practices of Spiritism, appropriating certain aspects of its rituals — prayers, invocations, ceremonies, and paraphernalia — while ignoring its scientific claims and philosophies. For example, when a member of the ilé community dies, a shrine known as a *bóveda* is erected on a table covered with white cloth. It consists of seven glasses of water, each representing an ancestor, with a cross or a rosary bead inserted in the largest goblet. The water for these glasses can consist of holy water from the local Catholic church, herbal water, or a cologne known as Florida water. Fresh flowers and a photograph of the dead person are also prominently displayed. By gazing at the water glasses and reciting certain prayers, individuals may be possessed by the dead family member.

Persecution of the Faith

Throughout Cuba's history Santería was linked in the minds of the white elite to antisocial behavior and was therefore persecuted. For example, in 1919 a *brujo* (witch doctor) craze swept the island. Mass lynchings occurred, fueled by rumors of devotees of Santería kidnapping white children in order to use their blood and entrails in religious practices. These reports began to circulate after a white girl was found dead, presumably cannibalized by brujos. White mobs descended upon blacks with "righteous indignation." One newspaper praised the lynchings, commending their violence as a "step forward that we take toward civilization." Blacks of the middle and upper classes abandoned Santería and internalized the myth that racism did not exist in Cuba, while disassociating themselves from the masses in the lower economic class in order to assimilate into the white mainstream. Santería was viewed by the dominant white Cuban culture as being primitive and satanic, a religion of the lower strata of society, unworthy of any serious academic investigation.

Fernando Ortiz, the famed Cuban cultural interpreter, was among the first during the early decades of the twentieth century to conduct ethnographic research under the rubric of racial theorizing, attempting to prove the moral inferiority of blacks to whites. The assumption of blacks' malefaction is evident in the title of his book, which primarily deals with criminality by focusing on Santería as a criminal phenomenon (the book is complete with police mug shots): *"Los negros brujos: Apuntes para un estudio de etnología criminal"* — "The Black Witches: Notes for a Study on Criminal Ethnology." Ortiz insisted that immorality was "in the mass of the blood of black Africans," a contamination also affecting lower-income whites. The fetishism of Santería had to be eliminated; he suggested lifelong isolation for its leaders. The movement away from "African fetishism" (and its white forms, palm-reading and Spiritism) and toward scientific reasoning could be accomplished by providing a solid scientific education for all blacks and also for low-income whites. Expressions of African culture (i.e., African festival dances) had to be heavily policed to prevent inciting lust, prompting immorality, and encouraging the (stereotyped) "black rapist." As a congressman during the 1919 brujo craze, he proposed legislation outlawing superstitious practices deemed antisocial.

Until 1940 Santería was a punishable crime in Cuba. Persecutions resumed in 1962 during the early years of Fidel Castro's revolution. Santería became subject to a growing number of restrictions, including bans against practicing its rituals or participating in its festivals. In the mid-1960s, santeros and santeras were arrested, imprisoned, and in at least one case, executed. Securing authorization from the CDR (an adjunct of the State Police) was needed to celebrate any ceremony, and such authorization was routinely denied. Lack of official authorization for worship resulted in arrest. The final declaration of the first National Congress on Education and Culture in 1971 stated that juvenile delinquency is partially caused by "religious sects, especially of African origin."[8] It was reminiscent of the days when Ortiz stressed the "criminality" embedded in Santería.

During the 1980s Santería was disparaged as "folklore" rather than as a legitimate religion, and persecutions began to soften. An increased interest in Santería developed because of the numbers of black Cuban soldiers returning from Angola and because of the 1985 publication of Castro's bestseller *Fidel y la religión* (Fidel and Religion). Added to this was the 1987 visit by his Majesty Alaiyeluwa Oba Okunade Sijuwade Olubuse II, the ooni of Ife. Furthermore, the Castro regime found economic value in the folklore of Santería: the bizarre and dangerous cultural Other was domesticated and commodified to produce badly needed tourist dollars. Hence the government initiated an unprecedented campaign to court the practitioners of Santería, and by

8. Carlos Moore, *Castro, the Blacks, and Africa* (Los Angeles: Center for Afro-American Studies, University of California, 1988), 100-102.

1990 the Religious Affairs Department provided economic and political support to state-friendly santeras and santeros.

Due to historical persecution, many of Santería's faithful maintained, as previously discussed, an outward appearance of Catholicism, in effect cross-dressing as Christians. With time, both faith traditions began to share quite similar sacred spaces. Some today see Santería as an authentic attempt on the part of the believer to grasp the reality of God, and Catholicism as a kind of check on the santera or santero to ensure that she or he can continue to be a member of the church. Others voice harsher criticism, claiming Santería adulterates "pure" Catholicism. For Pentecostals and some other Protestants, Santería is a satanic cult. Mainstream white Christians usually portray Santería as the dialectical product of Yoruba beliefs and Iberian Catholicism, in which a confused and idiosyncratic merging of the saints with the orishas occurred. In any event, the results are the same: our beliefs are pure, theirs impure. This relegates Santería to an inferior social position while elevating Catholicism or Protestantism to an authoritative location from which paternal correcting can originate. Such an approach continues the persecution of Santería by categorizing it as folkloric rather than as the legitimate faith of a people.

Santería in Exile

Worshiping the orishas has occurred on U.S. soil since slaves were first brought to work the southern plantations. However, unlike in the Caribbean, their religion did not flourish, mostly due to the process of "breaking in" African-born slaves as discussed above. A possible exception can be found in Louisiana, originally a Catholic French possession, where the African gods survived in the rituals of Voodoo. Santería, as described in this book, probably made its first appearance on U.S. soil in the late nineteenth century in New York, New Orleans, and Florida when large Cuban communities, many of which had African roots, were established in this country to work in the tobacco factories and to organize support for an independence war to overthrow Spanish rule. No doubt the greatest impact on the practice of Santería in the United States occurred with the advent of the 1959 Cuban Revolution.

Many religious Cubans were at first pleased with the 1959 pro-Castro revolution. The new revolutionary government's initial moves to end gambling, prostitution, and political corruption were well received as many churches supported the new regime. However, the early optimism of church and state cooperation gave way to disillusion as the new regime took a more leftist tilt. A closer relationship with the Soviet Union, the promoters of "godless communism," along with land and education reform (which curtailed church autonomy), led to the eventual break a few years after the Revolution's success. Catholics and Protestants became engaged in counterrevolutionary activities, openly struggling to protect their sacred space within the new political order. Many, mostly from the middle economic class, chose flight rather than fight.

From 1959 until 1962, approximately 153,000 refugees who could be considered "political exiles" crossed the Florida Straits for Miami. They usually left the island on their private yachts or booked rides on commercial planes or ferries. These refugees were quite homogeneous, mainly composed of former notables who were mostly white (94 percent), middle-aged (about thirty-eight years old), educated (about fourteen years of schooling), urban (principally La Habana), and literate in English. From 1962 to 1973, an additional 298,000 refugees who were predominantly white, educated, and middle class joined them. These Cubans had relied on direct economic links with the United States. As those links came to an end with Cuba's tilt toward Marxism, they primarily saw themselves as escaping communism as opposed to migrating.

Several first resettled in the Northeast, where jobs were available. However, the trauma of permanently finding themselves in a new country with different laws, traditions, customs, and language, along with the anxiety of being separated from the country and family they treasured and loved, as well as the stress caused by downward mobility, forced many Cubans, in an unconscious collective act of survival, to create community along religious practices. The Catholic Church in the northern states of New York and New Jersey failed them in their attempt to create this community. They found Irish- and Italian-dominated congregations uninviting due to language barriers and ethnic discrimination. The non-responsive Catholic Church led many of these refugees to seek spiritual fulfillment within Protestant churches, particularly among the Pentecostals.

For others, Santería became a viable alternative, one in which they could maintain membership in the Catholic Church while participating in a religious expression tied to their lost homeland. Santería made the move to the United States in large part because of its presence in La Habana, where most Cuban immigrants came from; other African forms of religious expression had little urban presence. While believers were reluctant to admit adherence to a socially objectionable religious expression while in La Habana, in the United States they embraced the faith as part of their cultural identity. Migration to the United States legitimized Santería among those who previously were ashamed by it because of its heavy African characteristics. Because refugees were mostly white, greater emphasis was placed on its Catholic and Spiritist influences, transforming it into a popular religion for exilic Cubans. Santería as a popular religion became an extended family wherein the dispossessed could find a way to survive their alienation. By participating in this most indigenous Cuban religious expression, the community was able to express and reinforce its devotion to the country its members lost while attempting to construct a new identity within an exilic space.

When we define "popular religion," of course, the term "popular" does not necessarily refer to popularity as indicated by the widespread practice of the religion. Rather, it focuses on its sociohistorical reality. A religion is "popular" because the disenfranchised are responsible for its creation, making it a religion of the marginalized, of the common people. The emphasis is on the community as opposed to those of the dominant culture controlling the official religion — in Santería's case, the Catholic Church. For example, when the Catholic Church during the 1960s disclaimed the authenticity of several saints, most notably St. Barbara and St. Lazarus, probably two of the most revered saints among Cubans, the Vatican was simply ignored as devotions to these saints continued unabated.

Worshiping the orishas with fellow Cubans in a mostly Cuban house-temple met more than just the spiritual needs of immigrants. They found spiritual leaders who spoke their language and understood their basic worldview, providing healing for the loneliness and isolation many Cubans faced in the northeastern United States due to their displacement. In effect, Santería functioned as a support group for these refugees. Because the vast majority of the migrating exilic Cuban community (about 99%) considered themselves white, Santería in the United States ceased being predominantly black, eventually developing into a white, middle-class religion practiced in the suburbs.

These exilic Cubans, tragically separated from the land of their birth, felt that they lost their patron saint, Our Lady of Charity, known to santeros and santeras as Oshún, when they were forced to flee Cuban soil. In 1973, in order to rectify this separation, exilic Cubans built on Biscayne Bay in Miami a tent-like shrine for Our Lady to serve as both a political and a sacred space. She faces the ocean, a beacon for those who cross over to the United States. She faces away from Cuba so that those who pray to her may look toward Cuba. In addition, Saturday evening masses are broadcast from the shrine to the island on Sundays. Upon this sacred ground exilic Cubans construct the image of a nation while living in a foreign land. For the older Cuban, the shrine embodies a unified and utopian Cuba that never was and can never be. Yet somehow, by simply worshiping in this space, one can be transported to that mystical place and time. For those who arrived as infants or children, and who are now busy paying mortgages and climbing career ladders, the shrine is a physical representation of the dreams of their parents, dreams to which they feel a strong if fading loyalty. The shrine provides a space where they can safely display this sense of loyalty without having to commit any required acts to make those dreams a reality. For their children, born and raised in this country, the shrine confirms that their parents' dreams of the island amount to little more than a fantasy island, a relic having little or no influence on the actions of the present.

The presence of Cuba's patron in the Miami shrine indicates that she, too, came from Cuba as an exile. Those who know Santería know that this is not the first time she is manifested as a wandering symbol of her people. As the deity Oshún, she journeyed from Africa when her children were forced by slave traders to go to Cuba. Powerless in preventing this catastrophe, yet deeply loving those who worship her, she decided to accompany them to Cuba. She first straightened her hair and lightened her skin to the color of copper, so that all Cubans might join together in worshiping her. Just as the Yoruba slaves found a source of support and comfort in Oshún when facing the difficulties of colonial Cuba, Exilic Cubans discovered the same support and comfort from Our Lady of Charity when facing refugee status in a foreign land.

By 1980, over 120,000 additional Cubans came to the United States through what became known as the Mariel boatlift. Unlike the predominantly whiter refugees of previous years, these Cubans were mostly of darker skin pigmentation and of the lower economic social levels, better representing the population's masses. Forty percent of these refugees were biracial, transforming the Miami exilic community from 99 percent white prior to the Mariel boatlift to 80 percent white, 5 per cent black, and 15 per cent biracial. A large portion of these new refugees were followers of Santería. Their numbers increased with the influx of approximately 40,000 rafters, known as *balseros,* during the 1990s. The arrival of these Cubans revitalized the Santería movement, bringing more adherents and providing a greater interest in the religion by the overall public.

Past and Future

The orishas' survival, first in Cuba and now in the United States, is probably due to the Yoruba religion's ability to adapt to new circumstances. The ability of adherents to reinterpret their beliefs based on the problems faced in their new social environment has allowed the religion to survive and thrive in a cosmopolitan culture like the United States. Resettlement to the Western Hemisphere, due to the vicious institution of slavery, introduced the orishas to what was for them a new world. In spite of the brutality of Cuban slavery, with time, white and black Cubans found themselves bending their knees to the orishas. What was at first the worship of separate orishas by different villages in Africa became, due to the slave trade, a unified structure wherein all of the orishas were worshiped in Cuba. Yet this structure never remained stable, for it constantly changed as newer shiploads of African slaves disembarked on the island. The further migration of Cubans to the U.S., mainly due to the 1959 Castro Revolution, introduced Santería to the larger Latin American community, as well as to African-Americans searching for a religious expression more indigenous to the African continent. With time, white Euroamericans, fascinated and attracted to what for them was a new religious expression, have also come to know the orishas.

This look at the historical roots of Santería is not intended to decry the loss of a "purer" form of African religiosity, but rather to demonstrate the changing nature of Yoruba spirituality, changing to meet the challenges its adherents faced and continue to face. An orthodox expression of Santería will never exist, for it is a way of life even more than it is a body of rituals or beliefs. How the orishas were known and worshiped in Africa changed when the Yoruba religion was transported to Cuba. It further evolved alongside and within Cuban history. And finally, with its introduction to the United States, due to the large Cuban migration caused by the 1959 revolution, Santería changed to adapt to the new challenges faced by refugees. Ironically, as Christianity and Islam make inroads in present-day Nigeria, orisha worship has declined. Islam, which is the dominant religion in northern and western parts of Nigeria, claims 47 percent of the population, while Christianity, which is dominant in the south and east, claims about 35 percent. The remaining 18 percent hold traditional religious beliefs, which includes orisha worship. Yet in the United States, orisha worship is growing and flourishing. And while this form of orisha worship, known as Santería, may differ from the original beliefs of those first slaves brought to Cuba, it remains a pre-modern religion that has survived in a postmodern world.

A Timeline of Santería

500(?)*   The city of Ilé-Ife is settled.
711   The invasion of Spain by Muslims begins.
900(?)   A trans-Saharan slave trade is established for the selling of Africans in Islamic markets.
1000(?)   The Yoruba migrate to the western coast of Africa, to an area which will eventually be known as southern Nigeria.
1100(?)   The Yoruba people begin to establish kingdoms, one in the savannah (northern Nigeria) and one in the forest (southern Nigeria). The Yoruba sacred culture begins to develop at Ife, which serves as the seat of the Yoruba kingdom through the 1600s. Also, the city of Benin is established in the rain forest area of southern Nigeria.

*? — indicates an approximate year

1200(?)	Mutual aid societies, known as hermandades (fraternities) are established in Medieval Spain. These guilds will eventual develop into cabildos in Cuba.
1300(?)	Islam becomes predominant in the northern region of Africa, among the cities along the trans-Saharan trade centers.
1300(?)	The Kingdom of Benin, consisting mainly of the Edo people group, is established when its people banish their corrupt king and request a new king from Ife, creating a new dynasty.
1350(?)	The Oyo kingdom is established by Oranmiyan, who, according to tradition, was a son of Oddudúa. By the 1400s Oyo establishes a hegemony over the other Yoruba kingdoms which lasts through the 1800s.
1441	First African slaves land in Lisbon, Portugal.
1450(?)	The Benin kingdom becomes an impressive empire under Ewuare, who expands his rule over parts of eastern Yorubaland.
1448	The Catholic Church provides its blessings to the Portuguese who begin to import slaves from the African west coast, bringing the first African slaves to Europe and introducing Christianity to the region. By 1472, Portuguese traders Ruy Seqira and Fernando Gomez visit the Bight of Benin, trading their goods for slaves. Eventually a slave-trade alliance with the kingdom of Benin is made, which continues to gain prominence with the introduction of European weapons.
1492	Christopher Columbus is discovered off the coast of Cubanacán (later to be renamed Cuba) by the native population who have inhabited the island since 1000(?) BCE.
1492	Spain is reconquered under the Spanish monarchs Isabella and Ferdinand. Among their first edicts is the "purification" of the land, calling for the expulsion or conversion of Jews and Moors.
1500(?)	Ilé-Ife begins to lose political power to the Oyo kingdom, although it retains its supremacy as a religious center.

1511   The first African slaves are brought to Cuba from the island of Hispaniola (present-day Haiti and Dominican Republic) to replace the decimated native population. These first African slaves brought the orishas with them to the island.

1521   The first African slaves are brought directly from Africa.

1532 & 1540 The Spanish crown prohibits the exportation of white, Jewish, Ladino, or Moorish slaves to Cuba. Only Africans could be used as slaves.

1553   The first British ship reaches the west coast of Africa, hoping to compete with the Portuguese for the lucrative slave trade.

1562   Sir John Hawkins transports the first 300 Africans from Sierra Leone to Haiti to sell as slaves.

1598   The first recorded African cabildo, formed by members of the Zap nation, is established in La Habana.

1650-1700(?) As the Benin kingdom wanes, the Oyo kingdom becomes a powerful military state thanks to its cavalry, funded with money from the slave trade.

1650-1700(?) The demand for sugar triggers a demographic revolution in the West Indies as more Africans are imported to work the emerging sugar plantations.

1698   Recorded history begins with the account of Oyo's cavalry invading the Allada kingdom in Dahomey.

1730(?)   Although the Dahomey kingdom is subjugated to the Oyo kingdom, it begins to become a major political power as the Oyo kingdom is weakened by internal monarchic rivalries. Dahomey begins to absorb Yoruba culture and religious influences.

1775-1800(?) Monarchic power is centralized in Dahomey as it becomes more dependent on the slave trade. The kingdom's wealth is due to the head tax levied upon the Atlantic slave trade.

1789   The Spanish Crown decrees the free trade of slaves in Cuba.

1790   State interference with and restriction of the cabildos' affairs in Cuba begins.

1807   England abolishes the slave trade and prohibits ships

	from engaging in the trade, using her mighty navy to patrol the African coast in an attempt to prohibit other nations from participating in the trade.
1815	The Atlantic slave trade becomes centered on the expanding sugar and coffee plantations of Cuba and Brazil.
1817	England signs a treaty with Spain declaring an end to the slave trade among Spanish colonies to take effect in May 1820.
1817-35	Oyo erupts in civil wars as rivals contend for the throne.
1818	Dahomey declares its independence from Oyo. This area would eventually become the Republic of Benin.
1820	The Owu and Egba civil wars begin, lasting throughout most of the century. Slave raiding flourished as a means to raise funds for the acquisition of firearms for the war effort. One of the tactics employed in this war was the total destruction of a vanquished town and the enslavement of the town's population en masse. This practice would end the worship of a particular orisha in Africa, while installing a large following of the orisha in Cuba. This was the case with Ochosi, divine hunter identified with all of the forest's wildlife.
1830	With the end of the slave trade, England begins to look for new commercial markets, using gunboat diplomacy to force local chieftains to agree to unequal treaties.
1831	The Oyo kingdom collapses when the Muslim Fulani conquer the northern Oyo region, cutting off its trading routes.
1850-70	Dahomey's economy changes from one dependent upon slave exportation to one based on the internal slave production of palm oil.
1850(?)	Spiritism, also known as Kardecism, makes its appearance in Latin America, with the first illegal Spiritist literature reaching Cuba by 1856. By the 1870s it becomes fashionable.
1861	On the pretense that England was unable to suppress the slave trade and ensure good government, H.M.S. *Prometheus* sails to Lagos and forces its king, Dosunmu,

to sign a treaty forming the British colony of Lagos. Hence the colonialization process of this region begins.

1865   England, through the West India Regiment, participates in the civil wars by battling the Egba to free the roads under their control so that England could have free access to trade with Africa's interior. With this act, British colonialist ventures expand in the region.

1865   Last official slave ship docked in Cuba, although the practice unofficially continued until the mid-1880s when slavery was finally abolished.

1867   British naval forces are able to, to a great extent, halt the transatlantic slave trade.

1870   Spain adopts the Moret law, which commits to the gradual abolition of slavery in Cuba.

1877   The Spanish colonial government begins to suppress the cabildos, fearing they could become a source for insurrection. By 1884, the Good Government Law will forbid all cabildos from meeting or organizing festivals.

1878   The Ten Year War for independence fails; however, Spain grants unconditional freedom to African slaves who fought for independence.

1880-86   Slavery in Cuba is gradually abolished through a tutelage program serving as an eight-year transition period; however, two years ahead of schedule, Spain totally abolishes slavery.

1882   Cabildos in Cuba are required to obtain a license, which is renewable on an annual basis.

1884   The Good Government Law is passed in Cuba forbidding all African cabildo meetings and the evening street celebration of religious feasts.

1886   What would eventually be called Nigeria becomes a British colony.

1888   Cuba passes a law prohibiting the formation of "old style" cabildos.

1895-1898   Cuba's War for Independence is fought. Within a month of the United States' entry into the war, Spain capitulates, transforming the local war for indepen-

	dence into the Spanish-American War, followed by several years of U.S. occupation of the island.
1897	Benin is partially destroyed and subdued by the British, who eventually bring it under colonial rule.
1910	Black Cubans who fought for independence create *El Partido Independiente de Color* (The Independent Party of Color) to force the government to consider seriously its rhetoric of racial equality and provide equal opportunities in power, employment, and services.
1912	Cuban blacks' protest against structural racism is labeled a race war. Thousands of black Cubans, mostly unarmed, are deliberately butchered by white Cubans, mostly for "resisting arrest." Yet no trace of the rumored uprising has ever been found: no cache of arms was ever discovered, no demonstration occurred outside the province of Oriente, no white woman was ever raped or cannibalized (contrary to newspaper accounts), and no destruction of valuable property occurred. Even so, thousands of white Cuban volunteers were given arms and paid by the government to rove across the nation putting down the revolt in any way possible.
1914	The British colonial venture in West Africa expands to the current national boundaries of Nigeria.
1919	A brujo (witch doctor) craze sweeps Cuba as mass lynchings occur, fueled by rumors of santeros and santeras kidnapping white children in order to use their blood and entrails in religious practices. These reports begin to circulate after a white girl is found dead, presumably cannibalized by brujos.
1940(?)	The term Santería begins to be used as a pejorative term by the Catholic clerics to describe the religious practices of the Yoruba in La Habana, Mantanzas, and the surrounding areas.
1940	Persecution of Santería in Cuba wanes.
1946	Francisco (Pancho) Mora (who changes his name to Ifa Morote) migrates to the United States. He is believed to be the first U.S. santero to establish an ilé and practice

Ifá divination in New York City. The center of orisha activities develops in the Upper West Side with the Rendezvous Bar on Lenox Avenue and the Illuminada beauty parlor being popular meeting places for believers.

1954   Mora initiates the first santera in Puerto Rico.

1956   The first public performance of orisha music and dance is organized by percussionist Mongo Santamaria at the Palladium night club in honor of Changó.

1959   Walter King (who changes his name to Oba Osejiman Adefunmi I) travels to Matanzas, Cuba to be initiated into Santería, becoming the first African-American to be fully ordained. Upon returning to New York he establishes the Changó Temple, incorporating it as the African Theological Archministry. By 1960 he moves the temple to Harlem, renaming it the Yoruba Temple. Also in 1959, Oba Sergiman and Christopher Oliana, two African Americans, travel to Haiti for ordination.

1959   Fidel Castro succeeds in his revolution against dictator Fulgencio Batista.

1959-73 Approximately 451,266 Cuban refugees, who could be considered "political exiles," cross the Florida Straits for Miami. Although mostly from the upper and middle economic class of the pre-Castro Cuba and predominantly white and educated, some were followers of the orishas. With them, the orishas are reintroduced to the United States — reintroduced because when the orishas first came with the African slaves, they were effectively eradicated by the slave masters.

1960   Nigeria becomes an independent nation.

1961   Leonore Dolme ordains the first African-American santera in Queens, New York, Margie Baynes Quiniones.

1961   Mercedes Noble (who changes her name to Oban Yoko) is credited with ordaining the first Cuban santera in the United States, Julia Franco. Until now, Cubans wishing to be ordained had traveled to Cuba for the rites. Yoko went on to establish a *casa de santo* (house of saints) in New York City to serve as a permanent home for the ordination of devotees.

1962	Persecution of Santería in Cuba resumes.
1964	Mora is credited with holding the first public Santería bembe in the United States, attracting over three thousand people.
1970	The Oyotunji Village is founded in Sheldon, South Carolina by Adefunmi I.
1971	The final declaration of the first National Congress on Education and Culture in Cuba states that juvenile delinquency is partially caused by "religious sects, especially of African origin."
1980	Mariel Boatlift brings over 120,000 Cubans to the United States, who unlike the predominantly whiter refugees of previous years, are mostly of a darker skin pigmentation and of the lower economic social levels. Forty percent of these refugees are biracial. A large portion of them are followers of Santería.
1980-85	An increased interest in Santería develops in Cuba due to the numbers of black Cuban soldiers returning from Angola. Persecution of Santería wanes.
1985	Castro publishes *Fidel y la religión* (Fidel and Religion).
1987	His Majesty Alaiyeluwa Oba Okunade Sijuwade Olubuse II, the ooni of Ife, visits Cuba.
1987	Ernesto Pichardo opens the church La Iglesia Lukumí Babalú Ayé in Hialeah, Florida, the first Cuban-based Santería church.
1992	The United States Supreme Court rules that the practitioners of Santería have a constitutional right to sacrifice animals in connection with their rituals.

Chapter 7

A Religion of Resistance

Usually scholars attempt to describe the faith of other peoples from their own perspective, one often radically different from that of the believers in terms of race, class, and so on. When this happens, even though the facts reported might be correct, the subject religion becomes an illusionary construct, often more grounded in the assumptions of the scholar than in the sociopolitical reality of the believers. This occurs when scholars attempt to superimpose their ideas of what a people, usually considered primitive, are supposed to believe based on how they practice their faith. All too often, the religion as a way of life is ignored.

If we want to understand Santería on its own terms, then we must reject any description of the religion that attempts to elucidate it only through its rituals or beliefs. Santería is a faith system that does not consider itself prophetic, that is, as directly mandated by God. As such, it does not promulgate the type of revelatory claims made by Jews, Christians, and Muslims. While these traditional religions are as a rule slow to change their rituals or modify their beliefs (although this does occur through the reinterpretation of sacred texts), Santería unapologetically discards beliefs and rituals that cease to be relevant while absorbing new beliefs or even new gods that can enhance the lives of its followers. Unlike Western religions, Santería is an amorphous and practical religion that promises immediate, tangible power in dealing with life's hardships, power that is manifested in a variety of ways depending on the believer's situation. The focus is not on understanding

189

the sacred forces like the orishas; rather, it is concerned with how these universal forces can be used for the betterment of humans. As a way of being and living, Santería, formed as a spiritual response to oppressive structures like slavery, developed into a symbol of protest. If we attempt to explain Santería only in terms of beliefs, we reduce the religion to a view of life, when in fact it is a way of life. This way of life has become a response against the societal forces bent on destroying the culture of the believers — a form of survival by way of cultural resistance.

Regardless of how academics attempt to describe, codify, and define Santería, in a very real sense, it exists beyond the explication of scholars. Santería must be understood by way of the everyday. Among Western religions, reality is commonly understood as two different worlds, one supernatural and ruled by metaphysical deities, and the other natural and ruled by the laws of science. Differences between sacred and secular, holy and profane, are emphasized. In the minds of the followers of Santería, such distinctions do not exist. All daily events are extraordinary and ordinary, miraculous and mundane. The common and the mystical are simultaneously normative within the life of the believer.

Consequently, any delineation of the religion's rituals — as we have done in this book — will prove insufficient on its own in depicting the faith. Since its inception, Santería has been an expression of a people's attitude toward finding harmony — harmony between one's life and one's environment, community, and the spiritual realm. For this reason, Santería can be understood only through the disharmony caused by the social and political climate of its adherents. Because situations change, the religion must also evolve to confront new struggles and challenges. Hence any understanding of Santería is subject to modifications depending on the changing social context of its believers. Each succeeding generation is encouraged to reinterpret, expand, delete, or add to the myths, proverbs, and traditions of the previous generation to meet the new challenges of today. When Africans were introduced to the hellish reality of slavery in Cuba, they reinterpreted their faith to help them cope with their new social context. When Cubans came to the United States as refugees, separated from everything that previously defined their identity, they too reinterpreted their faith to cope with their new context.

The Function of Faith

One of any religion's functions is to attempt to answer the "unanswerable questions" of existence. Who are we? How did we come to be? Is there a force greater than ourselves? What is our purpose in life? What is our role in the social order? Does anything exist after death? How these questions are answered indeed shapes the worldviews of individuals and communities. Yet, the function of religion also lies beyond how such questions are answered, answers which can never be proven beyond a shadow of a doubt. To be effective, religion's purpose in the life of a community must amount to more than simple claims concerning the nature of God, accounts of miracles, and speculation on what awaits human beings after death.

While belief systems are important, religion also serves a social function. It can either legitimize the sociopolitical power structures that exist, or it can protest and resist those structures. This function is usually accomplished by binding together like-minded individuals for the betterment of the whole. In times of crises and tragedies, or festivities and celebration, religion functions to create community which can provide assistance or companionship. During times of persecution, religion can serve and empower a people to survive the adversity they face. In the last chapter we saw how, in a very real sense, Santería was created by the disenfranchised to resist their annihilation, to be a religious expression that protested their subjugation.

Thus it was a source of strength for a persecuted people who searched for a means of survival while challenging the forces of colonialism that employed social mechanisms of power to enslave Africans. Like other belief systems of marginalized and persecuted people, Santería renders a counter-hegemonic challenge to the prevailing social and political order of the dominant culture. More than just a religion geared toward the survival of its devotees, Santería provides the disenfranchised with a source from which to champion social change. It is important to note that this inherent dimension of cultural resistance has been with the religion since its founding; it is not something that was appended when Yoruba religion arrived in the so-called New World. To attain a better understanding as to what this religion means to those who turn to it for strength to survive another day, we now turn our attention to some of the major social functions of the religion.

To Create Community and Prevent Assimilation

The ability to create community forestalled slaves' and exiles' assimilation into the dominant culture during their respective times of alienation, loss, and grief over separation from loved ones due to forced migration. The religion of the Yoruba slaves was at the heart of the cabildos they formed. And Santería house-temples offered a substitute family to Cuban refugees in the 1960s, who also found themselves separated from loved ones. Converts joined a house-temple in which the santero and santera functioned as godparents, and the different members of the congregation became brothers and sisters. Struggling with feelings of alienation brought about by migration, especially to nontropical cities like New York, Union City, and Chicago, the new converts became personally attached to the spiritual leaders who served as surrogate parents. The psychological and physical need of belonging, especially in an alien if not hostile environment, was met through the faith. It created a sense of binding solidarity within a varied community of individuals.

Émile Durkheim, the eminent social scientist, pointed out nearly a century ago that "The god of the clan . . . can therefore be nothing else than the clan itself, personified and represented to the imagination under the visible form of the [stone] which serves as totem."[1] He might well have been talking about Santería. Adoration, devotion, and fidelity to the orishas entrench followers' dedication to the faith community, and ultimately the two — the faith and the faith community — become one. Ceremonies and rituals become the means by which the faith community continues to bind its believers to itself. The belief in reincarnation only immortalizes the faith community by securing their continuation into the future while recognizing the death or loss of individuals. Individuals do not die, ceasing to exist; rather, they die to be reborn as the next generation of believers, hence continuously renewing the life of the faith community and securing its continuation from generation to generation.

The community created among Santería's followers helped the new Cuban refugees cope with the cultural upheavals occurring within the United States during the time of their migration just as it helped

---

1. Émile Durkheim, *The Elementary Forms of Religious Life*, trans. by Joseph Ward Swain (New York: The Macmillan Company, 1915), 206.

slaves centuries earlier. Most refugees left Cuba to escape communism and seek a safe haven for their children, only to find themselves in a country in the midst of the civil rights struggle, protests against the Vietnam War, and the sexual revolution, only to be followed in the 1970s with Watergate and the United States' defeat in Vietnam. The fear became that, rather than losing their children to communism, they might lose them to the tumultuous social upheavals of the United States. Santería became a way of creating insulation from the radical changes occurring outside the faith community.

In addition to the physiological trauma of displacement faced by these exilic Cubans, there existed an economic marginalization. Many who had traditionally followed the ways of the orishas were from the lower economic strata. Whether they historically lived in the slave quarters of the Cuban plantation, in the economically depressed segments of La Habana, or in the slum areas of New York City or Miami, they were accustomed to surviving in an environment devoid of privilege or opportunity. In Cuba, remaining faithful to the orishas became the means by which displaced Africans established a common identity amidst a social structure designed to extract their labor while destroying their personhood. In the United States, displaced Cubans from various socioeconomic backgrounds were forced to live in economically deprived areas, exposed to street violence, drugs, and gangs. Santería offered a holistic way of living in harmony with one's gods and one's hostile environment, an attractive alternative to what the streets had to offer.

The Santería community also provided an avenue by which to overcome the economic marginalization faced by exilic Cubans by contributing to the creation of an economic enclave, organized to serve the needs of the displaced Cubans. Doctors, dentists, electricians, plumbers, construction workers, and other professionals who lacked proper licenses or proper documentation from regulatory boards, continued to work in their profession, either from their homes or from the backs of their pickup trucks, diligent in avoiding the proper authorities. Little overhead, cut-rate prices for fellow exilic Cubans, and reliance on informal word-of-mouth networks, allowed these early entrepreneurs to establish themselves financially before eventually competing with the older Euroamerican firms. The Santería houses of worship became a marketplace where consumers and suppliers met, developed relationships, and helped one another establish themselves economically. At times money exchanged hands; other times the service was provided in the name of charity; others simply bartered their talents for other services or products.

Community is also created when like-minded religious people bind together against perceived or actual attacks from the community at large. A recent court case in which I gave a deposition as an expert witness illustrates how Santería creates community among people who perceive themselves as misunderstood. In 1997, an unknown person or persons hung a cow's tongue in front of a California social services office. The veterinary technician who examined the tongue stated that it was not the usual cut that could be store-bought; rather, the cow's mouth must have been pried open and the tongue cut out. Attached to the cow's tongue by 14 white pins were 14 pieces of paper; on each piece of paper was the name of an employee of the social services office. One of the employees whose name was not on the tongue identified herself as a priest of Santería. She was employed by the agency as a supervisor. It appears that her employees were planning a demonstration against her, scheduled to take place at noon on the day the tongue was discovered. The demonstration was to protest her alleged favoritism towards (among other things) fellow employees who were also involved with Santería. The demonstration was never held. In fact, it had been called off late the previous day, but the supervisor was unaware it had been canceled. According to County investigators, 11 of the 14 people whose names were on the tongue were outspoken in their criticism about the supervisor. The investigating official concluded that most had information that might have been harmful to the supervisor if known.

The opinion I gave to the court was that whoever hung the cow's tongue in front of the social service office was attempting to get an orisha to silence or repress the people whose names appeared on the pieces of paper attached to the tongue. While the overall reason of the sacrifice was for the practitioners of the faith to prevail in the dispute or argument with those whose names appeared on the pieces of paper, it was not meant to cause physical harm or death. No doubt, the cancellation of the demonstration only reinforced to the practitioners how powerful their religion was. After all, the tongues of their enemies, like the tongue of the cow, got nailed to prevent their wagging. Their success over against the forces outside of their faith community only served to unify and bind them closer together.

To Resist Oppression

Once enslaved, the first act of resistance for many Yoruba came in the act of suicide. Death appeared to be a preferable alternative to slavery. Not only did it deny the slave master his "property," but it reincarnated the slave as well — back in Africa, happy among his or her descendants. Others found a way to escape their enslavement, finding refuge in the dense forests and high mountains of Cuba, especially in the eastern portion of the island. They formed slave societies where their religious rituals could continue free from Christian domination. Formed as early as the 1500s, these communities lasted throughout the 1800s. Besides providing the former slaves, known as cimarrones, with a space to practice their religion, they also provided them the ability to resist the oppressive colonial system. A holy war was conducted against the slaveholders as these societies raided plantations to free slaves and kill slaveholders. They gave assistance to the enemies of Spain, specifically to pirates, joining them in attacking La Habana in 1539. At times, these ex-slave societies became the only form of resistance to colonial rule. At the very least, thousands of these communities provided safe havens for other runaway slaves. Their ability to resist oppression was in part fortified by their collective reliance on the orishas for guidance and spiritual fortitude.

To Subvert the Dominant Culture

Where there is power, there is resistance. Every oppressed group creates from its sociological location what political scientist James Scott terms a "hidden transcript," representing a collective critique of power. These hidden transcripts are usually expressed openly, although disguised so that the oppressors are kept in the dark. An outlet is found to express repressed feelings through a symbolic performance that can lead the disenfranchised to social stability. Although the practitioner of Santería may remain impotent, his or her orishas possess the power to protect the marginalized and humble the powerful. Santería as a resistance religion uses its rituals to critique the dominant power structures. For example, in the days of slavery, a decapitated white dove placed anonymously on the front steps of the "Christian" slaveholder might serve as a sign of forthcoming disaster. In response to it, the master might change his treatment of the slaves to elicit a reversal of whatever misfortune was about to come his way. The powerful was in effect given a warning that his behavior and attitudes toward those he oppressed were more grievous than could be tolerated.

Another example of subversion is the bembe, in which believers are mounted by the orishas. This form of spiritual possession creates a sacred space where the devotees are given the opportunity to express their hostility toward their oppressors. Through possession, the discharge of repressed feelings is allowed. Under normal conditions such outbursts would not be tolerated. Yet the voiceless can openly protest their existential locations by creating a hidden transcript of expression within the safe outlet of the possession. Because the ones mounted seldom recall what they did and said while possessed, they are usually absolved of their pronouncements and actions. The protest comes not from the subordinate individual but, under the cloak of possession, from the powerful orisha. The voicing of wrongdoings lends itself to the resolution of conflicts within the faith community as a controlled space is created, via the trance, where the plea for justice from the oppressed is voiced. At the very least, the acting out of repressed feelings of hostility, through the mask of possession, becomes therapeutic for the disenfranchised who, up until now, were forced to suppress those emotions.

As a catalyst for resistance, Santería has always played a role in the political development of Cuba. In the summer of 1958 Fulgencio Batista, Cuba's dictator, spent thousands of dollars to convene a meeting of santeras and santeros from throughout the island to summon the orishas to aid him against the forces of Castro's revolution.[2] For many Cubans, the battle between Batista and Castro was as much a spiritual war as a physical one, and in their view Castro won because of the ebbós (offerings) done on his behalf. Ebbós done by the vulnerable disenfranchised became a "safe" alternative to directly challenging the dictatorship of Batista, allowing them to participate safely in the triumph of Castro.

Castro's revolution, in turn, symbolically tied itself to Santería. The revolutionary guerrillas were based in Oriente, the colonial haven for runaway slaves and a stronghold for African religions. Many of these

---

2. Hugh Thomas, *Cuba: The Pursuit of Freedom* (New York: Harper & Row, 1971), 1122.

guerrillas, upon entering La Habana, wore elekes and waved the red and black flag of the 26th of July Movement. These colors are significant because they belong to Elegguá, the trickster, who determines destiny and fate. Elegguá is also considered first among the holy warriors. As these colors triumphantly arrived in La Habana, spectators familiar with Santería saw Elegguá (not an inappropriate symbol for what was to be a self-espoused guerrilla society) enter the city, ready to provide protection to Cuba and her people. Crucial was the date of the rebels' entry into La Habana — January 1, Niño de Atocha's Day, the holiest day of the orishas, when the course of history is set for the rest of the year.

The most often cited evidence of Castro's "designation" by the orishas occurred on January 8, 1959, during his first national speech from Camp Columbia. While he pleaded for unity and peace, a white dove landed on his shoulder. In addition to being a Christian symbol for the Holy Spirit, the white dove is also Santería's symbol of Obatalá. One legend states that during a skirmish between the brothers Changó and Oggún, Obatalá appeared as a white dove hovering over the combatants, bringing an end (however temporary) to the brothers' feuding. Castro symbolically occupied this ambiguous religious space. For Christians, he assumed the role of the Son of God, the Prince of Peace. For santeros and santeras, he appeared as Obatalá, the divine provider of peace. Even Cuba's oldest daily newspaper, the conservative *Diario de la Marina*, referred to the incident as an "act of Providence."

To Foster Wellness

All illnesses result from either external or internal conditions. Internal conditions are those whose origins are inside the sick individual — malfunctioning cells, for example, causing cancer. External conditions are those originating outside the body — in poisons, in spoiled food, in viruses, bacteria, and the like. To practitioners of Santería, evil spells, evil eyes, and evil spirits are also examples of external conditions. Santeros and santeras believe that even maladies that are not the direct result of spells have a spiritual component. Thus medicine, surgery, and other elements of Western healing may indeed be useful in alleviating symptoms, but for truly effective results it must be paired with a spiritual cure, to restore harmony to the whole person.

Santería has always been an alternative form of health care for those too poor to afford conventional medical services. As mentioned in the previous chapter, for most of Cuba's history the rural areas lacked any semblance of medical facilities. When black slaves, their masters, or local peasants needed medical attention, they turned to God for healing, seeking the assistance of the Catholic priest, the African healer, or both. These combined prayers and knowledge of herbal remedies in lieu of physicians' care. But as "modern" medicine developed on the island, mainly in the large cities and some rural areas, the religion willingly moved toward a supporting role in the quest for the individual's cure from sickness and disease.

While the Western-based health care concentrates on illnesses and infectious diseases, treating only whatever physically ails the body, Santería focuses on the spiritual cause of the illness. Santeros and santeras understand most illnesses to be psychological or physical manifestations of angry deities disciplining those who show disrespect toward them or the faith, or who neglect their dead ancestors. According to Dr. Mercedes Sandoval, professor of psychiatry and herself a believer, the majority of Cuban refugees who originally sought the help of a santera/o were suffering from psychosomatic disorders or stress-related symptoms, probably caused by migration and acculturation to a new country.[3] Studies indicate that supernatural beliefs increase during periods of insecurity — which migration certainly is. The supernatural becomes a means of coping with the feelings of frustration and aggression that come from being uprooted.[4] In this respect, Santería is a crude form of psychotherapy. Its leaders see themselves as working in partnership with medical doctors, at times insisting that their followers go to a doctor for healing after offering a sacrifice to the orisha who will bring about the healing through the physician. Of course, most medical professionals, especially Euroamerican doctors, remain unaware of the existence of their "partners." But to the followers of Santería, a dichotomy does not exist between the supernatural and medical science; rather they operate side by side, at times complementing each other.

3. Mercedes Sandoval, "Santería: Afrocuban Concepts of Disease and Its Treatment in Miami," *Journal of Operational Psychiatry*, Vol. 8, No. 2 (1977): 53.
4. Doris Gilestra, "Santería and Psychotherapy," *Comprehensive Psychotherapy*, Vol. 3 (1981): 71.

To Dignify and Empower

Santería also functions to provide self-determination for those who have little or no control over their lives. Those attracted to Santería have historically been the oppressed (slaves), the marginalized (poor people), and the disenfranchised (blacks and biracials). These groups were systemically excluded from the power structures that have been historically populated by slave masters, the socioeconomic elite, and whites in general. Society historically has defined those occupying the lower strata of society as sub-human. Yet in Santería the gods themselves choose to become one with these "outsiders" through the act of spiritual possession. Regardless of the difficulty of life or the challenges it presents, for a few hours, believers are one with their gods, allowing them to escape momentarily the marginality of their reality. They cease to be what those in power consistently define them to be. Quite the contrary, they become the earthly manifestations of deities, complete with all the power and dignity attributed to them. Even believers who are never possessed may become priests and priestesses, allowing them to occupy a position equal to, if not greater than, the Christian clerics attempting to convert them. In a very profound sense, believers in Santería are empowered to be more than their oppressors.

Santería's gods are not distant, perched on faraway heavenly thrones; rather, they live in solidarity with believers, aligning themselves with the devotees' gender, race, and class. As previously mentioned, the orishas appear as male or female depending on their paths (e.g., Changó the male warrior as St. Barbara, or Obatalá the father of the orishas as Our Lady of Ransom). Besides switching genders, many of the orishas — all of whom are black — put on white masks to appear European. It is also interesting to note that the saints whose masks they wear are in most cases not the major ones of the Catholic faith. They represent minor saints, often of the lower strata, who are closer to the people and are thus able to understand the practitioners' dilemmas and effectively communicate them upward. *Los santos* (the saints) fail to fit any neat male/female, black/white, or major/minor category. They inhabit a sacred area where borders are fluid and opposites are subverted and perpetually put in disarray.

Additionally, an immediate function of consulting the orishas through divination empowers the believer by removing doubt regarding which choice to make when facing a difficult decision. As previously mentioned, the devotee withholds information where the answer is obvious, or where the santera or santero through the use of deductive reasoning could arrive at an answer. This form of testing the validity of consulting the orishas provides the seeker with peace of mind, confidence, and reassurance that the course of action recommended by the orishas is indeed a communiqué especially for them from the gods. When the orishas indicate one should marry one's lover, take one job instead of another, or have the operation instead of waiting, the meekest find confidence to boldly take action — for the gods have spoken. The course of action taken becomes legitimized, shifting the responsibility and outcome of said actions from the devotee to the orishas, thus absolving the faithful believer of any culpability. But what if the consequences of the course of action prescribed prove to be disastrous? Because the answers to all of life's questions are found in Ifá, blame for ruinous consequences is given to the diviner, whose lack of knowledge obviously led to misreading the divination system.

To Relieve Guilt

The emphasis on the role of the orishas in everyday life has liberated some from assuming responsibility for the shortcomings, failures, and tragedies they face by relieving them of their guilt. At times, individuals develop debilitating guilt over the loss of someone or something. The death of a loved one can leave the surviving family member dealing with immense guilt, thinking maybe not enough was done to preserve the life of the dearly departed. Santería offers several ways of ministering to those grieving. By making offerings to the dead, and caring for them, the surviving family member remains connected to the departed loved one, abating any guilt they may be feeling. And through the belief in reincarnation within the next generation of family members, the living can have faith that the departed will return. Loss is replaced with rebirth, while guilt dissipates in the cycle of birth, death, and rebirth.

Besides alleviating guilt for individuals who lost a loved one, Santería has also provided a vehicle by which an entire community has dealt with the guilt of losing their country of birth. This is particularly evident with the migration of Cubans to the United States following the 1959 Castro revolution. Many who traveled to the safety of the

United States expected a short stay. As soon as Castro was toppled (most likely through U.S. actions), these Cubans would return to their homeland. However, as months turned into years, and years into decades, the hope of a quick return was replaced with the frustration and guilt of abandoning their country and their loved ones. Maybe if they had stayed and fought, some felt, they could have brought about the eventual downfall of Castro. The guilt of fleeing rather than fighting, of losing what they held dear, is deflected from the émigré community through Santería. Their predicament was caused not by their actions of fleeing, but rather by the orishas, the dead, or by the sorcery of their enemies. Consequently, they need not take full responsibility for it.

To Be a Theology of Liberation?

During the 1960s a Catholic reform movement known as liberation theology began to emerge in Latin America. Liberation theology is a systematic theology whose starting point is the experience and realities of the poor and oppressed within society. This theology reinterprets the Christian message from the perspective of those who are marginalized. Poverty is understood as a result of societal and systemic forces, and not solely of individual failings. To be saved is defined as liberation from societal structures of oppression, liberation to determine one's own destiny, and liberation through new life in Jesus Christ.

During the formation of liberation theology, emphasis was placed on how the grassroots understood God and their relationship to God. A concerted effort was made to move beyond theologies constructed in the halls of academia, specifically theologies that were eurocentric in nature. Rather, theologians found themselves articulating the faith of the indigenous people, the poor, the outcast, and the marginalized. Yet by focusing exclusively on Christianity, early theologians of liberation disregarded the possible contributions that could be made by those who were most marginalized within their society: the descendants of slaves who still followed the religious traditions of their ancestors. While claiming to represent the Latin American periphery, they concentrated exclusively on the members of that periphery who professed Christianity. Religious expressions grounded in the belief in the orishas, shared by so many of the oppressed in Latin America, were simply disregarded.

Since then, proponents of liberation theology have begun to construct theologies from the perspective of different religious traditions. Although originally a Catholic movement, there are now Protestant, Islamic, Buddhist, Hindu, and Jewish liberation theologians. While it is beyond the scope of this book to develop a Santerían theology of liberation, it should be noted that the social location of the religion's original followers, who suffered under oppression; the religion's present-day followers, who are mostly economically marginalized; and the societal functions the religion plays in liberating its followers from oppressive structures, both physically and spiritually, all make Santería a type of religion of liberation.

Creating Its Own Oppression

Like every other religious tradition, Santería is also in the ironic position of creating and sustaining its own forms of oppression. Historically this has most often taken the form of unscrupulous religious leaders (who are present, unfortunately, in every faith tradition) taking advantage of their positions, using their considerable power and prestige for personal gain. Although the fear of the orishas is supposed to be sufficient to prevent charlatans from bilking unsuspecting devotees, unfortunately there are those who prey on individuals desperate for solutions to the problems plaguing their lives. In the days of slavery, when black slaves practiced their faith under Catholic eyes, a system of domination within a system of domination developed as some priests of the Yoruba faith who were dishonest came to realize the extent of the power they wielded. In the sociopolitical vacuum created by slavery, the priest was religious leader, physician, and counselor. In short, he or she was the most important and powerful figure within the enslaved community. Priests eager to ensure their own relative safety and well-being in slavery were quick to see that the best way to do so was to take advantage of their position. Thus they suggested, subtly or otherwise, that displeasing them was tantamount to displeasing the orishas — and could, therefore, have disastrous consequences.

Another example of Santería perpetuating oppressive structures has developed in the United States, where religious practices are not immune to the influence of capitalist economic structures. Originally santeros and santeras bartered for their services: a chicken for a necklace, a pig for an initiation, and so on. Many santeros and santeras today preserve this practice, asking only to be reimbursed for the cost of what they provide. Thus, elekes might cost up to $25; an initiation ritual might cost a few hundred dollars. This fee, as we mentioned earlier, is usually referred to as the derecho, or "right." Not only is it the right of the santero or santera to be paid for services rendered, but no one should expect to receive anything from the orishas without being willing to give something in return.

During the Mariel Boatlift of 1980 a significant portion of the Cuban refugees who came to the United States were of African descent, and many of these practiced Santería. These newer refugees were dismayed at how materialistic the religion had become. Corruption was evident to them as they witnessed unscrupulous individuals charging up to $1,000 for a necklace or as much as $45,000 for an initiation, and santeros and santeras living in exclusive neighborhoods and driving expensive cars. This kind of inflation created a new form of religious oppression — one uniquely reflecting North American mores.

Concluding Thoughts

More than just a view of life, Santería offers its followers a way of life, a way of life that, while far from perfect, provides the means to cope with systems of psychological, physical, and socioeconomic oppression. It encompasses all aspects of life's daily struggle; it sees no dichotomy between sacred and secular. It gave enslaved Africans a sense of unity in resisting both despair and assimilation. Likewise it offered stability and identity to Cubans who found themselves exiled in the United States after the 1959 Cuban Revolution. These are some of the same aspects that continue to attract people, including Euroamericans, to Santería in the hectic, ever-changing United States of today. Thus Santería can truly be understood only from the underside of the dominant culture, from the perspective of those who every day resist and survive oppressive structures designed to benefit those who amass power and privilege.

Chapter 8 An Emerging Religion
within a Christian Environment

Open the Yellow Pages of any major city with a substantial Hispanic population and look under the heading "Religious Goods." There you will find several listings with either the word "botánica" or the name of an orisha as part of the business's name. In Miami alone there were over 87 such listings in the 2002 telephone directory. These stores, of course, are the ones that provide the necessary herbs and other paraphernalia for Santería's rituals. Animals for sacrifices can be located under the heading "Pet Stores" where the business name also contains the name of an orisha or the word "botánica." The proliferation of specialty stores geared to the needs of santeros and santeras is a clear indication of the growing presence of Santería. This presence is not limited to the commercial marketplace. Former Miami mayor Maurice Ferre acknowledged the importance of Santería as a growing social and political force when he said that when invited to attend a Santería feast or celebration, he is unable to decline the invitation. Refusing to appear, he says, "[would be like] telling a politician in Boston he shouldn't go to the St. Anthony's Parade or the St. Patrick's Day Parade."[1]

As Santería becomes more part of the mainstream, both it and the culture in which it finds itself begin to change in order to adapt to one another. Such changes do not mean that core beliefs of the religion

1. Sonia L. Nazario, "Sacrificing Roosters to Glorify the Gods Has Miami in a Snit — But Adherents of Santería Must Keep Their Orishas from Getting Riled Up," *Wall Street Journal* (October 18, 1984).

are altered, but that some of its views, practices, and rituals adjust to the new social environment, becoming more acceptable to the general populace. Since coming to the United States via Cuba, Santería has begun to distance itself from some of the traditional forms of Yoruba spirituality and from the heavy influences of Spanish Catholicism. For example, it used to be a prerequisite that santeros and santeras be baptized in the Catholic Church and that they attend the ilé Olofi (house of Christ) — that is, the local Catholic church — seven days after the asiento ordination. But such requirements are being challenged and even dismissed as more Jews, Protestants, and Muslims enter the faith. Although many santeros and santeras, when asked, still describe themselves as Catholics, others have no interest in aligning themselves with the Catholic Church.

Adapting for the United States

Most practitioners of Santería in the United States today are light-skinned, in large part because of the demographics of the Cubans exiled in the United States (80 percent white, 5 percent black, and 15 percent biracial). Few within the priesthood are of African descent. What was once primarily the religion of black slaves in Cuba is being transformed into that of white, middle-class suburbanites. If religion serves to bring together groups of people who agree on a particular concept of the sacred, then as those groups' demographics change, so too will the religion.

As Santería attracts more individuals of different ethnicities and socioeconomic classes, it will become less Cuban-centric. Spanish is already being used less, and specifically Cuban procedures are being discarded. For example, it was considered until recently that one could be ordained as a babalawo only on Cuban soil, because the stones of Olofi that were brought from Africa are still there. Many would travel to the island to be consecrated. Yet just as the orisha traditions survived the Middle Passage, so too are they surviving the Cuban exodus. The requirement of having to travel to Cuba is loosening as more seek initiation within the United States. The Americanization of Santería is redefining how the faith is practiced and understood. As middle- and upper-class non-Cuban and non-black adherents enter the faith, bringing with them more Eurocentric ideas regarding how to do "church,"

Santería is beginning to become a new religious expression, one which is changing to better adapt to the new social context where the faithful find themselves. To conclude this book, we will look briefly at a number of instances where Santería and mainstream American culture and faith are beginning to engage one another. Some of these engagements are for the better and others are less so; all of them are turning Santería into an expression of faith adapted to its new context.

Secrecy

Santería, as we discussed previously, has historically been a secretive religion, due in part to the persecution of its adherents who served as slaves for Catholic masters. The secretive nature of the religion has allowed it to survive since coming to the Americas some 500 years ago. But this secrecy was never part of the original African experience; it was adopted to protect the religion's systematic destruction by the Catholic hierarchy. Ironically, what was once an underground religion because of persecution became an underground religion in the United States because of embarrassment. For believers living in a modern world, the practice of what some classify as a pre-modern religion often led to ridicule, if not scorn. Because most believers in the States were of a lower economic stratum and non-Euroamerican, they often avoided exposure as a believer for fear of attracting another form of ethnic discrimination. They feared that the stigma associated with their beliefs might hinder their ability to become "normal" American citizens. Although religious liberties are technically protected in the United States, many believers continue to conceal their participation. At times, even friends or relatives may not know that one from their own family is a secret adherer. This helps explain why the religion continues to be shrouded in secrecy, wary of outsiders conducting investigations, and at times providing false information about the practices and beliefs of the faithful to ensure the religion's secrecy.

Nevertheless, since the 1992 United States Supreme Court decision protecting the constitutional right of the believers to offer sacrifices to the gods, some within the religion began to do away with its atmosphere of secrecy and attempt to bring it into the mainstream. The santero Ernesto Pichardo, whose case led to the 1992 Supreme Court decision, recognized the dissonance that existed between Santería and the dominant culture due to the secretive nature of the religion. Such secrecy provided followers of Christianity, Judaism, secular humanism, and so on, the opportunity to compare their own beliefs with what to them appeared primitive. Since the ruling, he has been working to create a broadly recognized organization that will help move the religion and its members from the margins of society toward "respectability." In the United States, public manifestations of religion are commonplace. Churches, mosques, or temples are routine manifestations of Christianity, Islam, Judaism, Hinduism, and Buddhism. By starting the first formal place of worship for Santería in the Miami area in 1987, he made a profound statement to the public at large — that santeros and santeras are also members of an acceptable religious group.

Along with the building came the formal organization of the congregation and the use of technology. Pichardo's American-style church now has databases, registration, dues, and membership. It also operates and maintains a well-organized website (http://www.church-of-the-lucumi.org) for members as well as interested observers. The member services page of the site offers information on workshops and courses, distance counseling, and general information on baptism, weddings, and funerals. Besides working to serve members of their congregation, the church also offers assistance to anyone from the media, academia, and law enforcement who needs to know about Santería. Hence Ernesto Pichardo has used the tools of a modern society to build credibility among mainstream Americans and to lead the faith out of its centuries of secrecy.

Media Representations

Most of what Euroamericans think they know about Santería is based on things seen or heard in the popular media — newspapers, television, film, and the like. These media have the power to present Santería either as a valid and sacred belief system, or as a strange and cruel cult. Unfortunately, the latter is the case far too often, as the media focus on the faith's premodern rituals, which make Santería seem exotic at best, malicious at worst. Though the United States' culture lends itself to being tolerant of diverse religious beliefs, still the trend exists to become concerned when the outward actions of a religion are not in accord with how the dominant culture defines civilization.

Let us look briefly at how print journalism has provided the dominant culture with a look at the religion. The earliest newspaper articles about Santería appeared in 1980 in the *New York Times*. Headlines from the May 24, 1980 and June 8, 1980 issues read, "Ritual Slaughter Halted in Bronx by a Police Raid" and "Police Seize Animals Prepared for Sacrifice by Cult in the Bronx." The articles that followed reported the increasing conflicts between the religion's devotees and local law enforcement officials. These headlines alone provided the reader with obviously negative images of Santería. And because the articles' focus was on the rituals and sacrifices of the religion, it was reduced in the mind of the public to just these aspects. According to the May 24th article, the police raided a Santería ceremony taking place in a South Bronx apartment. "[They] interrupted a primitive religious rite involving the ritual slaughter of animals." The scene encountered by the police was described as "blood-splattered confusion." They found twenty men and women in white robes "wailing and chanting" in an apparent trance. There were drums beating, chickens squawking, and goats bleating. This vivid description created a picture of Santería that was more a scene from a horror movie than from a legitimate religious ceremony.

Not only did the articles portray Santería as a strange cult, but also as one in constant conflict with the law and with animal rights activists. The owner of the apartment in the June raid was charged with 124 counts of cruelty to animals and harboring farm animals in the city. She could have been punished with fines up to $500 and one year in prison for each count. Since the 1980s, the majority of the newspaper and magazine articles about Santería have followed suit, focusing on events surrounding the practice of sacrifice. A sample of headlines from various news sources read, "Animal Sacrifices: Faith or Cruelty?" "A Chicken at Every Altar," and "Authorities Credit Animal Sacrifices to Santería Religion." If the media reduce Santería to the ritual practice of "cruel" sacrifices, and its practitioners to criminals, then the end result is a negative picture of the entire religion. This is true despite the fact that the Supreme Court declared these rituals legal.

When the media demonize Santería's animal sacrifices, few stop to think of the similarities between them and certain Christian practices. As Ernesto Pichardo points out, "You can kill a turkey in your backyard, put it on the table, say a prayer, and serve it for Thanksgiving, but if we pray over the turkey, kill it, then eat it, we violated the law."[2] Mainstream Americans tend to view the religion as exotic because they are looking at it from a culturally and socially different location. To believers in Santería, the sacrifices are as natural as a turkey dinner in a Euroamerican household — and as meaningful. According to Migene Gonzalez-Wippler, a follower of Santería, "To be on the receiving end of this type of cleansing is quite an unforgettable experience, and one that is likely to reshape the most skeptical mind."[3] To believers in Santería, ceremonies and sacrifices are ways of communicating with and honoring the gods. Yet the outside observer receives a very different message, since by and large newspaper accounts have failed to provide any serious or particularly accurate view of the religion.[4]

Animal Sacrifice

Animal sacrifices by practitioners of Santería may be a boon to journalists looking for sensational headlines, but they remain a bane to many Americans who live in places where the faith is practiced on a somewhat large scale. For example, Bill Bonner, who lives on a sailboat on the Miami River, noticed one morning two white-robed women chanting over a third by the riverbank while rubbing her naked body with a live chicken. The chicken was then slaughtered and its remains thrown into the river.[5] No doubt this was an offering to Oshún, goddess of love and the river. To the women making the offering it was an important expression of their faith, and to Bill Bonner it was probably somewhat strange and surprising. But to those who operate the county river cleanup boats, the number of decapitated chickens and doves left by the Miami River has become a significant problem.

Finding the remains of animal sacrifices is no longer limited to cities with large Cuban populations. For example, in Norfolk, Virginia, an area where Hispanics as a whole comprise only 3.12 percent of the

2. Bob Cohn and David A. Kaplan, "A Chicken on Every Altar," *Newsweek* (November 9, 1992): 79.

3. Migene Gonzalez-Wippler, *Santería: The Religion* (New York: Harmony Books, 1989), 155.

4. I am grateful to my research assistant Allison Sanders for her work on this section.

5. Michael Reese, "A Cuban Ritual Disturbs Miami," *Newsweek* (June 22, 1981): 44.

population according to the 2000 United States Census, a disembow-
eled lamb was found on the 200 block of East Ocean View Avenue in
August 2001. A month later, two cow tongues were found hanging from
Virginia Beach trees: one in the city park, the other behind the Holland
Plaza shopping center. The next month, headless chickens wrapped in
colored cloth were arranged in a ring around a flagpole at Mount
Trashmore. One of the carcasses had candy and toys in it, no doubt an
offering to Elegguá. The string of animal remains began to appear in
this community in April 2000 with the discovery of a headless chicken
on Little Creek Road.[6] While it is not certain that all of these animal
sacrifices were associated with Santería, it would not be surprising if
indeed they were.

All too often those with Euroamerican sensibilities cringe at the
thought of animal sacrifices, envisioned in their minds as something
primitive if not barbaric. When Ernesto Pichardo announced his plans
to open a Santería church in 1987 on a former used-car lot in the city of
Hialeah, an uproar ensued (see Figure 11 on p. 212). This was the first
time worship would occur in a building designated a "church" devoted
to the practices of Santería, since historically practitioners of the faith
met in one another's houses. Misconceptions flourished as neighbors
expressed fear that their pets would be stolen and offered up to the
gods. Reverend Edwin Diaz, pastor of the Joreb Baptist Church, while
defending freedom of worship, still opposed the church's right to carry
out its sacrificial rituals: "[T]hat there are still people in this era, in our
civilized society of the United States, still sacrificing animals in religious rituals is indefensible and repugnant." Marc Paulhus, director of
the southeast regional office of the Humane Society described Santería
as a "bloody cult . . . whose continued presence further blights the image of South Florida."[7]

Fear and misinformation led over five thousand individuals to
sign petitions urging the Hialeah City Council to prevent the opening
of the church. The local government responded by unanimously adopt-
ing an ordinance forbidding "animal cruelty," which, in effect, pre-

6. Steven Vegh, "Authorities Credit Animal Sacrifices to Santería Religion," *The
Virginia-Pilot* (November 8, 2001).

7. Rosalind Resnick, "To One City, It's Cruelty: To Cultists, It's Religion," *The National Law Journal* (September 11, 1989): 8.

Figure 11. Santería priest Ernesto Pichardo is here shown in this 1987 photo before the church he founded in the city of Hialeah. The Church of the Lukumí Babalú Ayé won a Supreme Court case in 1992, which allows believers of Santería to continue ritual sacrifice at ceremonies. Photo courtesy of the Historical Museum of Southern Florida.

vented Santería religious practice. But Ernesto Pichardo, who opened the storefront church, observed that the issue has little to do with animal cruelty concerns. As long as santeros and santeras kept the sacrifice of animals underground, no laws were passed. While almost everyone in this predominantly Cuban neighborhood knew about the existence of Santería, it was tolerated as long as it did not call attention to itself. When the church attempted to go public and become mainstream, public outrage erupted, going so far as to have politicians passing ordinances to suppress the religious expressions of the faith's devotees.[8] Although some santeros and santeras are beginning to emphasize non-animal sacrifices, by and large the spilling of animal blood continues to remain a crucial component of the religion even in America.

8. Jeffrey Schmalz, "Animal Sacrifice: Faith or Cruelty?" *The New York Times* (August 17, 1989).

Drinking Blood

Santería agrees with the biblical pronouncement that "the life of the flesh is in the blood" (Lev. 17:11). But while this makes drinking blood a necessary component to some Santería rituals, it has made it forbidden in the Judeo-Christian tradition. The biblical text states:

> If any person of the House of Israel or an alien residing in your midst drinks blood of any kind, I [God] will set my face against that person who has drank blood and will cut the person from my people. (Lev. 17:10)

In the Judeo-Christian tradition blood is shed, sometimes literally and sometimes symbolically, to atone for the sins of humans. In this tradition the price of sin is death, which is symbolized in the killing of the sacrifice. Santería does not focus on the shedding of blood for atonement purposes; rather, the spilled blood is used to feed and nourish the orishas. Through feeding, the orishas are empowered to assist their devotees. When a santera or a santero is possessed by an orisha, they will, at times, drink the blood of the sacrifices being offered to the orisha. Is this a violation of the biblical mandate concerning the prohibition of drinking blood? Not so, according to the devotee of Santería. A santero or santera would never drink blood unless they were possessed. And if they are possessed, it is not they who are drinking the blood, but rather it is the orisha who is drinking it. In a sense, what they are doing is faithful to the biblical text — for after all, all blood belongs to God, and as orishas they are only drinking that which already belongs to them. In this unlikely place, we may find a similarity between Santería and the dominant Judeo-Christian tradition: regardless of the theological differences, blood serves as a very important connection between the spiritual and physical worlds.

Jesus Christ

For Christians, regardless of the tradition or denomination of the believer, faith revolves around the believer's relationship with and understanding of Jesus Christ. Christianity teaches that God was incarnate in Jesus in a way not experienced by any other human being in history. But who is Jesus Christ in Santería? He is one of the masks worn by Olofi,

213

who is the embodiment of God on earth. Those who worship Jesus, therefore, are in reality worshiping Olofi. Santería considers Jesus to have been a great sorcerer, who, through esoteric knowledge and his total harmony with his environment and the spiritual world, was able to perform great miracles. The Gospels are testaments to Christ's knowledge of spells and ebbós (sacrifices and offerings). Today's santeros and santeras claim to know the secrets by which Jesus worked these miracles, and will repeat them for those who seek their assistance.

Adoration or Veneration?

For many Christians, especially Catholic Christians, practitioners of Santería are considered guilty of the sin of idolatry due to their worship of the saints as masks of the orishas. But where exactly is the line between worship and veneration? For the longest time, to worship something or someone meant simply to show it respect; thus in many ancient cultures rulers and heroes as well as gods were worshiped. But early on in the history of Christianity, scholars felt the need to clearly delineate what type of reverence was due to God alone and what could be bestowed on other human beings. Over time they concluded that certain individuals — particularly saints — were worthy of honor and remembrance, but only God should receive human adoration and worship. Thus, for example, to hold St. Peter in high regard for his closeness to Jesus and for the miracles he worked is perfectly acceptable. But to praise him in the same way that God is praised is considered inappropriate. From a Christian standpoint, Santería's emphasis on the saints often seems closer to the latter than to the former. Furthermore, what about the difference between worship and idolatry? Christianity understands idolatry to be the worship of any physical object as a god, and from this perspective the santera's or santero's veneration of otanes and other sacred objects looks alarmingly like idolatry.

From our learning the roles the saints and the otanes play in Santería, it is clear that accusations that santeros and santeras worship the saints and worship idols are dependent on how these practices are understood. In worshiping the saints, devotees of Santería see themselves as worshiping the orishas in disguise, and in worshiping the otanes they are worshiping the presence of the orishas in the stones. They are not crediting the stone itself with creating the earth, for example, or seeing St. Barbara or St. Francis as something more than human. Their view of the gods is simply different from Christianity's view of God. Thus it is right to say that Santería is not Christian, but not because it condones idolatry. It is not Christian because it rejects Christianity's main premise that salvation occurs through the work of Jesus Christ who was God incarnate, affirming instead a multitude of gods who guide humans through never-ending life cycles. A choice must be made on the part of the one who professes Christianity between the orishas and the God of the Bible — and this is a choice that both priests of Santería and ministers of Christianity seem to endorse.[9]

The Question of Christian Manifestations

Ernesto Pichardo recalls an ebbó he was making along with other santeras and santeros. When one of his assistants handed him a bottle of holy water taken from a local Catholic shrine, he recoiled, placed it on the ground unopened, and continued with the ceremony. Afterwards, he asked why he was given Catholic holy water. Because it is traditional, he was told. Yet Pichardo insists that this "tradition" is in fact an imposition on the faith. Catholic holy water, Pichardo reminds us, is consecrated to uphold the first of the Ten Commandments: that believers shall have no gods except Yahweh, the God of the Hebrew Bible. It is blessed by the priests in order to exorcize anything that is not consistent with that commandment. Santería, by its very nature, worships and honors a pantheon of gods. You cannot create an ebbó requesting the assistance and help of one of the orisha gods, Pichardo explained to his colleagues, and then invalidate the request by including water that exorcizes the very ebbó produced. Some of the other priests were offended by Pichardo's explanation, insisting on the need for Catholic holy water in the ceremonies and rituals. Those offended were not new to the faith; a few had been priests for nearly fifty years. While Pichardo laments their ignorance about their own faith, at a deeper level an argument can be made that Santería is simply in tension as it evolves into a new religious expression in the United States.

Another example of this tension between owning and rejecting

---

9. I am grateful to my research assistant Sarah Wilkinson for her work on this section.

Santería's Catholic manifestations can be seen in the way that the orisha Oshún is understood by the faithful. As La Virgen de la Caridad, Oshún has always been one of the most important icons for Cubans of all religious persuasions (see Figure 12 on p. 217). From her beginnings as the discovery of two native brothers and a slave boy, she has come to speak for an entire people. Originally she represented the orisha who traveled with her people from Africa to be with them in their slavery. For exilic Cubans in the United States, she became the god who left Cuba with them and waits with them to return home. For resident Cubans, she remains the hope for the marginalized who never left. As such, she reconciles diverse elements of Cuban society — Catholic and Yoruba, white and black, poor and middle class, exile and resident. She cannot be identified simply with one of these things, for she is all of them. La Virgen cannot be understood apart from Oshún; Oshún cannot be understood apart from La Virgen. The same might be said for Santería: it cannot be understood apart from either Catholicism or the worship of the orishas. As more non-Catholics enter the faith, they find a religion in the process of adapting to the social context of its new adherents and thus moving beyond both its Catholic and its African roots, becoming a truly United States–bred religious expression.

Myths

Originally, anywhere from 400 to 1,700 orishas were worshiped in Africa. Of these, only a few (about 20 to 25, with about 18 being highly popular) became renowned in the Western Hemisphere. As the orishas traveled to the United States, seven were singled out and given special attention: Obatalá, Elegguá, Orúnla, Changó, Oggún, Yemayá, and Oshún. They are referred to as *la siete potencias africanas,* the Seven African Powers.

The early Yoruba developed myths about the orishas in order to make sense of the dangers, uncertainties, and arbitrariness of the natural world that surrounded them. These myths, and the rituals that accompanied them, offered explanations for why the forces of nature operated the way they did. The orishas became sources of strength and security, in control of forces over which human beings had no power. Raging seas, violent thunderstorms, harrowing winds, even death did not have to be feared when they were identified with the orishas — the

Figure 12. This is one of the statutes of La Virgen de la Caridad used by the Shrine to our Lady of Charity located at 3609 South Miami Avenue, Miami, Florida. Religion and politics merge by embossing the Cuban national seal on the Virgin's white gown. Also of interest is the white Christ born to a *mulata* Virgin.

same orishas who cared for and responded to the offerings of their devotees. Thus Santería from its very beginning has strived to create harmony with the unpredictability of nature, providing security to people in an unstable world. The Judeo-Christian tradition, by contrast, has tended to downplay the power of nature, to "desacralize" nature, as the scholar Mircea Eliade put it. The great easterly wind may have parted the Sea of Reeds to allow the Hebrew slaves to escape their Egyptian masters; the prophet Elijah may have been able to withhold the rains from idolatrous kings; Jesus may have calmed a stormy sea with a word; but these events are retold in the Bible not in order to explain nature, but to explain God, who exists not in nature but above it.

The rise of modernity in the West in many ways sounded the death knell for pre-modern myths and legends. Explaining natural phenomena through the interactions of gods rather than by scientific inquiry ceased to be acceptable. Christianity, with its tendency to place God above nature, has fared better in such an environment than Santería has. Yoruba mythology was once predominantly accepted as literal fact, and attempts to read the legends of the orishas symbolically have not led to the religion being taken any more seriously in a highly technological culture influenced by the Age of Enlightenment. The tendency has been to dismiss Santería as exotic, primitive, folkloric — at the bottom of a kind of evolutionary scale on which monotheistic religions like Christianity occupy the top positions.

Of course, the dominant culture insists that the only way for a faith like Santería to rise in the rankings is to begin to conform to the Eurocentric Christian ideal. Consequently in the United States the myths of the faith have been downplayed, while the psychological and ethical frameworks have been emphasized. Thus the number of orishas worshiped has decreased by hundreds if not thousands, and practices once considered acceptable — fertility rites associated with the orisha Oko, for example — are now coming into question.

Body and Soul

Christianity also tends to see a dichotomy between flesh and spirit, between body and soul. The former is usually portrayed as weak, as an obstacle to individuals achieving their full spiritual potential. No less a Christian than the apostle Paul viewed the flesh as a constant stumbling block: "I know that within me, that is, in my flesh, dwells no good. . . . Wretched man that I am! Who will deliver me from this body doomed to death?" (Romans 7:18, 24). By contrast, the spirit connotes power. The spirit is responsible for producing fruits that lead to life. Devotees of Santería create no such dichotomy between body and soul. Indeed, to be embodied is so good and desirable that the orishas themselves participate in it by possessing their "children." It could even be argued that there are sexual overtones to these possessions. It used to be expected that individuals would abstain from sex for one year following their ordination, viewing their orisha as their new husband. Even the concept of possession, commonly referred to as "mounting," connotes this physical, spiritual, emotional, and sexual union. Elements of this exist in the Judeo-Christian tradition, for in the Bible, Jesus is often referred to as the bridegroom of the church. Likewise, the prophets described Israel as an adulterous wife when the people sought other gods to worship. But on the whole, Santería has affirmed the body to a much higher degree than Christianity has, and this continues to be true in the United States today.

Being Filled with the Spirit

One particularly striking similarity between Christianity and Santería can be found in the outward expression of those "filled with the Spirit" in Christianity's Pentecostal tradition and those possessed by an orisha in Santería. While Pentecostalism is accepted into American culture for the most part, it is at least to a certain extent disparaged as excessively charismatic and anti-intellectual. Both religious expressions occur along the margins of society, on the edge of what is deemed acceptable by mainstream religious groups, and both impact society from their position at the margins. Both also give an outlet for communication and a sense of authority to those who spend most of their lives in a powerless state.

Pentecostalism rose out of Protestant Christianity at the turn of the twentieth century. The aim of the earliest Pentecostals was to return to what they saw as the worship experience of the first-century church — a worship experience untainted by the cold rationalism of academia. Their focus came to rest on the salvation of Jesus Christ to those who believed in him. They also held a deep conviction that prayer for the sick and miracles of healing should be a prominent part of collective worship. Current statistics indicate that one in four Christians today participates in some form of Pentecostal worship.[10]

Both Pentecostals and devotees of Santería view faith healing as an important component of faith. The latter believe that the orishas heal people through possessions. The sick can approach an orisha-possessed individual and garner a direct healing. Migene Gonzalez-Wippler relates one such experience:

> The orisha singled out a young girl in the group and motioned her to come closer. "Omo-mi [my child], come to Oggun, you are poor, ill, sorrowful, and love always runs away from you. How is your leg? The one you broke last year . . . Oggun rub leg for you then you be well again." He motioned to one of the madrinas nearby who returned in a few moments with a small jar of yellow grease known as manteca de corojo. The orisha knelt on the floor in front of the girl, took off her right shoe, and massaged her leg with the corojo. He stood up swiftly and embraced the girl. He winked at her and laughed delightedly. . . . The girl moved away from the orisha, her face flushed with happiness.[11]

Healings are direct and very physical. The orisha knew just what to do and the girl left feeling better. Her faith allowed her to be freed from physical discomfort.

An important parallel between the two faith traditions in the area of healing is the aspect of looking at supernatural as well as natural causes for diseases rather than simply relegating them to the realm of science. Both groups believe that separation from God and God's will can lead to physical suffering, and that divine intercession can bring healing. Thus through possession or through intercessory prayer and the laying on of hands, those who are afflicted can be lifted from their pain and restored to communion with God. Yet Pentecostal healing is different from that of santeras and santeros in some significant ways. Pentecostals focus on the entire congregation having some ability to heal rather than just the one who happens to be possessed at the time.

---

10. Scott Richard and Allen Bergin, eds., *Handbook of Psychotherapy and Religious Diversity* (Washington D.C.: American Psychological Association, 2000), 159.

11. Migene González-Wippler, *The Santería Experience* (Englewood Cliffs, N.J.: Prentice-Hall, Inc., 1982), 142.

Taking their cue from the miracles performed by Jesus' disciples in the book of Acts, Pentecostals often lay their hands on the person who is afflicted and pray that God will heal them.

Another area of commonality between the two religions is that there are times during worship when both Pentecostals and devotees of Santería speak or act in ways very different from their normal behavior. In Santería, this is called possession; in Pentecostalism, it is known as being anointed by the Spirit (that is, by the Holy Spirit, the third person of the Christian Trinity). In Santería, there are many different deities that can take over the body of a practitioner, in addition to the spirits of the dead. As previously mentioned, several individuals can be simultaneously possessed by the same entity because the divine ashé is too great to all be housed in one human being. Possessions typically begin with mild hysteria and shaking from head to foot, followed by the whole body losing control as it shakes uncontrollably. Eventually, the characteristics of the orisha become manifested. For example, if the person becomes possessed by Babalú-Ayé, then they would most likely walk around as though using a crutch. Those at the ceremony press close to the one who is possessed, requesting healings. The touch of those who are possessed by the orishas is said to feel like a fraction of that of the actual orisha. When a believer was hugged by the orisha Obatalá, she described the experience as "[being] flooded with love. I leaned my head on his shoulder and his touch was bliss. I never before knew or felt such softness and warmth. I wanted to remain in his embrace forever." In like fashion, when this same person was touched by a person possessed by Oya, she described the experience as follows: "the hands of the orisha closed around mine, the feeling of unearthly power exuding from those glacial iron hands was so extraordinary I felt my arms tingle all the way up to the elbow. Her touch terrified me."[12] To feel the touch of the orisha is both wonderful and terrible.

Pentecostals take a different view of the Holy Spirit speaking through them. They believe that when they are baptized in the Spirit they are able to speak in tongues in the same way that the apostles did on the day of Pentecost in the book of Acts. This phenomenon is called glossolalia, and it entails the believer speaking in a language consisting of unintelligible syllables uttered in rapid sequence. It can happen pri-

12. González-Wippler, *Santería Experience*, 137, 142.

vately or during communal worship. Many describe it as a "perfect language" spoken by believers to God. It begins with the simple repetition of syllables and is often quite musical. As individuals become more experienced practitioners of this religion, they may be able to go in an instant from normal conversation with a human to divine conversation with God. Often speaking in tongues is accompanied by shaking, yelling, dancing, rhythmical movements, crying, laughing, and a feeling of intense rapture. As an ecstatic experience, it serves as a point of contact with God in which the individual may feel that he is personally talking with his Creator.

As already mentioned, in possession the santero or santera in essence becomes the god that they are worshiping. They deeply believe that a fragment of the power of this orisha has gone into them, and the mounted individual has the authority of the god for the duration of the possession. Pentecostals, on the other hand, are emphatic that when they speak in tongues they are still only human beings. Yet there are many clear ways in which these two phenomena are similar. Physically, they can be nearly identical. In both, individuals feel themselves touched by a higher power in such a way that they are intensely, immediately changed. Both religious expressions have a charismatic worship style that serves to give a voice to those whom society seldom hears. Possession and anointing of the Spirit both serve to work through feelings that may not always be socially acceptable to express in a more public venue, especially when those who are in a higher social class are present. They project individuals' frustrations with power structures into the supernatural realm and thus facilitate the resolution of believers' conflicts and problems.[13]

Concluding Thoughts

Since the 1992 Supreme Court decision legalizing the sacrifice of animals in connection with Santería, a movement among some santeros and santeras has been to bring the religion into mainline America. Ernesto Pichardo, whose case concerning his church in Hialeah led to

13. I am grateful to my research assistance Elinor Douglass for her work on this section.

the Supreme Court judgment, said shortly after the court victory, "The future is to institutionalize the Santería religion."[14] To this end, he has created web pages, written articles, and begun the arduous task of compiling a nationwide directory of priests of Santería. Nevertheless, over a decade after the Supreme Court decision, leadership within Santería remains fragmented even as the religion continues to attract new adherents.

Today, Santería has more devotees than do many mainline Christian denominations. In effect, it may be considered a mainstream American faith along with Christianity, Judaism, and Islam. Although this emerging religion is rooted in the religious traditions of the African Yoruba religion, Iberian folk Christianity, and European Kardecism, it is neither African, Roman Catholic, nor spiritist. Santería is, and will continue to evolve into, a uniquely American religious expression. Acceptance, however, requires some profound changes, some of which we saw are already taking place. For example, animal sacrifices are becoming less common as other forms of offerings are emphasized. As the religion is practiced in middle-class suburban homes, drum-playing during bembes is avoided to prevent angering neighbors. Likewise, fewer spiritual possessions occur, especially at celebrations that are open to the general public. Less emphasis is placed on the stories of the orishas, and those that remain popular are considered myth rather than fact. Additionally, the role of the babalawos is decreasing as santeros and santeras assume more priestly responsibilities. And finally, the African influences within the religion are minimized as the religion advocates more broadly "Christian" ethical perspective and principles.

Consequently, the definitive book on Santería has yet to be written, for the religion itself has yet to finish forming. The beliefs of the Yoruba people, brought to Cuba against their will to serve as slaves, took root in the Western Hemisphere. The process of acculturation that started several centuries ago has yet to achieve completion. Always ready to change in order to better equip its believers for the life-changing world they face, Santería willingly discards old beliefs, rituals, and gods which become obsolete while incorporating the beliefs, ritu-

14. Larry Rohter, "Santería Faithful Hail Court Ruling," *The New York Times,* June 13, 1993.

als, and gods of the society in which believers find themselves in order to resist and survive. Today, after centuries of secrecy and repression, Santería is on the verge of reformulating itself to become more mainstream, more "respectable," more acceptable as a belief system to the United States' largely Euroamerican population. What was once the religion of the uneducated black lower economic class is becoming the religion of educated middle-class whites. Consequently, as a growing religion in the United States, we can expect Santería to continue changing and adapting to the realities and challenges faced by its followers. For this reason, whatever Santería may be today, it will be quite different tomorrow.

Glossary

The Yoruba language is the mother tongue of approximately sixteen million people worldwide. It belongs to the Yoruboid group of languages, which includes several other West African tongues. Yoruba is a tone language where both the sound of the word and the integral tune (that is, the stress given to a syllable) must be considered in assessing the meaning of the word spoken. Although mainly concentrated in the western regions of present-day Nigeria, Yoruba is also the language used in the Western Hemisphere by the followers of Santería. Linguistic variations, in the form of dialects, exist in Africa, as in the case of the language spoken in the Oyo province as opposed to Lagos. Most of these differences are restricted to grammatical use.

When the Yoruba language was brought to Cuba, it was attuned to Spanish usage, altering how the African words were pronounced and defined. The language that developed became known as Lucumí. Below is a glossary of some terms used in the religion, many of which were highlighted in this book. Some of the words are Spanish words; others are Yoruba; still others reflect the mixture of these two cultures.

Abakuá: Secret, male-only societies formed by the Ekoi people of the Calabar Coast.

abikú: A transient spirit that possesses unborn children, bringing early death.

abofaca: A man who is ordained into Ifá or the Mano de Orúnla.

addele: Unread cowrie shells.

Glossary

adura: The Yoruba word for prayer.

Aganyú: The orisha who owns the volcano.

ahijado, ahijada: The Spanish word for godson or goddaughter, used for a person who becomes initiated under the tutelage of a santero or santera.

Ajé Chaluga: The orisha of health, luck, and fortune.

Alaaye: A name for Olodumare meaning "the living one who gives life to all of creation."

Ala ba la se: Title by which Obatalá is known, it means "the one who clutches the center."

alafia: Occurs during divination via coconut shells when all the sides facing upward are white. It indicates a tentative yes but requires that the coconuts be cast again.

Alamo rere: Title by which Obatalá is known, it means "the one who handles the chosen clay."

alaña: Owner of the consecrated batáa drums.

aleyo: Individuals who are not consecrated as santeros or santeras.

Aña: The soul or spirit that inhabits the ritual drums.

apotí: Throne on which the person being ordained as a santera or santero sits.

ara orun: Literally "the people of heaven," referring to those who came before us, the ancestors. The phrase can also refer to the orishas.

arun: Disease.

ashé: The supreme being as sacred energy that is the power, grace, blood, and life force of all reality, embracing mystery, secret power, and divinity. As a transcendent world force, it is absolute, illimitable, pure power, non-definite and non-definable.

asiento: Ceremony of initiation into Santería, also known as *hacer al santo*. The Spanish word for seat.

A-te-rene-k-aiye: Title by which Obatalá is known, it means "the one who covers the extension of the land."

avatar: Path or way of an orisha, also known as *camino*.

awo: Literally, "revealed secrets" via the study of divination.

Ayáguna: The orisha of pendency.

ayé: A long, small, white shell used during the diloggún ritual. It is held by the person seeking counsel and is used to determine whether the cowrie shells are indicating a positive or a negative answer.

Ayoba: Another name for Santería.

baba: Father.

babalawo: Literally, "father of mystery." A male high priest in Santería who is able to divine the future.

babalosha: A male priest or santero.

Babalú-Ayé: The orisha who governs the sphere of illness.

Baba Nkwa: One of the three aspects (along with Nzame and Olofi) of Olodumare.

baba-Oru: A person's heavenly father or ruling male orisha.

bajar a Orúnla: The Spanish phrase for "to bring down Orúnla," a ritual conducted by a babalawo in which seashells are consulted in conjunction with at least five more babalawos to determine the orishas of an individual being ordained.

balseros: The Spanish word for "rafters," used to describe those who fled Cuba by raft after the 1959 revolution.

batáa: Ritual drums played so that the messages of worshipers can reach the orishas.

batea: The wooden bowl where Changó's stones are stored.

bembe: A drum and dance festival performed in honor of the orishas.

bilongo: Witchcraft.

botánica: A religious goods store that caters to practitioners of Santería.

bóveda: A shrine for the dead consisting of seven glasses of water with a cross and/or rosary bead on a table covered by a white cloth.

brujería: Witchcraft.

brujo/a: Witch doctor.

cabildo: Social club set up along racial and linguistic lines; served as a mutual aid society in Cuba.

camino: Path or way of the orisha, also known as an avatar.

canastillero: Shelved cabinet where the santero or santera stores ritual paraphernalia.

Candomblé: An orisha-based religion practiced in Brazil.

caracoles: Spanish word for seashells.

Caridad de Cobre: A name for Cuba's patron saint, known as Oshún in Santería.

casa de santo: Literally, "the house of the saint"; the Spanish term for the house of a santero or santera.

casilla: Medium.

ceiba: Spanish word for a type of tree that is considered sacred in Santería.

Changó: The orisha who rules lightning, thunder, and fire.

cimarrón: A runaway Cuban slave.

Cofá de Orúnla: A woman's ordination into Ifá performed by a babalawo.

collares: Necklaces, the Spanish word for the elekes given as the first step toward entrance into Santería.

cowrie: The type of seashell used during divination rituals.

Cuanaldo: The ordination ritual that confers the usage of the sacrificial knife.

cuarto de los santos: A Spanish phrase for "room of the saints," which designates the room within the house set aside for conducting the rituals of the faith.

Dadá: The orisha of gardens and the newly born, specifically those born with curly hair.

dar coco al santo: Divination system that uses coconuts. Spanish for "giving coconut to the saint."

derecho: The fee charged by the santero or santera for their services; Spanish for "right."

despojo: A Spanish word that refers to the procedure of cleansing the individual from evil influences.

diloggún: A divination system that uses seashells; also known as mediloggún.

dueño de la cabeza: The Spanish phrase for "owner of the head," also known as the santo de cabecera; the orisha into whose mysteries the iyawó is ordained.

ebbó: A ritual involving a sacrifice to an orisha.

efún: A ball of husk held in the hands of the person seeking counsel during the divination process to determine if the answers to the questions asked of the cowrie shells are yes or no.

egun: The dead.

egungun: A person possessed by the spirit of a dead person.

ekuelé: Another name for opele.

eleda: Guardian angel inhabiting the iyawó's head. Possibly the individual's protector orisha, the individual's spiritual force, or a dead spirit who protects the individual.

Eleggúá: The orisha that is a messenger, the opener of ways, and a trickster.

elekes: Beaded necklaces, also known in Spanish as collares.

Elemi: A name for Olodumare meaning "owner of life who provides creation's nourishment."

elenini: Negative spiritual forces.

emí: The Yoruba word for "breath and soul," suggesting that Olodumare is the source of physical existence and human consciousness.

erí-aguona: A guacalote seed held in the hands of the person seeking counsel during the divination process to determine whether the answers to the questions asked of the cowrie shells are yes or no.

Espiritismo: Spanish word for Spiritism.

espiritista: Spanish word for Spiritist.

ewe: Plants, roots, trees, and flowers.

eyife: Occurs during divination via coconut shells when two of the pieces facing upwards are white, and the other two pieces are brown. It indicates a definite yes.

fundamento: Spanish word for foundation.

guerreros: Spanish word for warriors, a reference to the orishas Elegguá, Oggún, Ochosi and Ósun.

hacer el santo: Ceremony of ordination into Santería, also known as asiento. Literally "to make the saint" in Spanish.

hermandades: Spanish for fraternities.

Ibeyi: The orisha twins who protect children.

icofá: A woman who is ordained into Ifá.

idé: The green and yellow bracelet worn by men and women who are ordained into Ifá.

Ifá: The most prestigious of Santería's oracles.

Ikú: Death, a quasi-deity whose function is to dispose of life.

ilé: A home or spiritual community.

Ilé-Ife: "City of Origins" in Yoruba. The first city, where humans were created by Obatalá.

Ilé-Olofi: Literally, "the house of God," a Santería term for the Catholic Church.

Inle: Orisha of healing.

itá: Life and times of an individual or of one of the orishas.

itagua: Occurs during divination via coconut shells when three sides facing upwards are white and one side is brown. It indicates a tentative yes, but requires that the coconuts must again be cast because an error was made during the divination procedure.

italero: An individual who is highly regarded by the faith community for skill in reading the seashells.

Glossary

itótele: The medium-sized drum in the batáa.

itutu: A ritual performed to ease the transition of a deceased believer into the next phase of existence.

iyá: The largest of the three drums in the batáa.

iyalosha: Female priestess or santera who has ordained other santeras or santeros.

iyawó: Literally, bride; a name for the individual being ordained into Santería.

Jimaguas: Spanish for twins; sometimes used as a name for the Ibeyi.

Kadiempembe: A devil-type figure in Kongo mythology.

knife of Oggún: An ordination ceremony authorizing babalawos to sacrifice four-legged animals.

letra de año: A prediction made at the beginning of each year by a group of babalawos about events to come.

levantamiento del plato: The Spanish phrase for "raising of the dish," a ritual conducted a year after the death of a santero or santera to bid a final farewell to the deceased.

libreta: The Spanish word for notebook. Given to a santero or santera after ordination into the faith, it contains handwritten stories, legends, rituals, ceremonies, mysteries, and spells of the orishas, as well as the santera's or santero's itá, detailing future events, and prohibitions that the santero or santera needs to observe.

limpieza: The Spanish word for cleansing.

Los Guerreros: The Spanish word for "the Warriors" who are received by the believer for protection, specifically Elegguá, Oggún, Ochosi, and Ósun.

Lucumí: Another word for Santería. It also refers to any characteristic of Yoruba culture, as, for example, the language. Some scholars believe that the word is derived from the Yoruba greeting *oluki mi,* which literally means "my friend"; other scholars believe it refers to an ancient Yoruba kingdom called Ulkumi.

madrina: Spanish word for godmother.

Mano de Orúnla: In Spanish, "the hand of Orúnla"; refers to a man who is ordained into Ifá. Also known as the abofaca.

mayombero: Those ordained into a type of palo known as the regla de mayombe.

mediloggún: A divination system that uses seashells. Also known as diloggún.

medio asiento: Spanish for "half the asiento," which refers to the foundation rituals needed for eventually becoming a santero or santera. These rituals include the receiving of the necklaces, making Elegguá, and obtaining the guerreros.

meji: The Yoruba word for two.

Misa espiritual: The Spanish phrase for "Spiritism Mass," a Spiritist ritualism used by santeros and santeras.

necklaces: The elekes, which are known in Spanish as collares. Receiving them is the first step toward entrance into the faith.

ñáñigos: Members of secret societies known as Abakuá.

nganga: Also known as prenda; a bag or cauldron that contains ingredients that represent the elements of the world and the captured spirit of the dead. An important implement of those who practice palo mayombe.

Nzame: The aspect of Olodumare that created all that exists.

oba: Title for a ruler of an ancient Yoruba city-state.

Obakoso: Changó's title which means "the king did not hang."

Obatalá: Head orisha of the Yoruba pantheon; creator of humanity.

Oba-ti-ala: Title by which Obatalá is known, it means "the king who is dressed in white."

Oba-ti-o-nla: Title by which Obatalá is known, it means "the great king."

Obba: The neglected wife of Changó.

Obi: The Yoruba word for "coconut"; also the name of an orisha.

ocana-sode: Occurs during divination via coconut shells when three of the sides facing upwards are brown and one is white; it means no.

ocha: Saint.

Ochosi: The orisha of justice who also rules over the hunt.

Ochumare: The orisha of the rainbow.

ocóncolo: The smallest drum in the batáa.

Oddudúa: An orisha. Some believe that Olofi created a wife for Obatalá named Oddudúa. Others claim that Obatalá became two separate entities, one male known as Oddudúa, and one female known as Yemmú. In other legends, he is considered to be the founder of Ilé-Ife and the younger brother of Obatalá.

odu: A set of specific legends, proverbs, verses, or sacrifices associated with a particular throw of the cowrie shells in the diloggún ritual. Also known as letra.

Oggué: The patron orisha of the herds, specifically of animals with horns.

Oggún: The orisha of metals and war.

òjiji: Shadow.

Oké: The tutelary orisha of the mountains.

Oko: The orisha who oversees agriculture.

Olocun: Orisha who is the queen of the ocean's depths.

Olodumare: The supreme being, creator of all that exists.

Olofi: A name for Olodumare meaning "God on earth who serves as humanity's personal God."

Olojo Oni: A name for Olodumare meaning "Controller of daily actions who guides daily activities."

Olori: A name for Olodumare meaning "Universal Soul which exists within an individual's head."

Olorún: A name for Olodumare meaning "Owner of the heavens who lightens the day and provides the energy of life."

olosha: Another term for santeros and santeras.

oluki mi: Yoruba greeting which literally means "my friend." Possibly the origin of the word Lucumí.

oluwo: Highest level achievable by a babalawo.

omiero: A special mixture consisting of blood from the sacrifices offered during the ordination ceremony into Santería and juices extracted from herbs that are sacred to the orishas.

omo: Child.

Omo Oba: First, rebellious human created by Olodumare.

omo-orisha: Santero or santera who is the child of a specific orisha.

oñí: Honey.

ono-orishai: Literally, "child of the orisha."

Ooni: The spiritual authority of the Yoruba of Nigeria and all who worship the orishas in the Americas.

opele: A chain fifty inches long and interrupted by eight concave shell pieces, round pieces of leather, or pieces of coconut. Used for reading Ifá. Also known as ekuelé.

Oraniyán: The creator of land.

ori: Literally means "head"; however it is conceptually more like the soul. The very essence of an individual is contained within the ori. Once the body dies, the ori can be reincarnated into another body.

oriate: A type of master of ceremonies who leads several santeros or santeras in the making of an omiero.

orisha: Created by the supreme God Olodumare, they are quasi-deities which serve as protectors and guides for every human being, regardless of the individual's acknowledgment. They were the first to walk the earth, and from them all humans are descended.

Oroiña: The orisha who is the source of universal fire and solar energy.

Orúnla: The orisha who rules over divination and serves as the patron of babalawos.

orun rere: Good Heaven.

Osain: The orisha who oversees nature.

osainista: A herbalist.

oshe: Double-edged ax.

Oshún: The orisha in charge of rivers and love.

Ósun: One of the four warrior orishas; originally was the messenger of Obatalá and Olofi.

otá: A small rock held during the divination process by the individual seeking counsel, used to determine if the answers to the questions asked of the cowrie shells are yes or no.

otanes: Sacred stones which embody the orisha's ashé.

Oyá: The orisha in charge of wind, lightning, and ceremonies.

Oyé: The giant orisha of storms.

oyekun: Occurs during divination via coconut shells when all the sides facing upward are brown. This means no.

padrino: Godfather.

palero: A palo priest.

Palo: A popular form of spirituality that originated among the Congo or Bantu people.

Palo Mayombe: A form of palo.

Palo Monte: A form of palo.

pataki: Legend, myth, or story concerning the origins and interrelationships of the orishas, as well as the role they play in determining the destiny of humanity.

polvo de la justicia: The Spanish phrase for "justice powder," a special powder made to solicit the assistance of Ochosi by those facing the judicial system.

prenda: Another name for the nganga.

promesa: The Spanish word for vow.

rayado: The Spanish word for cut; used to refer to the person who has been initiated into palo.

Registro de entrada: Literally, "entry exam." A ritual that determines the guardian angel of an individual.

regla: Rule.

Regla de Ocha: Another name for Santería.

resguardo: Amulet.

rogación de cabeza: Ritual to feed the ori, the head.

santero, santera: Priest of Santería, consecrated to and the representative of a specific orisha.

santo de cabecera: The Spanish phrase for "the head's saint." Also known as the *dueño de la cabeza,* and refers to the orisha into whose mysteries the iyawó is ordained.

siete potencias africanas: Literally "the Seven African Powers," referring to Obatalá, Elegguá, Orúnla, Changó, Oggún, Yemayá, and Oshún.

sopera: Spanish word for "tureen," which is used to house the otanes.

Spiritism: A belief system involving the invocation of the dead through specific rituals.

Table of Ifá: The means by which a babalawo divines the future through the use of kola nuts or palm nuts.

tambor: Spanish word for drum.

trono: Spanish word for throne, used to refer to a display of an orisha's soperas.

Warriors: A reference to the orishas Elegguá, Oggún, Ochosi and Ósun.

Yemayá: The orisha who rules over the oceans and motherhood.

Yemmú: A feminine aspect of Obatalá.

yerbero: The Spanish word for herbalist.

Yewá: The orisha in charge of transporting corpses to Oyá.

Yoruba: People group who originated from what today is known as southern Nigeria. The name is believed to mean "cunning." Sub-ethnic groups include Oyo, Dahomey, and Benin.

Bibliography

This book has heavily relied on the material of many scholars who have written about Santería. Although "experts" on the religion disagree regarding the details of many of the myths and rituals of the religion, I have attempted to highlight those areas where most find agreement, while also providing dissenting views where necessary.

Agrupación Católica Universitaria. *Encuesta Nacional sobre el Sentimiento Religioso del Pueblo de Cuba.* La Habana: Buró de Información y Propaganda de la ACU, 1954.

Agüero, Sixto Gastón. *El materialismo explica el espiritismo y la santería.* La Habana: Orbe, 1961.

Aimes, Hubert H. S. *A History of Slavery in Cuba: 1511 to 1868.* New York: Octagon Books, 1967.

Balch, Phyllis A. *Prescription for Herbal Healing: An Easy-to-Use A-to-Z Reference to Hundreds of Common Disorders and Their Herbal Remedies.* New York: Avery, 2002.

Barber, Karin. "How Man Makes God in West Africa: Yoruba Attitudes toward the Òrìsà." *Africa,* Vol. 60, No. 3 (1981): 724-745.

Bascom, William R. "The Focus of Cuban Santería." *Southwestern Journal of Anthropology,* Vol. 6, No. 1 (1950): 64-68.

————. *Ifa Divination: Communication Between Gods and Men in West Africa.* Bloomington: Indiana University Press, 1969.

————. *Sixteen Cowries: Yoruba Divination from Africa to the New World.* Bloomington: Indiana University Press, 1980.

————. "Two Forms of Afro-Cuban Divination." *Acculturation in the Americas:*

Proceedings and Selected Papers of the XXIXth International Congress of Americanists. Edited by Sol Tax. Chicago: The University of Chicago Press, 1952.

————. "The Yoruba in Cuba." *Nigeria,* 37:14-20.

Beier, Ulli. *Yoruba Myths.* Cambridge: Cambridge University Press, 1980.

Benedictine Monks of St. Augustine's Abbey, Ramsgate. *The Book of Saints: A Dictionary of Persons Canonized or Beatified by the Catholic Church,* fifth edition. New York: Thomas Y. Crowell Company, 1966.

Bolívar Aróstegui, Natalia. *Los orishas en Cuba.* La Habana: Ediciones Unión, 1990.

Bourdieu, Pierre. "Genesis and Structure of the Religious Field." *Comparative Social Research,* Vol. 13 (1991): 1-44.

Brandon, George. *Santería from Africa to the New World.* Bloomington: Indiana University Press, 1997.

————. "The Uses of Plants in Healing in an Afro-Cuban Religion, Santería." *Journal of Black Studies,* Vol. 22, No. 1 (September, 1991): 55-76.

Cabrera, Lydia. *El monte.* Miami: Coleccion Chichereku, 1971.

————. *Yemayá y Ochún: Kariochas, Iyalochas y Olorichas.* Madrid: Edición C.R., 1974.

Camnitzer, Luis. *New Art of Cuba.* Austin: University of Texas Press, 1994.

Canizares, Raul. *Cuban Santería: Walking with the Night.* Rochester: Destiny Books, 1993.

Cardoza-Orlandi, Carlos. "Drum Beats of Resistance and Liberation: Afro-Caribbean Religions, the Struggle for Life, and the Christian Theologian." *Journal of Hispanic/Latino Theology,* Vol. 3, No. 1 (1995): 50-61.

Castellanos, Isabel. "A River of Many Times: The Polysemy of Ochún in Afro-Cuban Tradition." *Ósun Across the Waters: A Yoruba Goddess in Africa and the Americas.* Edited by Joseph M. Murphy and Mei-Mei Sanford. Bloomington: Indiana University Press, 2001.

Cortez, Enrique. *Manual del oriate: secretos del oriate de la religión Yoruba.* New York: Vilaragus, 1980.

Curtin, Philip D., and Jan Vansina. "Sources of the Nineteenth Century Atlantic Slave Trade," *Journal of African History,* Vol. 5 (1964): 185-208.

De La Torre, Miguel A. "Ochún: (N)either the (M)other of All Cubans (n)or the Bleached Virgin." *Journal of the American Academy of Religion,* Vol. 69, No. 4 (December 2001): 837-861.

————. *The Quest for the Cuban Christ: A Historical Search.* Gainesville: University Press of Florida, 2002.

De La Torre, Miguel A., and Edwin David Aponte. *Introducing Latino/a Theology.* Maryknoll: Orbis Books, 2001.

de Quesada, Gonzalo. *The Chinese and Cuban Independence.* Leipzig: Breitkopf & Hartel, 1925.

Durkheim, Émile. *The Elementary Forms of Religious Life.* Translated by Joseph Ward Swain. New York: The Macmillan Company, 1915.

Edwards, Gary, and John Mason. *Black Gods: Orisa Studies in the New World.* Brooklyn: Yoruba Theological Archministry, 1985.

Eliade, Mircea. *The Myth of the Eternal Return: Or, Cosmos and History.* Translated by Willard R. Trask. New York: Harper Torchbooks, 1959.

Elizondo, Carlos. *Manual del italero de la religion lucumí.* Self-published, n.d.

Espín, Orlando. "Popular Religion as an Epistemology of Suffering." *Journal of Hispanic/Latino Theology,* Vol. 2, No. 2 (1994): 55-78.

Fagbenro Beyioku, Akin. *Órúnmìlàism: the Basis of Jesuism.* Lagos: Tika Tore Press, 1943.

Fá'lokun Fatunmbi, Awo. *Awo: Ifá and the Theology of Orisha Divination.* Bronx: Original Publications, 1992.

———. *Ìwa-pèlé: Ifá Quest: The Search for the Source of Santería and Lucumi.* Bronx: Original Publications, 1991.

Fernández Olmos, Margarite, and Lizabeth Paravisini-Gebert. *Creole Religions of the Caribbean: An Introduction from Vodou and Santería to Obeah and Espiritismo.* New York: New York University Press, 2003.

Frazer, James George. *The Golden Bough: A Study in Magic and Religion.* New York: The Macmillan Company, 1951.

Frazier, E. Franklin. *The Negro Family in the United States.* Chicago: University of Chicago Press, 1966.

Geertz, Clifford. *The Interpretation of Culture: Selected Essays.* New York: Basic Books, 1973.

Gilestra, Doris. "Santería and Psychotherapy." *Comprehensive Psychotherapy,* Vol. 3 (1981): 69-80.

Gleason, Judith; Awotunde Aworinde; and John Olaniyi Ogundipe. *A Recitation of Ifa: Oracle of the Yoruba.* New York: Grossman Publishers, 1973.

González-Wippler, Migene. *Legends of Santería.* St. Paul, Minn.: Llewellyn Publications, 1994.

———. *Powers of the Orishas: Santería and the Worship of Saints.* New York: Original Publications, 1992.

———. *Santería: African Magic in Latin America.* New York: The Julian Press, Inc., 1973.

———. "Santería: Its Dynamics and Multiple Roots." *Enigmatic Powers: Syncretism with African and Indigenous Peoples' Religions Among Latinos.* Edited by Anthony M. Stevens-Arroyo and Andrés Pérez y Mena. New York: Bildner Center for Western Hemisphere Studies, 1995.

———. *Santería: The Religion.* New York: Harmony Books, 1989.

Bibliography

————. *The Santería Experience.* Englewood Cliffs, N.J.: Prentice-Hall, Inc., 1982.
Helg, Aline. *Our Rightful Share: The Afro-Cuban Struggle for Equality, 1886-1912.* Chapel Hill: The University of North Carolina Press, 1995.
Idowu, E Bolaji. *Olódùmarè: God in Yoruba Belief.* New York: Frederick A. Praeger, Publisher, 1963.
Izaguirre, Héctor. *Changó y el fuego cósmico.* Caracas: Editorial Panapo de Venezuela, 1998.
————. *Elegguá, Oggún, Ikú y Ochosi: Guardianes y guerreros.* Caracas: Editorial Panapo de Venezuela, 1997.
————. *Kori-Koto Yemayá.* Caracas: Editorial Panapo de Venezuela, 1998.
————. *Obatalá el padre creador del hombre.* Caracas: Editorial Panapo de Venezuela, 1998.
————. *Osain y la corte de los seis orishas.* Caracas: Editorial Panapo de Venezuela, 1997.
————. *Orula, Orugán, Chugudú: El triángulo adivinatorio en la Santería.* Caracas: Editorial Panapo de Venezuela, 1998.
————. *Palo Mayombe.* Caracas: Editorial Panapo de Venezuela, 1998.
Kirby, Diana González, and Sara María Sánchez. "Santería: From Africa to Miami via Cuba: Five Hundred Years of Worship." *Journal of the Historical Association of Southern Florida,* Vol. 48 (1988): 36-52.
Knight, Franklin. *Slave Society in Cuba During the Nineteenth Century.* Madison: University of Wisconsin Press, 1970.
Lefever, Harry G. "When the Saints Go Riding In: Santería in Cuba and the United States." *Journal for the Scientific Study of Religion,* Vol. 35 (September 1996): 318-30.
Manzano, Juan Francisco. *The Life and Poems of a Cuban Slave: Juan Francisco Manzano, 1797-1854.* Edited by Edward J. Mullen. Translated by R. R. Madden. Hamden, Conn.: Archon Books, 1981.
Martinez, Rafael, and Charles V. Wetli. "Santería: A Magico-Religious System of Afro-Cuban Origin." *The American Journal of Social Psychiatry,* Vol. 2, No. 3 (Summer, 1982): 32-38.
Masó y Vazquez, Calixto C. *Historia de Cuba.: la lucha de un pueblo por cumplir su destino histórico y su vocación de libertad.* Miami: Ediciones Universal, 1998.
Mason, Michael Atwood. *Living Santería: Rituals and Experiences in an Afro-Cuban Religion.* Washington, D.C.: Smithsonian Institution Press, 2002.
McClelland, E. M. *The Cult of Ifá among the Yoruba.* Volume 1. London: Ethnographica, 1982.
Medina, Tomás Pérez, and Eloy Herrera Hernández. *El camino de Osha.* Caracas: Editorial Panapo de Venezuela, 1995.
Moore, Carlos. *Castro, the Blacks, and Africa.* Los Angeles: Center for Afro-American Studies, University of California, 1988.

Murphy, E. Jefferson. *History of African Civilization.* New York: Dell, 1972.

Murphy, Joseph. *Santería: An African Religion in America.* Boston: Beacon Press, 1988.

————. *Working the Spirit: Ceremonies of the New African Diaspora.* Boston: Beacon Press, 1994.

Núñez, Luis Manuel. *Santería: A Practical Guide to Afro-Caribbean Magic.* Woodstock, Conn.: Spring Publications, Inc., 1999.

Ortiz, Fernando. *Los negros esclavos.* La Habana: Editorial de Ciencias Sociales, 1975.

Oyewole, Anthony, and John Lucas. *Historical Dictionary of Nigeria.* 2nd edition. London: Scarecrow Press, 2000.

Pals, Daniel L. *Seven Theories of Religion.* New York: Oxford University Press, 1996.

Pérez, Louis A., Jr. *Cuba: Between Reform and Revolution.* New York: Oxford University Press, 1988.

Pérez y Mena, Andrés Isidoro. "Cuban Santería, Haitian Vodun, Puerto Rican Spiritualism: A Multiculturalist Inquiry into Syncretism." *Journal for the Scientific Study of Religion,* Vol. 37, no. 1 (March 1998): 15-27.

————. *Speaking with the Dead: Development of Afro-Latin Religion Among Puerto Ricans in the United States.* New York: AMS Press, 1991.

Pichardo, L. Ernesto. *Oduduwa y Obatala.* Miami: St. Babalu Aye, Church of the Lukumi, 1984.

————. Personal interview. Miami, Florida. May 2000.

Pulleyblank, Douglas. "Yoruba." *International Encyclopedia of Linguistics.* Volume 4. Edited by William Bright. Oxford: Oxford University Press, 1992.

Raboteau, Albert J. *Slave Religion: The "Invisible Institution" in the Antebellum South.* Oxford: Oxford University Press, 1978.

Rahner, Karl. *Foundations of Christian Faith: Introduction to the Idea of Christianity.* Trans. by William V. Dych. New York: Seabury, 1978.

————. *Theological Investigations.* Trans. by David Bourke. London: Darton, Longman & Todd, 1973.

Resnick, Rosalind. "To One City, It's Cruelty. To Cultists, It's Religion." *The National Law Journal* (September 11, 1989): 8.

Richard, Scott, and Allen Bergin, editors. *Handbook of Psychotherapy and Religious Diversity.* Washington D.C.: American Psychological Association, 2000.

Rowlands, E. C. *Teach Yourself Yoruba.* New York: Hodder and Stoughton, 1969.

Sánchez Cárdenas, Julio. "Santería or Orisha Religion: An Old Religion in a New World." *South and Meso-American Native Spirituality: From the Cult of the Feathered Serpent to the Theology of Liberation.* Edited by Gary H. Gossen. New York: The Crossroad Publishing Company, 1997.

Sandoval, Mercedes. "Afro-Cuban Religion in Perspective." *Enigmatic Powers:*

Bibliography

Syncretism with African and Indigenous Peoples' Religions Among Latinos. Edited by Anthony M. Stevens-Arroyo and Andrés Pérez y Mena. New York: Bildner Center for Western Hemisphere Studies, 1995.

————. "Santería." *The Journal of the Florida Medical Association,* Vol. 70, No. 8 (August, 1983): 620-628.

————. "Santería: Afrocuban Concepts of Disease and Its Treatment in Miami." *Journal of Operational Psychiatry,* Vol. 8, No. 2 (1977): 52-63.

————. "Santería as a Medical Health Care System: An Historical Overview." *Social Science and Medicine,* Vol. 13B (1979): 137-51.

Schreiter, Robert J. *Constructing Local Theologies.* Maryknoll: Orbis Books, 1996.

Scott, James C. *Domination and the Arts of Resistance: Hidden Transcripts.* New Haven: Yale University Press, 1990.

Stevens-Arroyo, Anthony M. *Papal Overtures in a Cuban Key: The Pope's Visit and Civic Space for Cuban Religion.* Scranton: The University of Scranton Press, 2002.

Thomas, Hugh. *Cuba: The Pursuit of Freedom.* New York: Harper & Row, 1971.

Vega, Marta Moreno. "The Yoruba Orisha Tradition Comes to New York." *African American Review,* Vol. 29, No. 2 (Summer 1995): 201-206.

Verger, Pierre. "The Yoruba High God: A Review of the Source." *Odu: Journal of Yoruba and Related Studies,* Vol. 2, No. 2 (1966): 19-40.

Wetli, Charles V., and Rafael Martinez. "Brujeria: Manifestations of Palo Mayombe in South Florida." *The Journal of Florida Medical Association,* Vol. 70, No. 8 (August 1983): 629-34.

Index

Index

58, 65, 121, 197; as Saint Barbara, 8, 54-55, 66, 114, 199

Chicago, Illinois, 192

Christianity, xii-xiii, xvii-xviii, 1-3, 6-13, 15, 17, 28-29, 31-33, 47, 101, 160, 170, 172, 181-82, 189, 197, 199, 201-2, 208, 213-14, 218, 223; Catholicism and Santería, xii, 1-3, 7-13, 16-17, 104, 106, 161, 164-65, 167-69, 174, 176, 178, 186, 199, 202, 206-7, 215-16, 223; Christian saints and the orishas, xii-xiii, 3, 7-10, 13, 54-56, 59, 61-62, 64, 66-68, 71-75, 78, 81, 83-84, 86, 114, 167-69, 214-15; Protestantism and Santería, xiv, 1, 10-12, 104, 165-68, 176, 206, 219-22; and Syncretism, xiv, xvi, xiii, 1-2, 6-12, 176; Redemption, 18, 21, 213, 219

Christopher, Saint, 79. *See also* Aganyú

Church of the Lukumi Babalú Ayé, 103, 208, 211-12

Cleansing. *See* Rituals of Santería

Coconut, 60-61, 137, 164

Congo. *See* Africa

Cosmas and Damian, Saints, 86. *See also* Ibeyi

Corpus of Ifa. *See* Sacred Text

Cowrie shells. *See* Shells

Creation, 18-19, 33-40, 134-35, 139, 153

Cuarto de los santos. *See* House-temple

Cuba, xi, 167-71, 173-82, 184, 186-88, 193, 206-7; Africans in, xii-xiii, 2-3, 7, 19, 47, 67, 74, 135, 141, 154, 158, 160-67, 183, 185-86, 190, 193, 195, 203, 225; Chinese in Cuba, 140, 154; Matanza, xii, 186-87; practice of Santería, xvii, xi-xiii, 1-3, 8, 57, 74, 140-41, 157, 174-76, 186, 196

Dahomey Kingdom, 2, 70-71, 160, 183-84

Dead, the, 20, 34, 115, 118, 120, 142, 145-46, 172, 201, 221; as ancestors, 21-23,

173, 192, 198, 200; as tormentors, 22-24, 28, 118

Death, 20-21, 23-27, 191, 195

Dispojo. *See* Rituals of Santería

Divination, 8, 16, 21-23, 45, 47, 83, 110-12, 118, 126, 129, 131, 139-40, 156, 199-200; divination via Obi, 22, 141-43; regla de Ifá, 41, 62-63, 106, 140, 149-54, 187; regla de ocha, 26, 140, 142-50

Dogma of Santería, xv-xvi, 3-4, 10, 15, 102, 138, 140, 181, 189-90

Dutch Empire, 160-61

Durkheim, Émile, 192

Ebbós (offerings). *See* Rituals of Santería

Egun. *See* Dead, the

Eleda, 20-21, 115-16

Elegguá, 1, 42-43, 45-46, 48, 52-53, 59-60, 63, 68, 91-93, 108-9, 115, 122, 124, 126, 128, 142, 145-47, 211, 216; as Anthony of Padua, 54; as diviner, 60, 63; the great incest, 40-41, 81; as Holy Child of Atocha, 54, 61-62, 197; image of, 110-11, 113, 121; as messenger, 59-61, 63; as path opener, 60, 70, 109-10, 129; as trickster, 41, 60-61, 75, 77, 119, 141, 148; as warrior, 59, 81, 110, 112, 197

Eleke. *See* Beaded Necklace

Eliade, Mircea, 218

Evil, 15-16, 26-30, 50, 61, 110, 116, 139, 197

Ewe. *See* Herbs and plants

Flood, the, 43-45, 69, 72

Francis of Assisi, 64, 235. *See also* Orúnla

Frazer, Sir James George, 137

Fundamento, el. *See* Beaded Necklace

Geertz, Clifford, 31-32